100 Years of
Leeds United
Managers

The View from the Dugout

James Buttler

GREAT N-ORTHERN

Great Northern Books Limited
PO Box 1380, Bradford, BD5 5FB

www.greatnorthernbooks.co.uk

ISBN: 978-1-912101-07-8

Design and layout: David Burrill

CIP Data
A catalogue for this book is available from the British Library

*To everyone that has sung
'Marching On Together'
and meant it.*

Contents

Introduction

2019 is the 100th anniversary of Leeds United Football Club. Alongside around 10 million people worldwide, it is my club. The eleven guys running out on to the Elland Road pitch in that famous white shirt are my team. The results of their endeavours either make me smile broadly or devastate my mood. But, as the song says, through the ups and downs we march on together with a football club we all believe is the greatest there has ever been.

Pure hard stats don't necessarily back that assertion of constant greatness up. On 8 May 2004, I was one of 38,986 people in the stands at Elland Road as a 3-3 draw against Charlton Athletic was the full stop to the club's relegation from the Premier League. I remember the sound of amazing support as the crowd sang "we're going down, but we'll be back" throughout much of the game. As the final whistle blew, I don't think many of us thought it would take so long to retake our seat at England's top table.

The manager that takes Leeds United back to the promised land will be worshipped in West Yorkshire and beyond. The man in the dugout when promotion is won back to the Premier League, where Leeds United belong, will have turned often distant dreams into reality.

No manager ever falls short for want of trying. All of the men that have occupied the Leeds United dugout have recognised it as one of the best jobs in football. The potential for greatness has been there for them all. Few have taken that opportunity.

A successful Leeds manager will feel the strength of a passionate support. Vocal and the best around, when that wall of white noise is behind your winning side there can surely be no better feeling.

Recent seasons have fallen short of expectations, but the club we stand by through thick and thin has experienced the serious highs that only sport can provide. Don Revie, most people's greatest Leeds United manager ever, won the old First Division in 1968/69 and 1973/74 and led the side to a second placed finish on five other occasions. Howard Wilkinson took his side to Leeds United's third English title in 1991/92.

The Club lifted the FA Cup in 1971/72 under Revie, who also led them to League Cup success in 1967/68 and to UEFA Cup glory in 1967/68 and 1970/71. Jimmy Armfield took Leeds United to the European Cup final in the 1974/75 season.

A rich history is one to be proud of, but it can also cast a long shadow over present realities. Every man who has answered the call to be the next Leeds boss will have dreamt of replicating former glories. They have all been eager to achieve, we are desperate for them to do it and one day, hopefully soon, our time will come again.

If you've never been to a game at Elland Road, then do it. Sit in the stands and listen to the crowd. Hopefully a goal will go in the opposition's net and you'll be dragged to your feet by those around you and it will not be very long before you are swept along with the magic and madness of it all.

This book chronicles the history of Leeds United through the eyes and actions of the men that have occupied the dugout trying to achieve their own slice of greatness. The managers who have hoped the indomitable support from the stands will inspire their signings to win matches and take them on to glory.

Riding the crest of a large and victorious Leeds United wave must be the greatest feeling for a manager. Standing alone on the touchline as the defeats mount up and the chairman's eyes burn into the back of your neck, the loneliest.

Managers may come and go, yet they embody our hopes and are the target of our frustrations. It's a thankless task, but they have all contributed to making Leeds United the club we call our own. And we should thank them all for their efforts, whether they yielded silverware or not.

LEEDS CITY

1902–1919

From small acorns...

It is hard to believe that Leeds was not always a football hotbed. In fact, it took a seriously long time for the sport to make any impact on the city at all.

Sheffield was Yorkshire's football front-runner with Sheffield FC the world's first football club, founded on 24 October 1857. When the English Football Association began work in 1863 it had a southern focus and didn't recognise Sheffield, leading the steel city to establish its own Sheffield Football Association.

For a while the English FA and Sheffield FA played the game under their own different rules and it wasn't until 1863 that Sheffield FC became members of the English FA. In true Yorkshire style they still insisted on retaining their own 'Sheffield Rules' until 1878.

The first match ever staged in Leeds saw two Sheffield sides stage an exhibition match at the Holbeck Recreation Ground on Boxing Day 1877. It was a financial flop. Organisers rubbed their hands when a decent crowd showed up, only to find that the majority were season ticket holders of the Holbeck Rugby Club and had watched the game free of charge.

Hunslet Association Football Club was formed in 1878 and folded five years later when only three people showed up at the AGM. They reformed in 1889, playing as Leeds Steelworks, but ended once again in 1902, without a ground to host their matches.

In August 1904, the men behind Hunslet got together at the Griffin Hotel in Boar Lane and agreed 'the time was ripe to for a good Association club in Leeds'. Leeds City Association Football Club was born and those gathered agreed the purchase of Holbeck Rugby Club's Elland Road ground.

Leeds City began life in the West Yorkshire League, reformed in 1902, as a replacement for the disbanded Hunslet side. They hadn't been able to fully complete the purchase of Elland Road before the league fixtures got underway and instead played at the Wellington Ground in Low Road.

On 17 September 1902, Leeds City played their first ever FA Cup match with a preliminary round game away defeat at Rockingham Colliery, who led 2-0 at half-time and 3-1 by the end.

On 13 October 1902, officials at Leeds City finally approved the lease of Elland Road at a cost of £75 a year. They retained the option of purchasing the ground the following March at a maximum price of £5,000.

A month later, when all was signed and sealed, the purchase price had dropped to £4,500. Football in the city of Leeds finally had a home. Elland Road hosted its first Leeds City match on 15 October as Hull City won a friendly game 2-0, played in front of 3,000 supporters.

The first home win came a fortnight later when Harrogate were soundly beaten 5-1 in a friendly. It was, however, well into December when the first home win came in the West Yorkshire League, but the early results were a mere sideshow as Leeds City officials had bigger fish to fry and high aspirations. They had set their stall out to gain admission to the Football League, Leeds being the largest city in the country that did not have a Football League club.

Big name players represented City as they bid to raise their profile by playing invitational matches against some of the biggest clubs in the country. If games against the glamour sides clashed with their West Yorkshire League fixtures, City would often play weakened sides in the league as they opted to impress against more famed opponents.

Another signpost that Leeds City were thinking of bigger things ahead came when Gilbert Gillies was appointed their first manager. Over 100 applicants had applied for the position after it was advertised in February 1905, before the days of spoof CVs built around expertise playing 'Championship Manager'.

Gillies' arrival was announced on 7 March 1905 and it was obvious that his previous experience of taking Chesterfield into the Football League was a key factor. He had also just guided the Spireites to their best ever finish of 5th in Division Two.

A club statement said that Gillies: "has been connected with Association football for over sixteen years and has played an active part in all departments of club management. During his association with Chesterfield, the club has grown from a very small junior organisation, and much of its success is due to the skill and energy which he has brought to bear in its management. He has attended the meetings of the League for the past six years, and is well appointed with club secretaries, whilst his knowledge of players and the arrangements to be made for securing admission to the competition will be of great service to the Leeds Club."

Leeds City was alive and kicking, they had a ground, a manager and Norris Hepworth, a local clothing manufacturer, and AW Pullin, a renowned journalist who wrote under the pseudonym 'Old Ebor' in the *Yorkshire Evening Post*, became deputy chairman.

The club had big aspirations, but this was all set against a backdrop of football, or 'socker' as it was known back then, punching on the periphery of activity in the city.

"Leeds holds a unique position in the world of football," the *Leeds Mercury* reflected. "It is the only city in Great Britain with a population of over a quarter of a million which does not possess a first-class Association team, and indeed, prior to the dribbling code being taken up with such tact and foresight at Bradford, the latter place, together with Leeds and Hull, were for many years the only cities in the British Isles of over 150,000 inhabitants where Association football of the highest class was not firmly established.

"The fact that the three great Yorkshire cities mentioned have lagged behind other large cities of the kingdom has to be attributed, of course, to their connection with the Northern Union code," the article continued as it hinted at the financial rewards on offer if clubs like Leeds City could make their mark.

"But the Bradford City Association club, with average attendances approaching 10,000 and gate receipts of nearly £200 per match, have shown what may be attained in one season with a surrounding population of 280,000. What, therefore, may be expected of a club conducted with the same amount of tact and foresight in the area of Leeds, with its 440,000 inhabitants?

"Professional Socker has never been tried in any large centre of population where it has not been a gigantic success. For instance, in 1892, when the two junior Association teams of Manchester — Newton Heath and Ardwick — were just coming to the fore, they had to fight their way, as Bradford City did last season and as Leeds City will have to do, in a district where the Rugby code was paramount, and at a time when such organisations as Swinton, Swinton Hornets, Salford, Sale, Manchester, Manchester Rangers, and Broughton Rangers were a power in the land. Yet the young Associationists prospered in a way which soon outgrew all their rivals. Ardwick became Manchester City, and Newton Heath Manchester United, and the clubs marched from the Alliance into the Leagues. As showing what strides the dribbling code rally has made in Manchester, it may be mentioned that on Christmas Day, 1902, the two premier clubs met in the Second Division, and on the same day, with the same weather and the same local interest, Broughton and Salford also met. There were 17,000 spectators at the latter contest, and no fewer than 49,000 to see the former, constituting a League record which stands to this day; while attendances of over 40,000 have been recorded at Clayton both this season and last.

"Leeds can and ought to have a status in this pastime. It is the fifth largest city in the country, but as a football centre, compared with Birmingham, Sheffield and Manchester, it is a nonentity. The Association game is proving itself week by week to be a sport which in its appeal to human interest has no rival except cricket, and it is a pastime in which the amateur can and does play side by side with the professional without losing caste. The strides it is making suggest that sooner or later Socker will capture the whole of Yorkshire, and Leeds, as the geographical centre of the county, will have to play its part in the movement."

Leeds City officials were keen to take their slice of this northern socker pie. History would show that the *Mercury* had underestimated the riches the sport would bring, but also the hands holding Leeds's purse strings were not always the best equipped to take advantage of what was on offer.

Leeds City became a Football Association associated limited company with an initial launch of 10,000 £1 shares and on 10 April 1905 elected a board at the Griffin Hotel with Norris Hepworth elected as the first chairman.

At the annual meeting of the Football League on 29 May 1905, the number of places in the League was extended from 36 to 40 with Leeds City topping the vote to gain election alongside Burslem Port Vale and Chelsea. The club officially became a limited liability company on 5 June 1905.

"The managers of the Leeds Club have been very energetic, and their work on securing an eleven which will meet all demands is in a forward state," the *Mercury* reported on City's work towards building a team that would compete in the League.

"In this connection Mr G Gillies and Mr F Jarvis, the manager and secretary respectively, are to be congratulated on the result of their labours. Though the team which has already been got together is fairly satisfactory, it is probable, now that a place in the competition has been obtained, that it will be strengthened."

The club brought in players that had shown their worth elsewhere. Only centre-half Jack Morris was a local boy. Among the new acquisitions were goalkeeper Harry Bromage from Burton United. Dickie Morris, an inside forward, who would become the first City player to gain international recognition, for Scotland. He would move on to play for Grimsby Town after only a year at Elland Road.

The capacity of the Elland Road ground was increased to 22,000 and work done to improve the surface, ensuring more grass than had been the case when used for rugby.

Dick Ray, a 29-year-old defender, had played under Gillies at Chesterfield and was installed as Leeds City's captain to lead the team out for their first ever appearance in the Football League on 2 September 1905 against Bradford City in front of 15,000 at Valley Parade.

"To be candid, even those in the best position to appraise the capabilities of the eleven men who have been drawn from the four corners of the country to constitute the side, did not go so far as to anticipate victory — the advantages of Bradford City were so very pronounced," the *Leeds Mercury* previewed. "When it is remembered that Bradford have already experienced two years of strenuous League football, and that they were able to place in the field the strongest team they have yet possessed, with the additional advantage of playing on their own ground, the difficulties which confronted the Leeds men will be fully appreciated."

A cagey first half saw the game goalless at the interval and then Bradford's superior fitness told in the second half. With 15 minutes to play a goalmouth scramble ended with Bradford's forward Jimmy Conlin slotting past Bromage to register the only goal of the match.

Leeds were beaten 1-0 after failing to take their chances in front of goal. The first ever City team to represent Leeds in the Football League lined up like this: Harry Bromage (from Burton Albion), Charlie Morgan (Tottenham), Harry Stringfellow (Swindon Town), James Henderson (Bradford City), Jock MacDonald (Blackburn Rovers), Dick Ray (Chesterfield, capt), Fred Parnell (Derby), Bob Watson (Woolwich Arsenal), Dickie Morris (Liverpool), Harry Singleton (QPR) and Fred Hargreaves (Burton United).

The *Leeds Mercury* wrote of City's "surprising performance" that "Leeds City have undergone their baptism with flying colours. It is true they did not succeed in gaining their first competition victory over Bradford City, but their performance was so entirely meritorious , considering the whole of the circumstances that their 'trial step' must be regarded in the light of a highly meritorious performance… Directors of the Elland Road organisation were more than pleased with the display of their men. Every confidence has been placed in the manager of the club, Mr G Gillies, and that he has been able to achieve so much in building up the team must have strengthened his position materially. Taking everything into consideration, he has gained a great triumph."

The *Yorkshire Evening Post* commented, "Truth to tell, the Leeds City were fully entitled to share the honours. They played the better game, and it was only a certain lack of finish in front of goal which prevented them scoring."

And the *Mercury* added, "Ray, the captain of the Leeds team, ... played a sterling game, being cool and collected, and overcoming many difficulties by his sound judgement."

The disparate nature of a recruitment policy that had drawn players from across the country meant it took Gillies time to blend a cohesive team.

The club adopted the nickname of 'The Peacocks' due to their long association with the Old Peacock Inn, but were also popularly referred to as 'The Citizens'.

Singleton was misfiring up front and it was substitute Tommy Drain who scored City's first two goals as they collected their first point in a 2-2 draw with Lincoln City.

On 16 September, Gillies' team won their first match in the League as they beat Leicester Fosse 1-0 with Singleton hitting the back of the net with what the *Yorkshire Post* referred to as a 'somewhat lucky goal'.

Leeds had been lurking at the bottom end of the table in the early weeks of the season, but gradually grew in confidence to climb the table. The attendances at Elland Road were steadily growing, with 20,000 watching a 0-0 against Chelsea on 25 November.

Hargreaves had not settled up front and Gillies signed David Wilson from Hull City for £120 to add goals.

When one looks back at team photos from that era it is hard to see the men pictured as youngsters. Heavy moustaches and slicked back hair were the order of the day and Wilson, in particular, despite being only 22 could pass for a man 10 or 15 years older. He was an instant hit with supporters as his appetite for attack saw an upturn in results. On 3 March, Leeds City hammered bottom side Clapton Orient 6-1 with Wilson scoring four, having another disallowed and also hitting the bar. City had risen to sixth in the table.

Wilson, however, suffered a torn ligament in an away game with Grimsby Town and missed eight games, although he still ended the season with 13 goals from 15 appearances.

A 1-1 draw at Grimsby saw some fierce tackling as the hosts sought revenge for their defeat earlier in the season. With Wilson out and a number of injuries sustained against Grimsby, Leeds struggled to maintain their bid for promotion.

The battle at the top of the table involved Chelsea, Bristol City and Manchester United. When Leeds lost 2-0 in the West Country it secured Bristol City's promotion as champions.

When Manchester United won 3-1 at Elland Road the following week it meant they also won promotion. Wilson returned to the Leeds attack after injury as they beat Glossop 2-1 to finish their debut season sixth in the Second Division.

Leeds had arrived. An area dominated by rugby league was opening its heart to soccer and heroes were being born.

Wilson was the star attraction. The impact the former soldier had made in his first season at Elland Road had been immediate and well received. In goal Bromage had put in some fine displays. But far from being the disparate team of individuals that Gillies had assembled at the beginning of the season, they ended their first League campaign as a strong unit, playing attractive football and with the public excited for the future.

The rugby league attendances at Headingley had fallen from over 9,000 to less than 6,000. The average attendance at Elland Road to watch City had been over 9,000 with matches against Bradford and Chelsea seeing 20,000-plus crowds flocking through the turnstiles. The club generated a profit of £122 in its first year in the Football League.

The 1906/07 season saw the arrival of Billy McLeod, who signed from Lincoln City for £350 plus a game's gate receipts and he replaced Wilson up front. McLeod scored 15 goals in his first season as Leeds City finished mid-table and would go on to score 171 goals in 289 games for the club.

Wilson's time at the club had ended in tragedy. During a game against Burnley in October 1906 he had been winded in a robust first half challenge. During the second half he collapsed after heading a ball. After leaving the field he was found writhing on the floor complaining of chest pains. Doctors were called and Wilson began to feel better and returned to the field of play against medical advice. His return lasted three minutes before he retired from the match once again in considerable distress.

PC John Byrom recalled: "I assisted him to the dressing room and helped him to undress. He said he would have a hot bath, but all at once after getting into the bath he laid down and started kicking his legs violently. I took hold of him and held his head out of the water, but he seemed to lose consciousness, and never spoke again."

Results didn't improve for Gillies and after another mid-table finish the following season his contract was not renewed.

In March 1908, Frank Scott-Walford took charge after being released by Brighton. Despite bringing in new players from Brighton and Ireland, the club spent the 1909/10 season at the bottom end, in 1910/11 finished in mid-table obscurity, followed by having to apply for re-election in 1911/12. Scott-Walford was forced to resign.

Leeds City would exist for a total of 15 years, playing all of their football in the Second Division and always struggling with debt.

Chairman Hepworth was forced to put his hands in his own pockets on a number of occasions to keep things afloat.

Former Spurs player, Herbert Chapman, was appointed manager after a successful managerial stint at Northampton. He took charge in 1912 and performances improved. If it had not been for the advent of World War One, the side may have pushed for a place in England's top tier.

In the 1913/14 season the club missed promotion by a mere point and recorded their best ever league result, an 8-0 victory against bottom of the table Nottingham Forest on 29 November 1913.

Scottish international Jimmy Speirs had been signed from Bradford City and linked up with Billy McLeod to forge an intelligent forward partnership. A rejuvenated McLeod ended the 1912/13 season with 27 goals in 38 games.

Ivan Sharpe came in on the wing from Derby County. Chapman had also shored up his defence by signing John Hampson from Northampton Town.

Leeds City were 4th in the Second Division table, with games in hand on the leaders, and on a five-game unbeaten run when Forest came to Elland Road.

The *Leeds Mercury* wrote: "In just over half an hour they were three goals to the good, and the match, to all intents and purposes, was all over bar the shouting. They played against the wind, and even with this handicap they always did well. When the forwards had the ball, they attacked with headlong impetuosity, and with no mean skill."

McLeod opened the scoring and Price notched twice as City were 3-0 up by half-time. A 14,000-crowd watched as Hampson headed a fourth goal from a Sharpe corner and McLeod added the fifth. Despite Mick Foley missing a penalty, Speirs made it 6-0 before another two goals from McLeod completed the destruction.

"The City forwards, especially McLeod and Price, were a brilliant lot, who displayed fire and resolution in all their attacks," enthused the *Leeds Mercury*. "They were supported by a trio of halves who did their work excellently, while Copeland and Affleck were a puissant pair of backs."

The club record scoreline for Leeds City had come in an 11-0 trouncing of Morley in a 1905 FA Cup preliminary round match. The previous best league result had been a 6-1 win over Clapton Orient in 1906.

McLeod's supreme form saw him selected for the Football League XI against the Southern League on 9 February 1913 and again against Scotland on 21 March. He was named a reserve for England in March, didn't play and was never called up again.

City had finished 4th in 1914 and hopes had been high for promotion the following year. The 1914/15 season began with four straight defeats, however, and by December the team were in the relegation zone and facing the prospect of being forced to apply for re-election for the second time in three seasons.

Leicester Fosse were the opponents at Elland Road on 12 December and were fairing worse than City, fresh from a seven-goal battering by Wolverhampton Wanderers on 14 November 1914.

Tony Hogg started in goal for City as George Affleck, Fred Blackman, George Law, Jack Hampson and Mick Foley formed his defence. Simpson Bainbridge, John Jackson, McLeod, Arthur Price and Sharpe were the forward choices.

Price, signed from Worksop Town in December 1912, was in for Speirs who had been ruled out with injury. He had been a fall guy for City's poor form and the game against Leicester Fosse gave the 28-year-old a chance to re-stake his first team claims on an atrocious day of high winds and rain.

The gate was the lowest of the season as a mere 5,000 turned out with public opinion opposed to the continuation of the football league calendar.

"The question of whether football should be abandoned during the War is being much debated in sporting circles, and opinion appears to be divided on the matter," stated the *Yorkshire Post*. "While many people think it would be a disgrace to this country to have thousands of able bodied players devoting themselves to the game, and hundreds of thousands of men watching them, when there is an urgent need for volunteers, others declare that, like other amusements, football will provide a much needed release for the large numbers who must be left at home and serve to divert their attention."

During the same week that Leeds hosted Leicester Fosse, the four home nations met to abandon international matches for the season. The Scottish Football Association also suggested that domestic cup competitions should also be cancelled, but that was rejected because "there is no evidence in fact that the playing of football has hindered or is hindering recruiting. On the contrary, there is good reason to conclude that football has encouraged and assisted recruiting... Further, the meeting is of the opinion that to deprive the working people of our country of their Saturday afternoon recreation would be very unfair and very mischievous."

The Germans attacked Allied forces near Ypres in Belgium, the French made advances in Alsace, there were fierce battles in Poland and a German cruiser was sunk in the Baltic. A conflict many had predicted would be over quickly was showing no signs of abating.

The Peacocks kicked off into the wind and were ahead after 10 minutes as Bainbridge fired home. Billy Mills put Leicester Fosse level from distance, before Bainbridge added his second and then turned provider for McLeod. Leeds were 3-1 up at the break.

Price took advantage of Leeds's dominance in the second half. The inside-forward scored a hat-trick as his trickery undid the Fosse backline. Leicester pulled back with a consolation from George Douglas before McLeod added his second of the game to secure a 7-2 win.

"Considering the heavy state of the ground, the game was as good as one could expect, but the home players adapted themselves to the conditions far better than their opponents," reported the *Leeds Mercury*. "All the City goals were the outcome of cool and clever forward play, and it has been many a day since the City players scored so prolifically or shot so often as they did on Saturday."

Leeds failed to build on the win, however, losing 2-1 to Barnsley a week later as the conflict in Europe raged and the official league programme was officially abandoned. There had been signs that manager Herbert Chapman was getting it right, but the war prevented his push for a place in the First Division as City flourished during the unofficial war years.

During wartime, as with other clubs around England, the practice was to recruit famous guest players, enlisted to boost the team. England internationals Charlie Buchan and Fannie Walden were two players that represented the city as guests. Guests were supposed to receive expenses and nothing else. The vast majority of clubs ignored that rule, but it would only be Leeds City that would pay the price. Those payments made to some of the guest performers would ultimately lead to the club's demise.

In 1916, City won the Subsidiary tournament of the Midland Section and finished top of the full Midland Section in 1917 and 1918. It had been decided that the Midland winners would meet the top side from the Lancashire Section over two legs, home and away, to be determined the unofficial title of League Champions. Proceeds from the games would go to the National Football War Fund.

Leeds City had scored 75 goals in 28 games in 1917/18. Guest player Clem Stephenson had been the key player during the season but was unable to partake in the two play-off matches due to his duties with the RAF at Crystal Palace.

33-year-old Newcastle forward Billy Hibbert, who had been capped by England in 1910, was brought in to replace Stephenson. Skipper Jack Hampson was missing through injury, and in his absence, Bob Hewison continued to captain the side.

City took on Lancashire Section champions Stoke who had pipped Liverpool to the title on goal difference. The first leg was played at Elland Road on 4 May 2018 and Leeds were ahead after 10 minutes as Cawley struck the crossbar and after a scramble Billy Hibbert headed home.

Stoke responded strongly before Jack Peart broke clear after 30 minutes, beat the Stoke defence and finished clinically. Leeds reached the end of a frenetic first half 2-0 up and then showed their resilience as they withstood severe pressure to hold their advantage to the full-time whistle. The 10,000 attendance saw £435 go to the Football National War Fund.

Ahead of the second leg in the Potteries, the *Leeds Mercury* warned: "There could be no question as to the superiority of Leeds City over Stoke in the first of the League Cup final matches at Leeds on Saturday, and their two goals lead must be considered a useful one. It is quite conceivable, however, that Stoke will improve their form under home influences. Leeds City's task is by no means over."

15,000 watched a barnstorming opening spell where both sides had chances and the keepers were never far from the action.

After half-an-hour, City's chances were dealt a major blow when right half-back Hewison, the City skipper, was carried off with a broken leg, which effectively ended his career. Arthur Price filled in at the back as Leeds managed to reach the break 0-0 and 2-0 up on aggregate.

"It had been anything but a good exhibition of football in the first half, more especially after the first quarter of an hour, but certainly the best combined movements had come from Leeds City, whose endurance had now to be tested owing to the fact that they were a man short," reported the *Evening Post*.

Stoke came close to being awarded a penalty as the second half got underway as Leeds were pegged back. Stoke scored from the penalty spot via Parker after 78 minutes and City battled manfully to preserve their lead until the final whistle.

"For an hour the City's defence had an uphill fight, but they never wavered under the series of keen attacks which the Stoke forwards levelled on their goal," confirmed the *Leeds Mercury*. "So resolutely did the City meet all these efforts that Stoke were too fatigued to derive material benefit from their belated goal."

Leeds City had won the League Cup and had claimed the unofficial crown as England's champion club.

After World War One, competitive football resumed in England for the 1919/20 season. Supporters had undergone hardships, loss and required fresh hope in their lives. The resumption of sport was a much-needed distraction.

It was all change. The First Division, the sport's top league for many years before Sky 'invented' football in 1992, was expanded from 20 to 22 teams with Chelsea reprieved from relegation and Arsenal promoted to the top flight despite only finishing fifth in the 1914-15 season. The Second Division was also expanded to 22 sides with Stoke City becoming a league side again, while Coventry City, South Shields, Rotherham United and West Ham all joined the English Football League for the first time.

As the 1919-20 season got underway on 30 August and a new era of sport began, all members of the 44-team league structure were intent on making their mark on post-war Britain. For Leeds City that hope was short-lived as what became known as the Leeds City Scandal hit the headlines. It had in fact been brewing behind the scenes for years.

Chapman had relinquished his managerial position to take charge of a Leeds munitions factory during the war and recommended that his assistant, George Cripps, took administrative control, whilst new chairman Joseph Connor and another director, looked after on-pitch affairs.

With the leadership Chapman had provided over the preceding three years gone, the club lacked the cohesion it had experienced under his guidance. Connor did not think Cripps was up to the job he'd inherited, and their relationship became particularly fractious. The board insisted an accountant be hired to oversee the club's accounts.

Cripps was responsible for managing the team and correspondence, which did not serve to ease tensions, which by 1918 had become so bad the Board were seriously considering terminating the club altogether. The financial situation was worsening, but John McKenna, the chairman of the Football League, urged Leeds City's directors to fight on.

Cripps had become a universally unpopular figure throughout the club, but, with the war over, Chapman resumed control, and everyone hoped that harmony would return. It didn't.

Cripps threatened to sue for wrongful dismissal when he was told to return to his former position as Chapman's assistant. He demanded £400 and told his solicitor that Leeds City had made illegal payments to players during wartime. A £55 deal was swiftly negotiated with Cripps in return for a written pledge that he would not spill the beans on club affairs. He also passed back any club documents in his possession. Leeds City's solicitor, Alderman William Clarke sealed all of Cripps's papers away in a strongbox in his city centre office.

Chapman had signed full-back Charlie Copeland in 1912 and he had made his debut in a 4-0 win over Glossop on 9 November that year. Copeland had only nailed down a regular first-team start during the war years and found himself in dispute with club officials when he requested a pay rise. In reaction to the club's refusal to meet his demands, he threatened to make allegations to the Football Association and Football League about illegal payments that had been made to guest players during wartime. The club called his bluff and instead gave him a free transfer to Coventry, but Copeland did not forget his grievance and made his allegations formal in July 1919.

Leeds were not the only club to have made such payments, but the authorities were unable to ignore Copeland's official complaint made in July 1919.

Copeland was also represented by the same solicitor that had represented Cripps and in response to their claims the Football Association and the Football League set up a joint inquiry.

The Commission hearing was held in Manchester on 26 September 1919 and Alderman Clarke was asked to present the club books. When Clarke refused the club were given until 6 October to produce the documents.

Leeds City beat Wolverhampton 4-2 on 4 October as Billy McLeod scored a hat-trick, but that would turn out to be City's last ever game. The deadline for producing documents passed and their next game was suspended. After a meeting on the inquiry at the Russell Hotel in London, City were expelled from the Football League and disbanded.

"The authorities of the game intend to keep it absolutely clean," said John McKenna. "We will have no nonsense. The football stable must be cleaned and further breakages of the law regarding payments will be dealt with in such a severe manner that I now give warning that clubs and players must not expect the slightest leniency."

City officials would face further punishment as their silence and failure to produce financial documents was deemed to be an admission of guilt.

The Leeds players were out of work and had never contemplated that proceedings would provide such an abrupt end to their City careers. The Football League stepped in to pay their wages until they found new clubs. In order to facilitate that process, an auction was held at the Metropole Hotel in Leeds on 17 October.

30 League clubs arrived in Leeds to not only bid for players, but the club's nets, goalposts, boots, kit and physiotherapy equipment.

The squad went on the cheap as all players combined were sold for just over £10,000. Star striker McLeod fetched £1,250, whilst the lower echelons of the squad went for £100 apiece as the bidding clubs found themselves very much in a buyers' market.

Five City officials were subsequently banned for life — Connor, Whiteman, fellow directors Mr S Glover and Mr G Sykes and, rather surprisingly, manager Herbert Chapman. The board promptly resigned, but Chapman earned a reprieve after evidence was later given that he was working at the munitions factory when the illegal payments were allegedly made.

Leeds City had played only eight matches of the 1919/20 season when they were hastily replaced by Port Vale in the League. Vale went on to finish 13th after inheriting the 10 points that City had previously won. There was some bitterness in the mouth with many in the city feeling that Port Vale had exerted pressure behind the scenes in a bid to accelerate Leeds City's demise and promote their own existence. The football Gods would throw down the irony a few months later of Vale being Leeds United's first Football League opponents.

Leeds folk have a reputation for stubbornness and belligerence, and these were qualities that would ultimately serve them well as they followed football in the city over the next 100 years.

For, as Leeds City crumbled into memory, moves were afoot in the city to create Leeds United. A new football club, a new beginning and one that would take the city into the future. The football lovers in Leeds were not prepared to take the death of their club lying down.

On the same day as the players that they had cheered from the stands were being auctioned off, more than 1,000 Leeds City fans met in the Salem Hall in Leeds. A local solicitor, Alf Masser, chaired the meeting at which it was unanimously agreed to form a new club and a supporters' club.

And Leeds United Association Football Club was born, with a seven-strong management committee which included Masser, along with Joe Henry junior (son of the Lord Mayor of Leeds who had fought extremely hard to save Leeds City, including an offer to take control of affairs himself — an offer the inquiry had declined), Mark Barker, R.E.H. Ramsden, Charles Snape and former players Dick Ray (appointed manager) and Charlie Morgan.

Leeds United joined the Midland League upon invitation to replace Leeds City Reserves and the club moved into Elland Road. Yorkshire Amateurs had been using the ground after Leeds City's demise, but only temporarily.

The rebirth of a team in Leeds had been led by the supporters and that is a large part of where the pride and passion come from today. The people of Leeds were not prepared for football to die. They didn't stop believing.

And fair play to them for it. Leeds fans today have a lot to thank them for.

Huddersfield Town can be equally proud of the actions taken by their support-base around the same time. For a considerable time, it appeared that the Huddersfield club would become the team to play as Leeds United from Elland Road, bringing their players with them.

With attendances down and finances stretched beyond the limit, the chairman of Huddersfield, J Hilton Crowther, believed taking his Second Division club to be part of the Leeds revolution was the only viable option. Leeds United officials agreed at a meeting on 7 November 1919 and both parties, together, approached the Football League so that the transference could be rubber-stamped. But for the reaction of the Huddersfield supporters it was a mere formality.

Huddersfield fans demonstrated at the next match. They agreed collectively to demand that the Huddersfield Town directors not to be party to the transference until the local public had been given the chance to show their support of the club through increased attendances. They asked that immediate steps be taken to increase the capital of the company from £10,000 to £30,000 by an additional issue of 20,000 £1 shares. It was also proposed that the company should be converted to public ownership, allowing supporters to invest in shares.

A ten-man committee was to be appointed to examine ways of finding the money to pay off the debentures held by the Crowther brothers.

Efforts were begun to raise the funds required by the club from the Crowthers and an application was made on 10 November 1919 to send a deputation representing Huddersfield Town shareholders to a vital meeting of the League Management Committee to present their case for rejecting the transference. They were permitted to attend, and it was ruled that Huddersfield Town would be given one month's grace, until 8 December 1919, to raise £25,000, to meet the sum of the debt deemed payable to J Hilton Crowther. In return, he would forego his interest in the club. If the money was not forthcoming, Huddersfield Town would move to Elland Road and become part of a new Leeds United.

At the next meeting at the Euston Hotel in London on 9 December 1919 the deadline was extended to 31 December 1919.

Interest in the club had been raised and performances on the pitch were much improved. They say, 'You don't know what you've got 'til it's gone' and the Huddersfield supporters didn't want to see their team gobbled up by Leeds. Some gave little amounts, bigger supporters and businessmen reached deeper into their pockets.

Supporters were then informed that 'three Huddersfield gentlemen' had undertaken to resolve the settlement terms. Those three were Joseph Barlow and his two Liberal Club companions, Alderman Wilfred Dawson and Rowland Mitchell.

Barlow had been breakfasting at Merseyside's Adelphi Hotel when J Hilton Crowther and Arthur Fairclough, the new Leeds United manager, walked in and proceeded to talk about the events of Huddersfield Town. Overhearing the conversations, Barlow was riled and spoke to his two friends and agreed to invest. Barlow took £1,000 worth of shares and the other two £500 apiece.

They had talks with D Stonor Crowther before finally persuading him to desert his quest for £25,000 in favour of accepting £17,500 plus the allotment of 12,500 shares in the club, which he would give them the option of purchasing, at 10s (50p) each in the future.

The supporters had saved Huddersfield Town and on 17 June 1920, after three months of personal negotiations with their creditor, the terms were settled. The agreement was made permanent the following month.

On the pitch Huddersfield Town won promotion to the First Division as well as reaching the FA Cup Final. They would appoint former Leeds City manager Herbert Chapman and enjoyed huge success through the 1920s, winning the League Championship three times.

Crowther had invested his intentions on Leeds United and became the new club chairman. He loaned Leeds United £35,000, repayable when United gained promotion to the First Division.

He brought with him Arthur Fairclough, who had won the FA Cup with his Barnsley side in 1912. Fairclough was appointed Leeds manager on 26 February 1920 and Dick Ray became his assistant for a while, until he left the club in 1923.

The resurrection of football in Leeds was complete when United successfully applied to enter the Football League. When the vote was carried out on 31 May 1920, the club came out on top of the votes with 31, followed by Cardiff City with 23, and both clubs were admitted to the Second Division season for 1920/21.

A Third Division was added to the league structure in the following season and the expansion allowed the Football Association to elect the newly formed Leeds United, joined by Cardiff City in the Second Division.

1

RICHARD 'DICK' RAY

1919–1920 and 1927–1935

The epitome of loyalty

Born: 4 February 1876, Newcastle-under-Lyme, Staffordshire
Died: 28 December 1952, Leeds, Yorkshire (aged 76)

Matches	Won	Drawn	Lost	Points	Pts/Match	Win %
341	142	72	127	498	1.46	41.64%
				RANK	15th/36	12th/36

The man destined to be the first manager of Leeds United was Dick Ray. He'd been Leeds City's first captain and was a very large influence on football in the city of Leeds in those early days.

Ray was a confident man, not bashful about voicing his opinions. Respected for his loyalty, he made 38 league appearances as a left-back and became a committee man, club secretary and manager.

Born in the Potteries, he'd begun kicking a ball with his local club Audley, before signing as a 17-year-old for Macclesfield in 1893. He earned a reputation as a solid and effective left-back, winning the Cheshire Senior Cup in his first season at the club.

In May 1894, he moved on to Burslem Port Vale. He returned to Macclesfield where he won the Cheshire Senior Cup for the second time in the 1896, and then, over the next few years, he played for Manchester City, Stockport County and Chesterfield, winning a Second Division Championship medal with Manchester City in the 1898/99 season.

He played with Non-League Macclesfield from 1900 before re-joining Manchester City, back in the Second Division, in September 1902. He then played for Coventry City (February 1903), Stockport County (July 1903), Chesterfield (June 1904) and then the city of Leeds came calling in 1905.

Gilbert Gillies had been the Chesterfield manager that had taken Ray to Saltergate, but he was then installed as the first manager of Leeds City in March 1905. Ray joined him four months later and captained the side through their inaugural season, but when the board didn't renew Gillies' contract after three years in charge, Ray moved on too, this time to Huddersfield Town. He had a brief return to Leeds City in April 1909 and Mirfield United (November 1910), before retiring as a player in 1912.

When he served in the Royal Army Service Corps during World War

One, he maintained a close contact with friends and colleagues in Leeds. When Leeds City were expelled from the Football League in October 1919, Ray became a member of the seven-strong committee that was elected to manage the formation of Leeds United.

Ray took on the role of secretary-manager, responsible for both team selection and playing policy. With precious little money to spend, he did a fine job as he took the side through part of the 1919/20 Midland League season. But when the new Leeds United chairman Hilton Crowther recruited Arthur Fairclough in February 1920, from his old club Huddersfield Town, Ray became his assistant.

He moved in to manage Doncaster Rovers in June 1923 when the South Yorkshire side were elected to the Third Division (North), but his success there was limited to mid-table or below.

Fairclough, however, resigned when Leeds United were relegated to the Second Division at the end of the 1926/27 season and Ray was asked to return to Elland Road in July 1927. His remit was extended to include overseeing all team and football affairs, including selection and tactics.

Fairclough had left a solid squad and Ray took advantage by steering the club back to the First Division at the first attempt in 1927/28. He made few changes from the team inherited from Fairclough, although he did sign Charlie Keetley in July 1927. He plucked the striker from non-league football and Keetley would score over 100 goals in a Leeds shirt over the next seven seasons, beginning well with 19 from 16 appearances in a good first season.

A 13th placed finish followed in 1928/29 and then, in 1929/30, the club had its best season to date with a top five First Division finish, the best return until Don Revie's mid-1960s team.

The joy was short-lived, however, as Leeds tumbled to relegation with a 21st placed return in the 1930/31 season. Again, the club showed fortitude by bouncing back at the first attempt, finishing runners-up to Wolverhampton Wanderers in 1931/32.

Back at the top table in 1932/33, Leeds would finish the season in 8th position, and there were a couple of extraordinary matches.

On 27 December 1932 at Elland Road, the official crowd was 56,796 watching a 0-0 draw between Leeds and the best team in the country, Arsenal. The teams had played at Highbury on Boxing Day, just 24 hours earlier. Surprisingly, Leeds had beaten the Gunners 2-1, with Charlie Keetley bagging a brace in front of a huge 55,876 crowd. Joe Hulme had scored for Arsenal.

Arsenal had been six points clear at the top of the table. With the lead diminished the crowds flocked to Elland Road. The gates had been locked for safety reasons and hundreds climbed on house roofs, watched from the top of the Peacock Public House and from Beeston Hill. The record attendance would stand for 35 years.

Supporters were desperate to see Leeds repeat the previous day's win and narrow the gap to just two points. Regardless, Leeds were in contention, for a while anyway.

Arsenal went on to take the title and repeated their success in the 1933/34 and 1934/35 seasons. United's team lost form and slipped down the table as 1933 arrived, although they did have an FA Cup shock left in them.

Newcastle had won the Cup in the previous season, beating Arsenal in the final, and had beaten Leeds 3-1 at St James' Park a month before. On 14 January, two goals inside three minutes from Arthur Hydes shocked the defending champions and he added another goal in the second half to complete a superb hat-trick.

Leeds finished 9th in the First Division during the 1933/34 season and memorably, on 7 April 1934, beat Leicester City 8-0 at Elland Road to record their biggest ever win. The result equalled Leeds City's best result 20 years before and was a record that stood until 1969 when Leeds beat Lyn Oslo 10-0. Arthur Hydes was the club's top scorer over the season with 16 goals, but Leeds's prolific hitman missed the Leicester mailing through injury.

In 1934/35, the Leeds defence had been strong and determined with England internationals Willis Edwards, Ernie Hart and Wilf Copping occupying the half-back line.

Copping was then sold to the financial might of Arsenal and the repercussions of his loss in the back line was there for all to see. In the second game of the season they were thrashed 8-1 at Stoke, they lost 6-3 to West Brom in November and were battered 7-1 in Chelsea in March.

Leeds results worsened markedly, and they finished 18th, just avoiding relegation, but Ray felt he'd taken the club as far as he could. Ray, by now 59 years old, resigned his £1,000 a year job on 5 March 1935. He'd done well on a limited budget and had brought through a number of young talents. Bert Sproston, Wild Copping, Billy Furness, Willis Edwards, Ernie Hart and Eric Stephenson had all progressed to England international honours. Arthur Hydes, Tom Cochrane and George and Jimmy Milburn became outstanding first-team performers. His best signing, in July 1927, was Charlie Keetley, who would become the club's most prolific goalscorer.

The Football League appointed Ray to manage the first league representative team in February 1934, which played out a 2-2 draw with the Scottish Football League at Ibrox Stadium. Ray was presented with a gold medal to mark the occasion.

He became Bradford City Manager in April 1935. They avoided relegation from Division Two at the end of that season but were relegated in 1937. Ray left the club a year later when he was relieved of responsibility for team selection. He was a man who liked to do things his own way and having someone else meddling in who played was a step too far. By this stage he was 62 and spent some time scouting for Millwall before retiring from football altogether a couple of years later.

He ran a garage and invested in a number of billiard clubs. He died in St James' Hospital in Leeds on 28th December 1952, aged 76. His footballing association with the city of Leeds had spanned, on and off, 30 years.

He goes down in history as an influential and loyal figure who played a huge part in the formation of Leeds United. He had laid down a firm foundation for the Leeds United managers that would follow.

2

ARTHUR FAIRCLOUGH

1920–1927

First taste of the top flight

Born: March 1873, Barnsley, Yorkshire
Died: 18 March 1948 (aged 73), Sheffield, Yorkshire

Matches	Won	Drawn	Lost	Points	Pts/Match	Win %
306	109	77	120	404	1.32	35.62%
				RANK	23rd/36	25th/36

Barnsley-born Arthur Fairclough was a football fanatic. His playing career stalled before it got going because of ill-health, so he invested his younger days in becoming a referee. He was then elected to Barnsley Football Club's management committee in 1896 and became club secretary in 1898 as they secured their place in the Football League.

He managed his hometown club between 1898 and 1901, although his other business interest, running a public house in Barnsley, got in the way. So much so that he stood down as manager. He was replaced briefly by John McCartney until 1904, when Fairclough came back as manager-secretary until 1912. He'd not been able to stay away from football completely in the interim, winning election to the Sheffield Football Association in July 1902.

When Fairclough began his second spell in charge of Barnsley, they had become an established Second Division side, battling it out for mid-table obscurity with Leeds City.

He took Barnsley to the FA Cup final in 1910 but lost out 2-0 to Newcastle, after a replay. Two years later, he went one better as his side beat West Brom to lift the FA Cup.

After steering The Tykes to silverware, Huddersfield Town came calling and he became secretary-manager on 24 April 1912 and established the club in Division Two. Much of the work he had done for the Terriers, operating on a minimal budget, shaped the club in readiness for Herbert Chapman who picked up the baton and took them to the very top of the English game. Chapman collected the league titles, but Fairclough had laid the groundwork and created a side that was ready to blossom.

Fairclough was in charge of Huddersfield during the proposed and highly controversial transfer to Elland Road. Fairclough was in full support of Hilton Crowther's desire to transfer the operation to Leeds.

He was present at the 7 November 1919 meeting at the YMCA Hall, Albion Street in Leeds and addressed the meeting along with Crowther to support the amalgamation proposals. He also accompanied Crowther to the Football League Management Committee on 9 December 1919, where the deadline for transference was extended as Huddersfield Town supporters were raising money in, what would ultimately be, a successful bid to halt proceedings.

In a time of anxiety and turmoil he maintained his focus on football and came out of the financial crisis and period of huge doubt with dignity intact and reputation enhanced. Ultimately, the financial malaise the club had found itself in would be Fairclough's undoing.

At an emergency board meeting on 23 December 1919, it was unanimously agreed to accept Fairclough's resignation. He had embarrassed the club he had worked for, and Huddersfield elected Ambrose Langley to replace him immediately. An appeal seeking the club's continuance until the end of the season, giving it time to sort out its finances, meant court proceedings were adjourned. But Fairclough was out of work.

When the amalgamation of the Huddersfield and Leeds clubs ultimately didn't happen, Crowther had already thrown his lot in with the new Leeds United, who had been elected to the Football League at the end of May 1920. He had been appointed to head the board of directors and persuaded Fairclough to follow him and take over from Dick Ray as team manager at Elland Road. Ray became Fairclough's assistant.

'Mr Arthur Fairclough, than whom there is probably no more astute team builder in the country, has been given a free hand in the signing on of players,' stated the *Yorkshire Post*. 'Leeds United should, with ordinary luck, qualify for the First Division within three years.'

Fairclough steered Leeds United through its first full season in the Football League. With Ray, he assembled a squad by recruiting a number of players from local junior football clubs along with players with league experience.

Robust defender Jim Baker followed Fairclough from Huddersfield and Jimmy Frew came south from Hearts.

For Leeds, the 1920/21 season began on 28 August with an away trip to play Port Vale at the Old Recreation Ground, Bryan Street, Hanley. Recognise the irony? Vale had been the team to replace Leeds City when they were expelled from the Football League after only eight games of the season before.

Leeds wore blue and white vertical striped shirts, white shorts and white socks as they were led out by captain Jim Baker.

Watched by a crowd of 15,000, Leeds United's first competitive side lined up as follows: Billy Down, Bert Duffield, Arthur Tillotson, Robert Musgrove, Jim Baker, Jimmy Walton, George Mason, Ernie Goldthorpe, Bob Thompson, Jack Lyon, Jerry Best.

Port Vale won 2-0, but Leeds United were up and running as a Football League side.

Their first home match at Elland Road was played on Wednesday, 1 September. Leeds lost 2-1 to South Shields and there is still debate about who scored the club's first Football League goal. In the *Official History of Leeds United*, the goal is credited to Jack Lyon who, it says, scored from a cross provided by Len Armitage. Newspapermen at the game accredited the goal to Armitage. Who knows? 16,958 people were in the crowd that day, someone must have been paying attention. Leeds had opened their account but were still without a league point.

Three days later at Elland Road, they had their first win, 3-1 against Port Vale, with a goal from Jerry Best and a brace from Matt Ellson. The quick feet of Rob Thompson scored the club's first hat-trick against Notts County at Elland Road on 11 December 1920. Thompson scored a club-high of 12 goals as Leeds began life in the Football League with a 14th place finish in the Second Division.

Tommy Howarth top-scored with 13 goals as the club ended the 1921/22 season in 8th, and there was improvement again in 1922/23 with 7th in the second tier and 16 goals for Percy Whipp.

Dick Ray moved on to take up challenges elsewhere and Fairclough replaced him with Blackpool boss Dick Norman, a reunion with a man that had worked with him at Barnsley.

The pair combined well. In 1923/24, Fairclough steered his side towards promotion to the First Division as they topped the table as Jack Swann banged in 18 goals. After six matches they had one win to their name, then they won nine and drew two of the next 11 matches.

On 26 January 1924, Leeds hosted Sheffield Wednesday at Elland Road in front of 15,000 supporters. They had drawn 0-0 at Hillsborough the week before and Fairclough's side went into the match with one win in eight games, but they needed to dispose of 8th placed Wednesday to stay on track for promotion.

Leeds had not beaten their Yorkshire rivals in five attempts, but that January day, after a hard-fought encounter, a goal from Swann won the game and steadied Fairclough's team for the remainder of their promotion push. Swann ended with a tally of 18 league goals that season, topping the Leeds charts.

On 26 April 1924, Leeds beat Nelson 1-0 before a bumper 20,000 Elland Road crowd. Nelson were at the wrong end of the table, but put in a spirited display and enjoyed the better moments of the first half, but Fairclough's half-time talk did the trick.

The *Yorkshire Post* commented: "By sweeping passes, the Nelson goal was often in jeopardy, but good approach play was missed by faulty shooting from scoring positions," as Leeds attempted to make their pressure tell in the second half.

With three minutes left to play, a Joe Harris corner found Walter Coates to score the only goal of the game and sent Leeds United up to the First Division for the first time. Leeds supporters poured on to the turf in celebration.

Fairclough and Norman had worked wonders on a small budget to create a side that had won the Second Division by three points from Bury and Derby County.

It will come as no surprise that during the celebrations and speeches that took place after the final whistle a common theme raised its head. The club appealed for financial help to those that had stayed behind. Financial malaise and Leeds United have never been far apart.

Fairclough signed high profile players in a bid to compete in the First Division. Tom Jennings and Russell Wainscoat came in to add further attacking firepower. Ernie Hart and Tom Townsley were added to strengthen the defence and Willis Edwards and Bobby Turnbull were recruited to make an impact.

The next few seasons tested the team to the full as they just managed to cling on to their Division One status. 1924/25 saw them finish 18th with Swann top-scoring again with 11 goals. 1925/26 and Leeds ended their second season in the top flight in 19th with Tom Jennings scoring 26 goals as he formed a potent strike-force with Russell Wainscoat.

Despite Jennings breaking the record again with 37 of Leeds's 69 goals in the 1926/27 season, Leeds conceded 88 times at the other end and finished 21st and were relegated and Fairclough resigned in the close season.

Fairclough will be remembered as the manager who gave the city its first taste of top-flight football. Despite relegation, he left behind a team that was able to win promotion straight back to the top division a year later under the returning Dick Ray. He had done some wonderful work at Elland Road and his fingerprints were on the club's success throughout the period between the two wars.

Fairclough returned to Barnsley briefly in 1929, but resigned after a year back at Oakwell. Five years later, he made another return, this time as a director. He died in a Sheffield nursing home, aged 72, on 18 March 1948.

BILLY HAMPSON

1935–1947

Don't mention the War

Born: 26 August 1882, Radcliffe, Lancashire
Died: 24 February 1966 (aged 83)

Matches	Won	Drawn	Lost	Points	Pts/Match	Win %
217	70	47	100	257	1.18	32.26%
				RANK	29th/36	29th/36

The Second World War can't ever be said to have come at the right time for anyone. In Billy Hampson's case, it robbed him and his team of a chance to build on the momentum that had been gathering pace at Elland Road.

Hampson, after initially turning to experience to consolidate, developed young talent. It was a strategy threatening to bear fruit.

He was born in Radcliffe on 26 August 1882 and had come to football late. He had played full-back for Rochdale, Bury and Norwich before being signed for £1,250 by Newcastle United in January 1914. After his big money move and, as would happen to his managerial career over 20 years later, a world war got in the way.

The outbreak of war saw Newcastle close its St James' Park ground and a 31-year-old Hampson, who wanted to carry on playing, joined Leeds City as a guest player. He played 91 games between December 1916 and April 1919 and was part of the side that won the unofficial League title in 1918.

He was 37 when the war ended and bizarrely lost his place in the Newcastle side to Billy McCracken, who was even older. McCracken left in 1923 to try his hand at managing Hull City. Hampson became the oldest FA Cup finalist ever, at 41 years and eight months old, in the 1924 final where Newcastle beat Aston Villa 2-0.

In 1927, he moved on to South Shields and played for another three years until, aged 47, he took over as manager of Carlisle United in March 1930. He didn't take to management easily. Carlisle leaked 101 goals as they finished 15th. Two members of his team may ring a bell — Bill Shankly and Bob Batey.

He left Carlisle in May 1933, had a short stint out of the game before a spell in charge of Ashington back in the north-east after they had dropped out of the Football League in 1929.

He returned to Newcastle after the war, aged 37, but had to play second fiddle to the even older Tyneside legend Bill McCracken, who is credited with getting the offside law changed in the 1920s. McCracken became so adept at catching forwards offside that it forced a change in the rules of the game to give attackers a chance.

Hampson had taken over from Dick Ray at Leeds United in March 1935. Leeds were loitering in the bottom half of Division One and finished 18th that season. Hampson sought out some experienced heads to add backbone to the team. He brought in goalkeeper Albert McInroy and forward George Brown, both former England players.

In terms of duration, he would hold the post of manager of Leeds United for longer than anyone. His 12-year period of service spanned the Second World War, although his tenure lasted for five seasons of peacetime football.

In 1935/36 they finished in 11th place and then 19th the following season, avoiding relegation by two points. Back up to 9th in 1937/38 and then 13th in 1938/39.

That season, on 1 October 1938, Leeds hammered Leicester City again, this time 8-2. What was notable that day at Elland Road was the performance from striker Gordon Hodgson.

Hampson had rung the changes up front and brought in young wingers David Cochrane and John Hargreaves. Both scored, but also set up a multitude of chances for Hodgson, who scored five times to enter the record books with United's best-ever haul.

Hodgson had signed from Aston Villa in March 1937, after enjoying success with Liverpool. Leicester City keeper Sandy McLaren had picked the ball out of his own net eight times four years before. This time he caught his studs in the turf mid-way through the first half and tore tendons in his instep. Fred Sharman, a centre-forward, replaced him in goal and soon conceded. Full-back William Frame had a go in goal and struggled too.

Leeds were 3-0 up by half-time and tore through City's defence in the second half. Although Leicester would get their revenge at Filbert Street in February where they won 2-0.

Hampson built a side that blended experience and youth. Goalkeeper Jim Twomey was bought from Newry Town, winger David Cochrane from Portadown and wing-half Bobby Browne from Derry City. All three of the young recruits would go on to represent Ireland.

The club were weak financially and Hampson did well to steer the team through the number of seasons in the First Division he achieved. He often had to sell his better players and ensure young talent was sourced to keep the ship afloat. It was never easy. Right-back Bert Sproston was sold to Tottenham Hotspur for a near record £9,500 in June 1938.

His managerial style ensured a good team spirit and players wanted to stay and fight for their manager. He had their respect.

There are so many stories of tragedy in the 1939-45 World War that a few young footballers in Leeds not fulfilling their potential seems a minor detail. So many sportsmen never came home, including the great spin bowler Hedley Verity from just up the road in Leeds at Yorkshire County Cricket Club. These were young men cut off in their prime.

When the War was over, and football resumed in 1946/47 many of Hampson's team were past their peak. He made the mistake, however, of sticking with many of his pre-War picks. It simply didn't work. It may not have been a sound football decision, but it illustrated the bond that had developed between the manager and his squad. There are worse qualities to be remembered for than misplaced loyalty.

The Football League had resumed and was divided into north and south with Leeds finishing the season bottom of the northern teams.

As sport got back to normal for the 1946/47 top division, Leeds did not improve, collecting 18 points from their 42 matches, with six wins and six draws. Only one point had been won away from Elland Road as they conceded a Leeds-low of 90 goals (the only season where the team has conceded more was 92 in 1959/60) and finished 18 points adrift of safety. It was an unwanted record low that stood for 30 years.

Hampson resigned in April 1947, before relegation had been mathematically confirmed. Many at the club felt he didn't need to go. His resignation was accepted by the club, who appointed him chief scout, which he kept until October 1948. He would go on to work as a coach for Northumberland Schools Football Association.

Hampson died on 23 February 1966 in Congleton, Cheshire.

4

WILLIS EDWARDS

1947–1948

Too much Mr Nice Guy

Born: 28 April 1903, Newton, Derbyshire
Died: 27 September 1988 (aged 85)

Matches	Won	Drawn	Lost	Points	Pts/Match	Win %
47	13	8	26	47	1.00	27.66%
				RANK	30th/36	31st/36

Willis Edwards' association with Leeds United lasted between 1925 and 1960. You could not find anyone more loyal to the cause.

He had played for the club for 18 years before joining the backroom coaching staff and then becoming manager in 1947, when he replaced Billy Hampson. He will be remembered far more fondly for his wonderful play than for his disappointingly brief spell as manager.

After hanging up his boots in 1943, Edwards had become trainer Bob Roxburgh's assistant and took responsibility for the reserves. Toward the end of the relegation season of 1946/47, Hampson had resigned and Edwards was put in temporary charge of the team for the remaining games.

He worked on the team's fitness and skills, but results did not improve in the second tier. He was known as a nice guy and perhaps lacked the grit to make the harsh decisions required in times of strife.

"He seemed to be picking the team with the directors and trainer," full-back Jimmy Dunn would later say. "I think he was just a figurehead; not management material. There was a sense of the club drifting."

By the end of the 1947/48 season, Leeds had just held on to their second-tier status with an 18th placed finish and the board took action, realising they needed a more ruthless hand on the wheel.

Edwards was demoted to assistant manager where his 'yes man' tendencies would be of more use. The plain truth was that Edwards simply wasn't cut out for management, but was a football man to the bone. He was happy to serve under the new manager and give his all to Leeds United and remained at the club for another 12 years.

Born in Derbyshire on 28 April 1903, he began working life down the pit and played football for local club, Newton Rangers.

After unsuccessfully attempting to land a contract with First Division

Blackburn Rovers, he was taken on by Chesterfield on 30 shillings a week. The Spireites had lost their Football League status in 1909 and managed the career of the fledgling young talent of Edwards with patience and an eye on his long-term development.

He made his debut at half-back at the age of 16 against Grimsby in 1919. His talent was immediately obvious, but not enough to impress the scouts of Sheffield United who labelled him too small to make it at a higher level.

Sheffield United got that call very wrong. Edwards would go on to play for England 16 times between 1926 and 1929. Leeds United made a better decision, signing the fledgling talent for £1,500 in March 1925 after he had played 70 times for Chesterfield.

Edwards was thrown into Leeds United's battle against relegation from the First Division alongside Arthur Fairclough's other new signings Tom Jennings and Russell Wainscoat. Edwards was technically gifted, with superb control and the ability to pinpoint his passing. In an era of crunching challenges, he was swift to nip into a tackle and was never booked or sent off in his career.

One clearance he made goes down in Leeds folklore. Instead of jumping to head the ball away from goal he made a handstand and back-heeled the ball away from above where his head would have been.

Arsenal and England's Eddie Hapgood described him as, "An ideal half-back who could go forward or back at any time and all the time." Alan Morton of Rangers and Scotland said Edwards was "a really grand all-round player, so firm on the ball yet so light on his feet and accurate in his passing."

He made his England debut against Wales in March 1926 in a 3-1 defeat and missed only five games until 1929. He played three of his last four internationals alongside Leeds teammate Ernie Hart and the pair were joined by Wilf Copping at Elland Road in 1930. The trio united to provide Leeds with a formidable half-back line until Copping moved to Arsenal in 1934.

Edwards made the last of his 444 Leeds appearances in 1943, aged 39. After ending his long association with Elland Road in 1960, Edwards saw out his working life in a jam factory. He died in October 1988 in Leeds, aged 85.

5

MAJOR FRANK BUCKLEY

1948–1953

The Major

Born: 3 October 1882, Urmston, Lancashire
Died: 21 December 1964, Walsall, West Midlands (aged 82)

Matches	Won	Drawn	Lost	Points	Pts/Match	Win %
225	88	63	74	327	1.45	39.11%
				RANK	17th/36	16th/36

There may have been more successful Leeds managers, but none as interesting or flamboyant as Major Frank Buckley. He carried a Victorian authority in the dressing room and arrived at Leeds United with a huge reputation.

Buckley left Hull to replace Willis Edwards at the end of the 1947/48 season. Whereas Edwards had been too timid to sort out an ailing side, Buckley was not so reserved. He took the tough decisions with relish and relit the fire in bellies. Buckley was in charge and everyone knew it.

The son of Sergeant John Buckley, Frank followed him into the forces in 1900 at the age of 17, signing a 12-year agreement to fight in the Boer War. He was instead sent to Ireland and became a gymnastics instructor and rose from Corporal to Lance-Sergeant before buying himself out of service for £18 in 1903 to play for Aston Villa.

He'd played a lot of sport while at school in Manchester and continued to play cricket, football and rugby. A Villa scout spotted him and recommended that he attend a trial in Birmingham.

Villa had won the English Championship in 1900 and were recognised as one of the biggest sides in the country and the 20-year-old six-foot centre-half found breaking into the first team an impossible task. He also found first-team chances tough to come by at Brighton, Manchester United and Manchester City.

He'd spent four years in football, but had only made 39 first-team appearances, but his career received a boost with a move to Birmingham City where he played 55 games in two seasons.

Buckley played very much like he would manage. He was a down to earth defender with few thrills, he drove his side forward from the back and it would be with Derby County from 1911 that his talents would come to the fore.

He played 92 times for the Rams and earned his only England cap in 1914 when he was 30 years old. England were shocked 3-0 by Ireland and Buckley was never called up again.

Derby were promoted to the First Division in his first season at the Baseball Ground and he played 92 times, but he wanted away. He took out a newspaper advert offering himself to any other club. Bradford City stepped in and bought him for £1,000 and paid his £50 release fee.

He only played four times for the Bantams before heading to Fulham Town Hall to sign up for active service.

When at Derby, his no-nonsense style was reinforced when he was hauled in front of a Football Association disciplinary committee for punching a member of an opposing side. He offered no apology, instead telling the committee he would do exactly the same again.

"The other man, he said, used filthy language every time he came near an opponent," a committee member recalled, "and as he persisted after being warned he 'let him have it'."

The football powers that be had agreed to continue playing football during the conflict, but the general public were largely of the opinion that these young, fit men would be better utilised in the war effort. The Home Secretary, William Johnson-Hicks, founded the 17th Service Battalion of the Middlesex Regiment, better known as the 'Football Battalion'.

Buckley was the third man to sign on the dotted line at its launch at Fulham Town Hall in December 1914, but had actually been the first man to step forward, volunteering his services a few days before the meeting. Of 1,800 footballers eligible to join him, only 122 had by the end of 1915, although many footballers had chosen to join other regiments instead.

Buckley's previous army experience saw him start the war as a 2nd Lieutenant and he was in charge of No 1 Platoon which was entirely made up of professional footballers. He was in France by January 1916. In the Battle of Delville Wood at the end of July 1916, he was hit by shrapnel, which tore into his shoulder and punctured his lungs.

"The stretcher party took Major Buckley, but he seemed so badly hit you would not think he would last out as far as the casualty station," remembered George Pyke, the Newcastle United centre-forward after the war.

Buckley was taken to a military hospital in Kent where surgeons removed the shrapnel and saved him. Despite badly injured lungs he was back with his men by January 1917. He was mentioned in dispatches in 1917 after the 17th Middlesex were involved in hand-to-hand fighting. He was gassed in the conflict and his lungs suffered again, so much so that he was sent home.

His wounds ended his playing days and his regiment suffered heavy losses and produced many tales of gallantry with Cardiff City's Lyndon Soe awarded the Distinguished Conduct Medial.

Having survived the war, and aged 36, Buckley opted to return to football as a manager. He took charge at Norwich City in 1919, where, strapped for cash, his aptitude for spotting young talent proved very useful. He used the many contacts he had made during the war to widen his network. He even played one match himself in September 1919.

He left the Canaries in 1920 after a series of disagreements and financial issues. It hadn't been the successful managerial baptism he'd been hoping for and he opted to work as a commercial traveller for Maskells, a confectionary maker, a role he performed for three years.

But then by chance he bumped into Albert Hargreaves, a director at Blackpool. He was enjoying his job with Maskells, but the promise of transfer funds and a decent wage persuaded him to join the Seasiders in 1920.

He brought in a youth system and redesigned and changed the colour of their playing shirt to tangerine as he wanted his side to be "bright and vibrant" for a "new age".

He donned a tracksuit and took part in training, which few managers did at the time. He introduced physiotherapists, encouraged good nutrition and a strict fitness culture. He was fifty years ahead of his time and certainly the first in British football to incorporate such regimes into football management.

Buckley oversaw the emergence of strikers Harry Bedford and William Tremelling, but soon lost them to Derby County and Preston North End respectively.

After four years in the seaside town, he moved on to Wolverhampton Wanderers, taken to the West Midlands by a board that had been impressed by his transfer record of buying low and selling high. At Wolves, he recruited from further afield by employing an extensive scouting system that operated nationally to scoop players from under the nose of other clubs. His ability to uncover talent on the cheap and sell it on for profit further down the line made Wolves over £100,000 during a single season.

The Major was forward-thinking, unconventional and a little bit bonkers. After an embarrassing loss to Mansfield, he made his players train in Wolverhampton town centre and put them through their paces with a tough set of drills in front of their supporters.

He was ruthless, driven and massively ahead of his time. Every player was given a booklet which detailed exactly what was expected of them. The rules were made public and supporters were encouraged to report anyone they saw breaching the disciplinary standards.

The use of psychologists was incredibly uncommon, but Buckley wasn't afraid to do anything to maximise the squad at his disposal. When Wolves striker Gordon Clayton considered giving up the game after a goal drought led supporters to mercilessly barrack him during games, Buckley sent him to see a psychologist.

Clayton scored 14 goals in the next 15 matches and wrote to Buckley's wife: "The very name of Wolverhampton Wanderers was a nightmare to me. I detested the place. I do not think I was liked or respected by a single person with the exception of Major Buckley."

It was common knowledge that Buckley gave his players "pep pills", likely to be some kind of amphetamine, and then there were the monkey testicles.

Buckley first met the chemist Menzies Sharp in 1937. Sharp had studied under renowned French surgeon Serge Voronoff who had developed theories about grafting monkey testicles. The controversial 'Monkey Gland' treatment required 12 injections and was said to improve strength and confidence.

Ultimately, it was found that they only had a placebo effect and Voronoff's reputation never recovered.

"To be honest, I was rather sceptical," Buckley said. "And thought it best to try it out on myself first. The treatment lasted three or four months. Long before it was over I felt so much benefit that I asked the players if they would be willing to undergo it."

Only two Wolves players refused to take the injections and it seemed to have an incredible effect. Wolves went on a superb run. They beat Everton 7-0 and Leicester City 10-1, results which prompted both sides to register complaints with the Football League. A doping scandal ensued with questions asked in the House of Commons.

The 'Monkey Gland' treatments began to lose credibility when Wolves lost 4-1 to Portsmouth in the 1939 FA Cup Final, which had been dubbed the 'Monkey Gland Final'. The humans had won.

The complaints made by Everton and Leicester were rejected at the end of the season because the injections had not been forced on the players. But, after a number of other clubs also tried the treatment, the Football Association issued guidelines but stopped short of banning the process.

Wolves had finished second in the First Division for the second year running, this time just one point behind Arsenal. It was the closest Buckley would ever get to silverware, although Wanderers did lift the 1942 Football League War Cup.

Buckley took no rubbish from his team. His emphasis on fitness, diet and behaviour stayed with him throughout his managerial career. Players were not permitted to smoke, he arranged for them to stay overnight in hotels before matches and told them to have two early nights before every game. He also resisted signing players that were married, believing that wives would "get in the way". Of his 1937 squad at Wolverhampton, all 40 were single.

"If you had a rotten game you'd hardly dare go in at half-time," recalled his keeper Don Bilton. "You were going to get the biggest bawling at. He cursed and swore at you. So, from that point of view he was a terrible chap."

In 1939, aged 56, Buckley had tried to re-join the army, but was told that he was too old. Instead, he ran a Home Guard unit and marched his men to Molineux for training.

It was a surprise to all at Wolves when, after the war, Buckley chose to join Notts County. The groundwork had been done at Wolverhampton Wanderers for the side which won three league Championships and two FA Cups in the 1950s.

He'd been lured into the Third Division by a massive wage of £4,500 a year and repaid that when he signed Jesse Pye on a free transfer to then sell him a year later to former club Wolves for £10,000. Buckley moved on quickly to Third Division Hull City.

Two years after moving to Boothferry Park, he joined Leeds United. By this time, he was 65 years old and moved to Elland Road in 1948 with the target of restoring the West Yorkshire side's Division One status.

A young man on the groundstaff had asked the manager to pay him 30 shillings for six buckets full of weeds he had removed from the Elland Road surface.

"Get out of here!" the Major yelled from behind his office desk. "You're already getting paid to do that. Don't ever let me see you up here again with your buckets!"

That youngster was Jack Charlton who would go on and win the World Cup with England in 1966.

Buckley was the first professional manager appointed by Leeds that had experience of success elsewhere. Leeds, who had struggled financially for many years, turned to Buckley with a track record of profitability in the transfer market.

Welsh giant John Charles signed for the club on his 17th birthday and would become one of the biggest British stars of his generation. Buckley built the side around him.

Buckley did his customary financially sound deals in the transfer market. Centre-half Roly Depear came in from Boston for £500 in May 1948 and was sold for £8,000 to Newport a year later. Con Martin and

Aubrey Powell were both sold for five figure fees.

But despite Buckley's willingness to strengthen Leeds United's coffers, he resisted selling on Charles who was pivotal to the side.

The new boss raised admission prices, got rid of all of the club's older players and in his first season led the club to a 15th place finish. The decline had been halted. Tommy Burden had been signed from Chester on the recommendation of Willis Edwards and would become a very popular captain.

He also tried the monkey glands again but this time via a combination of injections and capsules. The success of this strategy was unproven.

"I didn't take them," said John Charles. "But the smaller people took them. He thought it was good for them. It was in his mind that those monkey gland treatments would do the players well and they would play better. I don't think it did, but that's what he thought."

Despite his hard work, promotion with Leeds eluded Buckley. In five years at the club, he recorded finishes of 15th, 5th, 5th, 6th and 10th and they made it through to the FA Cup sixth round for the first time in the club's history in 1950.

That FA Cup run had seen Leeds beat Carlisle 5-2 away in the Third Round. Bolton required a replay after a 1-1 draw with Bolton at Elland Road saw the Whites through 3-2. A Fifth-Round win over Cardiff had set up a quarter-final tie with Arsenal which saw 150 coaches travel from West Yorkshire to London to be part of a 62,000 strong crowd that saw Leeds beaten 1-0.

Ken Chisholm played for Leeds in the 1948/49 season. He was a Scotsman who was not afraid to voice an opinion. He'd been a fighter pilot in the war and had scored 17 goals in 40 games

"Ken was a character, a good poacher who liked to go out with the lads for a drink," Jimmy Dunn, an inside-forward for Wolves, remembered. "Buckley told him, 'This city's not big enough for both of us and I'm not going.' So ultimately Chisholm went — to Leicester City in an exchange deal that brought Ray Iggleden to Elland Road."

After five years at Elland Road, Buckley decided he could take the team no further and resigned in April 1953. He left before the fruits of his youth policy became evident.

He had not stopped innovating. He played ballroom dance songs over the PA system during training.

"We used to have to dance across the pitch," remembered John Charles. "He'd have us all running round and he'd stop you and he'd say 'right, take your partners and start dancing. One, two, three. One, two, three'. We used to go right across the field and back again."

Buckley liked a contraption too. He tried a few but was best known for the 'shooting box' which fired balls towards players at different angles to improve their control, agility and balance.

"Beneath the gruff exterior he was a kind man," said Jack Charlton. "My shoes must have been a sight and he asked me if they were the only pair I had. I nodded. The next morning, he handed me a pair of Irish brogues, the strongest, most beautiful shoes I'd ever seen. And I had them for years."

Tommy Burden had played under the Major at Wolverhampton and Leeds. "At Leeds, there were never training sessions such as they had at Wolves where players would come in the morning and go out running in spiked shoes," he remembered. "In his last season, Tom Holley only used to train at night.

"Buckley was a shock to Leeds United. He couldn't bear a player who only had one foot. He felt that if you earned your living at football you should be able to use both feet. He had a go at me about it in front of the rest of the players. I remember him looking at his little Welsh terrier and saying, 'You've got a better left foot than him, haven't you?'

"The new Leeds manager cut an extraordinary figure. He spoke like an upper-class gentleman. I remember him bawling out Len Browning one day for not saying good morning. He always wore Oxford bags and his shoes were hand welted, shining to perfection. You didn't call him Frank, you called him Major."

Buckley, who had built his reputation on a scouting network that was hugely bolstered by his many connections in the game, found his powers diminished as those allies around the game got older and either retired or died.

He moved to Walsall and saw his side relegated in his second season. He retired at the end of the 1954/55 season and spent the last decade of his life in Walsall, where he died aged 82. His ashes were scattered on the Malvern Hills.

Major Frank Buckley was a pioneer and revolutionary in the game, perhaps before it was completely ready for that advancement. His influence, however, has shaped the game ever since. Many of the players under his charge went on to become successful managers and his practices are now commonplace.

In the 2013 Football League 125-year celebrations, Wolves fans voted Buckley as the club's third greatest ever manager and in April 2015, he was awarded the prestigious 'Contribution to League Football' award by the Football League.

6

RAICH CARTER

1953–1958

The Silver Fox

Born: 21 December 1913, Hendon, Sunderland
Died: 9 October 1994, Walsall, West Midlands (aged 80)

Matches	Won	Drawn	Lost	Points	Pts/Match	Win %
217	90	51	76	321	1.48	41.47%
				RANK	12th/36	13th/36

Horatio, or Raich as he was known, Carter was an exceptional sportsman and one of the few to have played professionally at both football and cricket.

Carter was an inside-forward blessed with a huge amount of skill. Nicknamed the 'Silver Fox' because of his grey hair and cunning play, he was also known as 'The Maestro' because of his talent and ability to control a game with his trickery.

His father, Robert, had played football for Port Vale, Fulham and Southampton and Raich would follow him into the sport in 1931 when, at the age of 18, he became a Sunderland player.

He made 245 appearances and scored 118 goals and became the youngest man to captain a side to a league title in the 1935/36 season. A year later, he lifted the FA Cup as he scored in the Black Cats' 3-1 win over Preston North End at Wembley.

Biographer Frank Garrick, likened Carter's style of play to Paul Scholes. A player of exceptional quality, he was a string-puller, threading the killer pass and as happy being creative as he was banging the goals in.

Although he occupied a place in midfield, Carter was Sunderland's joint top scorer in their Championship winning season as the Mackems ended Arsenal's domestic dominance. The Gunners had won three titles in a row, but Carter scored a memorable hat-trick against them in a league-clinching 5-4 win. He would pop up to score a last-minute winner against the same opposition in the Charity Shield the following season.

It had been Sunderland's sixth title, but the FA Cup win in 1937 was their first. Carter assisted two goals and scored one as his side won 3-1 against Preston. He climbed the Wembley steps to receive the trophy from the Queen in her coronation year.

Such was the standard of his play for both Sunderland and England that Madame Tussauds made a waxwork of him.

When war broke out, Carter was 26. When peacetime returned, he was 32 and his peak years were behind him. He had served in the RAF and would appear as a guest player for Derby County whilst rehabilitating as an injured airman at RAF Loughborough.

During the conflict, he was awarded 17 unofficial international caps and scored 18 goals.

Sunderland viewed him as pivotal to their post-war hopes. But Carter wanted a longer deal than was offered as his wife was ill and so much of his career had been taken from him.

"Sunderland were silly to sell me for that price and Derby were lucky to get me," Carter said modestly after the Black Cats' offers were insufficient and Derby swooped in with an £8,000 transfer. Together they enjoyed immediate success.

Back at Wembley for the 1946 FA Cup final, Derby beat Charlton 4-1. "I knew we'd win the cup because Raich said so," said teammate Reg Harrison. Carter is the only man to have won the FA Cup on both sides of the war.

He also dovetailed a short spell as a cricketer for Derbyshire when he was playing football for Derby County.

To say Carter was a successful professional cricketer would be an overstatement. His career in county cricket was short-lived, but that he had one at all illustrates what a talented all-round sportsman he was.

He represented Derbyshire in 1946 and would later play for Durham briefly in Minor Counties cricket. To begin with he was asked to play for Derbyshire's 2nd XI. He top-scored with 47 against Nottinghamshire 2nd XI and accepted an offer to play professionally.

Carter would only play three County Championship matches. His batting wasn't tight enough technically and his shot selection would let him down. He only made eight runs in four innings and found playing a full day of county cricket exhausting. His bowling stood up to the challenge. His best bowling was 2-39, but he was too old at 32 to have the desire to improve as a player. Cricket's top level was beyond him and he settled for turning out for Derbyshire in benefit matches.

Carter, now in his mid-thirties, was keen to move into management and realised he was going to have to move elsewhere to get that opportunity. Many clubs were interested in signing one of the best players in England and it was a blow to a number of big clubs when Carter opted to join Third Division side Hull City.

Carter was impressed with the ambition of the Hull directors and their manager Major Frank Buckley. The signing, for £6,000, saw Carter installed as a player and assistant manager to Buckley. It was a major triumph for the Tigers and posters were plastered all over the city telling everyone 'Carter Will Play'.

Carter won the last of his 13 England caps in 1947 in an international career that had seen him score seven goals and span 13 years and was cruelly robbed of his peak powers. He played his final game for England in 1947 in a 6-0 thrashing of Switzerland at Highbury.

Most football fans will have heard the name Stanley Matthews, but not so many Raich Carter. Carter, however, can be referred to very much in the same breath and it's a cruel twist that he isn't held in higher esteem. Matthews certainly classed him as an ideal foil for his own legendary play.

He said that Carter "was the ideal partner for me. Carter was a supreme entertainer who dodged, dribbled, twisted and turned, sending bewildered left-halves madly along false trails. Inside the penalty box with the ball at his feet and two or three defenders snapping at his ankles, he'd find the space to get a shot in at goal... Bewilderingly clever, constructive, lethal in front of goal, yet unselfish. Time and again he'd play the ball out wide to me and with such service I was in my element."

It wasn't long after Carter's Hull debut that Buckley resigned to move away to manage Leeds. It soon became apparent that, despite his lack of managerial experience, Carter would be installed as Hull's new boss. He was given full control of the team and excitement was at fever pitch that such a superb talented player was operating at Third Division level and was going to take Hull to new heights. Even opposition fans were heard to cheer his arrival at their grounds.

Attendances were approaching 50,000 and when the Tigers drew Manchester United in the FA Cup Sixth Round tickets were gold dust. A 55,019-crowd watched United struggle to get past Hull as they man-marked Carter out of the match. A 73rd minute winner saw Hull eliminated but their performances were taking national headlines.

Hull were promoted at the end of the 1948/49 season and Carter established them as a solid Second Division side.

Don Revie, then a 22-year-old, jumped at the chance to sign for Carter and Hull in November 1949. To play in the same team as his schoolboy hero was something that Revie couldn't refuse.

Revie moved from Leicester City for £20,000 after Carter had been impressed with the inside-forward when he had played against Hull earlier in the season.

Carter played on until 1953 when aged almost 40. He had long earmarked Revie as his replacement as Hull's creative dynamo. Revie loved playing with his mentor and was inspired by the way Carter found space on the pitch and find the killer pass.

As a partnership they were too similar and Carter said later, "I think he let me down. I was expecting too much too soon. Revie didn't play as well as I thought he would. I always thought he was an inside-forward, but he didn't have the punch an inside-forward should."

Carter retired as Hull boss in 1951 and began a new life running a sweet shop in Hull. Revie moved on to Manchester City a month later for £25,000 and without them both Hull's form worsened. Carter was begged back at the end of the season and managed to steer the club clear of relegation.

In the English Football League, Carter had played 451 games and scored 215 goals. In January 1953, he was back as a player-manager for Cork Athletic in Ireland, leading the team to an Irish Cup win that same year. Carter went out with a bang, scoring the winning goal in Cork's Cup final replay. But that was as far as his ageing legs would take him and he hung up his boots for good.

And that's when Leeds United took him to Elland Road in 1953, where just as he had done at Hull, he replaced Major Frank Buckley.

The Major had come close to promotion back to Division One, but hadn't delivered top-tier football to the city. It was Carter's task to complete the job. The script was the same for Carter, as with managers before him. He had some terrific players, John Charles the star, but little money.

Leeds finished 10th in Carter's first season, which was exactly the same as Buckley had achieved in his final season before moving on. But Charles was magnificent as he hit a club record 42 goals in 39 league matches.

Carter had been at the very top of the English game and did not lack belief in his own abilities. Some of the Leeds squad interpreted that as arrogance. He'd been the same as a player. He would parade around the midfield as if he owned the place, and, more often than not, he did. A peacock, the game would flow through him, at his pace. He was the leading man that brought his supporting cast in when he saw fit. He took shots with both equally strong feet and was in control, complete charge, and looked like he knew it.

Perhaps it was that ability to be magnificent that made him resent the mundane. The admin, paperwork, the day-to-day tasks bored him. It had seemingly come so easily to him that he found it almost impossible to understand a mere mortal's struggle. It is difficult to argue with his arrogance, because he'd been good enough not to have to argue his own defence.

Tommy Burden left Leeds for Bristol City early in the 1954/55 season. A free-kick routine had gone awry in a 5-3 defeat to Bury. "Carter was blaming the goalkeeper John Scott. I thought 'This isn't fair' so I turned around and said, 'You're the one who's bloody well to blame'. We fell out. I think Raich suffered from thinking that there weren't many better players than he."

Jack Charlton wasn't a big admirer of Carter's managerial abilities either: "Raich Carter wasn't a coach, and he didn't employ coaches. Everyone respected him as a great player of the past, but he didn't understand that you might need help to work on your game. Maybe Raich was such a good player that he didn't understand how things that came easily to him might be difficult for other people.

"The only training we used to do at Elland Road in those days was to run down the long side of the pitch, jog the short side, sprint the long side, and so on. We used to have five-a-side and eight-a-side matches on the cinder surface of the car park. But no one ever coached you, there was nobody you could talk to about your game, we never went out and practised free kicks or corner kicks or anything like that. We never really had any team talks, and we never had a run down on the opposition.

"Leeds United wasn't what I would call a professional club in those days. You trained in the morning — you went home — nobody bothered what you did the rest of the day."

Considering Carter was following Buckley, a manager acknowledged for his authoritarian style of management, Carter was categorised by John Charles as being similar, but without sufficient substance to back up his viewpoint.

"Carter was very opinionated," said Charles. "He had the view 'I do it this way, so you do it this way, whichever way I say'. He wouldn't let you argue. He was a nice man, but he loved himself. He would take the credit for what you'd done."

Yet Carter was well placed to pass his own skills on to Charles's game and undoubtedly made him a better player.

The 1955/56 season delivered the promise of First Division football as Carter's side gained promotion after nine seasons in Division Two. Ending their campaign in second place, the team scored 80 goals and won 23 of their 42 games played.

John Charles was top scorer with 29 goals, and he'd increase that tally the following season in the First Division. His 39 goals included 38 in the league and enabled Leeds to finish in 8th place.

Charles was the club's prized asset and a fine line had been walked for some time when it came to his future. It was always seen as a balancing act. A huge component of the team that contributed massively to any success, against Leeds's perpetual financial struggle. To cash in or not was the conundrum.

At the end of the 1956/57 season, the board finally decided the time had come to take the money and a world record fee of £65,000 was agreed with Italian giants Juventus. Carter had believed he would receive all, or the majority, of the money to invest in new players. That was not to be.

The manager always maintained he received less than half of Charles's fee and, without their goal machine, Leeds plummeted to a 17th place finish at the end of the 1957/58 season. Carter's contract was up for renewal and he was stunned when the board confirmed that his time was over.

Carter had gained the club promotion, had not received backing in the transfer market, but had still reinforced their status as a First Division side. He was understandably devastated not to be given more time to rival the best of English football.

Disillusioned, he stayed away from the sport for a while, but eventually it was always going to lure him back. He became manager of Third Division Mansfield Town in January 1960. By the time of his arrival, the descent to relegation had been established and the following two seasons were spent struggling to get back.

Carter had moved on to Middlesbrough by the time Mansfield's promotion back to the Third Division had been confirmed. He took charge of Second Division Boro in January 1963, but Brian Clough's prolific scoring power had left for Sunderland and Carter found it difficult to inspire any kind of improvement.

Three years after arriving at Boro, Carter was dismissed as the team plummeted towards relegation to the Third Division for the first time ever.

Carter was a laid-back character who had been an incredible player and assumed everyone he managed would have his mindset and talent. It was patently not the case and Stan Anderson, one of his coaches at Middlesbrough, remembers a coach journey that, to him, epitomised Carter's laid-back manner.

"On the coach going to the match, I had a word with Raich and told him that he needed to give the players a strong team talk before the game," Anderson recalled. "He really needed to gee the lads up, because we were dropping down the league like a stone. So, the coach pulls to a halt in the car park. Raich stood up and said, 'Right lads, here we are, safely arrived at our destination. Look at this man sitting next to me who drove us here.

He got us here correctly, safely and did a smooth professional job. That's what I want from you tonight lads. Give me a professional job. Right, over to you Stan.'

"I was speechless," Anderson exclaimed. "I had to get up and follow that! I did my best, but of course, we lost the match. The problem was that because Raich was such an exceptionally gifted footballer he couldn't understand that most players would never be as good as he was no matter how hard they tried."

That was Carter's last position in football, and he returned to Hull to run a retail sports outlet and then a credit business. He suffered a stroke in September 1994, and passed away at his home at Willerby, near Hull, aged 81, leaving a widow, two daughters and a son.

Carter is remembered as a hero in Sunderland where there is a Sports Centre named after him. In Hull, they named a road after him. In Leeds, few would now know his name.

7

BILL LAMBTON

1958–1959

Iron Man Bill

Born: 2 December 1914, Nottingham
Died: 16 September 1976, Sherwood, Nottingham (aged 61)

Matches	Won	Drawn	Lost	Points	Pts/Match	Win %
24	10	2	12	32	1.33	41.66%
				RANK	22nd/36	11th/36

The Leeds United board's unwillingness to offer a new contract to Raich Carter had not only surprised the outgoing manager. It had taken the supporters and media by surprise also.

If as a board you decide to part company with a manager that isn't quite cutting the mustard, there must be confidence that the replacement will make tangible improvements.

Bill Lambton, a former army sergeant major, had been recruited by Carter as a trainer-coach in November 1957. He had replaced Bob Roxburgh, who had been at the club for over 20 years. The veteran was moved to oversee physiotherapy and Lambton took his place.

John Charles had been gone for a full season and the team were struggling without him. The methods that Lambton employed were found a bit peculiar by the Leeds players, who struggled to warm to his lack of football prowess.

When Carter left the club, Lambton was made manager, initially on an interim basis, which already seemed a strange decision considering he'd never been in such an elevated position before.

There are few positives about Lambton's tenure and he certainly didn't deliver success to Elland Road, although he found two men that would. He signed a teenager called Billy Bremner and a 31-year-old Don Revie.

He wasn't the right man. If the same scenario played out in modern times there would be thousands of words written speculating, hypothesising and ridiculing the choices made. It's unknown who the target was for chairman Sam Bolton and his Leeds board, but it is certain that Lambton wasn't the number one on their shortlist. And then Lambton stayed on longer than was originally intended.

Lambton began with a 4-0 away defeat at Bolton on the opening day of the 1958/59 season. It was a struggle and by early November Leeds had gained only 12 points from 16 games. They were third from bottom of the table and Lambton was forced to delve into the transfer market and Revie was brought in from Sunderland for £14,000.

Revie was a former England international and came into the team as Leeds strung four wins together to move up to 11th in the table. It was a run that convinced the board that Lambton was worth a punt in the role full-time. He was made permanent manager on 9 December 1958.

Whoever had been on the shortlist, the bigger names the support and playing staff had been waiting for, hadn't materialised and the cards were stacked against Lambton from the outset. When one hears that a certain manager had 'lost the dressing room', it would seem Lambton never held the complete respect of the Leeds players.

"Bill was a nice enough man, but he wasn't a player, he wasn't a coach, he wasn't anything," stated Jack Charlton. "If you ever saw Bill walking about he always had a piece of paper in his hand — nobody ever found out what was written on that paper, but it made him look as though he was doing something.

"Bill was a fitness fanatic," Charlton added. "I remember one windy day, when we complained about the balls being too hard during a training session, Bill told us that anyone worth his salt ought to be able to kick balls in his bare feet and never feel it, so one of the lads said, 'Well, go on then.' Now Bill wasn't a pro, he'd probably never kicked a ball in anger in his life, and yet here he was running up to kick the ball in his bare feet, and of course you could see him wincing afterwards. This is the manager who's just been appointed, and he's making a fool of himself in front of his players. He finished up hobbling off the pitch, with all of us laughing at him. Bill never recovered from that day."

Lambton had attempted to be a professional footballer, but barely made a ripple. As a goalkeeper, he had joined Nottingham Forest in 1935, but he wasn't a talented player and hardly featured. He moved on to Exeter City and then Doncaster Rovers, but again limited statistics on a limited player suggest he made a total of four first-team appearances across an 11-year career spanning the war.

He moved into coaching in Denmark where he was given the opportunity to work at KB Copenhagen. During his time overseas, he gained some attention when working as a fitness trainer with British boxers.

His coaching style concentrated more on fitness than football and he was soon back in England with Scunthorpe where he had players trampolining.

And then the call from Carter had taken him to Leeds with a CV as thin as Jack Charlton's brother's hairline.

After the brief run of success that met Revie's arrival, results returned to disappointing once again. Wilbur Cush had stood down as Leeds captain with Revie the unanimous and obvious choice to succeed him.

Grenville Hair and Jack Overfield had lost patience with Lambton and asked him to put them on the transfer list. Leeds travelled to Wolverhampton and were thumped 6-2 and the board were getting fidgety.

As Charlton had intimated, the writing was on the wall. The players and directors met, and everyone present openly expressed their dissatisfaction and complete lack of faith in Lambton.

"A few weeks later we had a meeting, and after some of the lads had their say, the chairman asked if we wanted the manager to leave and every one of the players said yes. Bill said pathetically, 'If you let me stay, we'll have a new start,' but nobody said a dicky bird. He was sacked that same day.

"I felt sorry for Bill. I didn't take him seriously as a football man, but I got on alright with him. I used to see him later from time to time when he was running a pub on the Leeds-Grimsby road, and he seemed much happier."

Lambton resigned after that February 1959 meeting and claimed "interference" in his training methods had been the reason for his failure to achieve positive results. He had been in charge for only four months.

The man that Lambton had initially come to Leeds to replace, Bob Roxburgh, was put in temporary charge for the final 10 games of the season, where Leeds finished 15th in the First Division.

Lambton should never have been put in a position where he was patently out of his depth. He moved back to Scunthorpe where he spent an unwanted record of the then shortest ever managerial career. He was in charge for three days in April 1959, although it was said later the appointment had only ever been verbal and not contractual.

It seems bewildering that some people, with a zero-track record of any success are given opportunities. The men with genuine claims for managerial positions must have been banging their head against brick walls the length and breadth of the country.

Lambton moved on to take caretaker charge of Grimsby Town until February 1960. He resurfaced as manager of Chester between November 1961 and July 1963 and then quit football and returned to live in his native Nottinghamshire until his death, aged 61, in September 1976.

8

JACK TAYLOR

1959–1961

Beans on toast management

Born: 15 February 1914, Barnsley, Yorkshire
Died: 22 February 1968, Barnsley, Yorkshire (aged 64)

Matches	Won	Drawn	Lost	Points	Pts/Match	Win %
78	26	17	35	95	1.22	33.33%
				RANK	26th/36	28th/36

If you are going to ever be asked to 'follow that' into the Leeds United dugout, jumping into the shoes of Bill Lambton would not be the most daunting of tasks.

Jack Taylor arrived at Elland Road in May 1959 full of hope and belief that he would be the man to take Leeds to the very top of the English game. Taylor inherited a club that was rudderless, had been deemed a joke for taking a hapless punt on the inexperienced Lambton and the players needed a lift in morale and discipline.

He was third choice for the position. It wouldn't take him long to see why others had turned the job down. There was a mountain to climb.

Leeds chairman Sam Bolton thought he had got his first-choice candidate only for Arthur Turner, the manager of Headington United and former Birmingham City boss, to change his mind at the last moment. He was persuaded to stay at Headington, a club that would become Oxford United. Turner would help them gain admission to the Football League.

A familiar face at the club was former skipper Tommy Burden, but he also turned down the offer to return to Elland Road. It was not a tempting job for many after Lambton's amateur hour reign had turned the club into a poisoned chalice.

Over to you Jack Taylor…

Taylor, from Barnsley, had joined the Wolverhampton groundstaff in 1931 as a 17-year-old. He became a professional in January 1934 for the First Division club and made his debut on 1 February 1936 in a 5-0 defeat to Bradford City. When Cecil Shaw left at the end of 1936, Taylor became a regular and formed a solid full-back partnership with his younger brother Frank.

He was part of Major Frank Buckley's promising side of the 1930s and was ever-present throughout the 1937/38 season as Wolves missed out on the League title by a solitary point. He made 79 League games for Wolves before being transferred to Norwich City in Division Two where he played 34 league games during one full season before the suspension of the Football League due to the outbreak of World War Two.

Taylor played for Barnsley and Watford as a guest player during wartime before re-joining Norwich who had fallen into the Third Division South and were forced to seek re-election after ending the 1946/47 season in 21st.

He reunited with Major Frank Buckley at Hull City in July 1947, before seeing out his career with the Tigers under another future Leeds manager, Raich Carter. Taylor hung up his boots after making 72 league appearances for Hull and helping them win the Third Division North in 1948/49.

As a manager, Taylor cut his teeth with Weymouth in the Southern League before being picked up by Queens Park Rangers in June 1952. QPR had finished bottom of the Third Division (South) under former Leeds United forward Dave Mangnall. He was in charge at Loftus Road for nine years doing nothing more than a solid job, steering QPR from relegation fights to mid-table anonymity. He often returned to the Leeds area to scout and sign the local talent.

He walked into Leeds United in May 1959 with spirts low and discipline poor. Dominant dressing room figures needed effective management or there would have to be consequences. Both Eric Kerfoot and Jimmy Dunn had been outspoken opponents of Bill Lambton and if left to their own devices, as two popular figures on the terraces, could quickly turn the tide against Taylor too. Both men, after loyal service, were coming to the end of their careers and Taylor wisely opted to move them on.

On the pitch, however, the season was not going well and Taylor's move to get rid of Kerfoot and Dunn hadn't curried favour with the supporters, particularly as neither had been effectively replaced.

He brought with him Syd Owen, who arrived from Luton Town, and trainer Les Cocker came with him to facilitate the nurturing of new talent.

The new manager needed to consolidate Leeds's position in the game, certainly not continue to let them slide, but a porous defence resulted in relegation. It would be unfair to point the finger squarely at Taylor. Lambton had metaphorically left a prawn behind the radiator and the smell of his mismanagement overpowered Taylor's efforts.

Jack Charlton and Grenville Hair remained solid at the back, but there was little or no support for them. Taylor sold striker Alan Shackleton to Everton in May 1959, which again made fans scratch their heads. He successfully recruited a replacement in John McCole who came in at a price of £10,000 from Bradford City with the powerful frontman banging in 22 goals in 33 league games, although contributions from elsewhere on the park were few and far between.

With goals flooding into their own net, Taylor signed defender Freddie Goodwin from Manchester United for £10,000, but it was far too late to make a difference.

They were already condemned to relegation. Leeds had scored 65 goals and conceded 92 and were relegated on 34 points.

"We got a manager called Jack Taylor, and his brother Frank joined the club as coach," recalled Jack Charlton. "In those days, managers didn't wear tracksuits, but Frank did. He was the first guy who ever took me out on a pitch and taught me how to kick a ball properly — following it through, keeping it low, chipping balls, that sort of thing. One thing he did was to lay down two bricks and place the ball between them, then ask you to run up and hit it full on. You soon learned to keep your eye on the ball! I could talk to the Taylors about the game, and suddenly I felt I had kindred spirits within the club.

"But the other players didn't respond well to the new approach," Charlton continued. "Their general attitude was that they came into the club to do their bit of training, played their matches, and then buggered off. They just weren't interested in developing their own skills or any theory or anything like that."

Physiotherapist Bob English had been working at the club since 1957 and had been hoping for more dynamism from a new manager.

"The club was not in a good state before Don Revie took over," he stated. "There wasn't much enthusiasm, I didn't think. Jack Taylor was a nice man, don't get me wrong, but he didn't crack the whip enough. Training was slack though Don Revie, as a player, was a great fellow as far I am concerned... he was one of the ones that really did train.

"But Taylor never came out to watch people training. I think I remember him only once getting out his tracksuit and coming out to join us," English recalled, in stark contrast to the memories of Charlton.

Taylor inherited Billy Bremner from Lambton and found a player that was growing increasingly frustrated by what he had found in Leeds.

"It just wasn't run as a professional football club," Bremner said later. "To go to see Mr Taylor: Christ, you had to go through one secretary, then another, and finally you would get to the third secretary and she would say he couldn't see you. The only time you ever saw the manager was if you travelled with the first team on a Saturday. Training was just doing laps... a kickabout with a ball... no ball on a Friday... just sprints.

"We went to play a crucial game towards the end of the season at Blackburn Rovers," Bremner recalled. "I remember wondering where we were going to eat. In the end we stopped at a cafe and had beans on toast. It was all a bit of a rush... yet this was the most important game of the season."

Taylor ousted United stalwarts Archie Gibson, George Meek and Jack Overfield in the close season. Irish international and former skipper Wilbur Cush was also moved on.

The Whites' struggles continued in the second tier as the loyal support was growing impatient.

Taylor was struggling. He recruited a number of new players, but nothing changed, and injuries quickly disrupted any initial momentum.

Goodwin had combined effectively in defence with Jack Charlton in the Second Division. Eric Smith was signed from Celtic, but the Scottish international suffered a broken leg in the second game and was out until after Christmas. Smith was surprised with the atmosphere he found within the squad.

"The players were undisciplined," Smith would remember. "It wasn't their fault. Jack Taylor was the manager but had let things go. I certainly didn't expect what I saw in the first three or four days. We would go on long training runs and players would walk in with ice lollies in their hands."

Former England international winger Colin Grainger arrived, but never excited and the team was far too dependent on John McCole's goals. The striker hit 20 goals in 35 league games, but again no other player got past 10 goals and they sat in the relegation zone for the entire season.

Leeds were in freefall and the board had to act. Harry Reynolds had taken over as chairman from Sam Bolton and he summoned Taylor to give him notice that his recommendation to the board would be dismissal. Taylor resigned on 13 March 1961 with a year yet to run on his £2,000 per year contract.

Taylor's last match in charge was a 1-0 win over Norwich, but that couldn't mask the apathy, malaise and depths the team had sunk to. Leeds had lost the previous four games, conceding 13 goals in the process.

Taylor was required to work wonders to redress the downturn in Leeds fortunes. It had been a challenge completely beyond him. After his departure, he stayed in Yorkshire and died in his hometown of Barnsley on 22 February 1978, aged 64.

Jack Charlton was going nowhere fast as a defender at Leeds. He would tell the ITV cameras for their *Leeds, Leeds, Leeds* documentary, "There was nothing happening at Elland Road. Nobody told you anything.

You trained and you ran and played five or seven-a-side on the car park.

"Every time you opened your mouth, if you said anything about the game, 'shut up, it's got nothing to do with you, you mind your own business and do the job you're told to do'.

"We weren't taught anything, we weren't coached. It was a club that I would have been quite happy if somebody had come in and said, 'would you like to leave'. I would have said 'yes'."

The board acted quickly to replace Jack Taylor and after making some poor choices they made the best decision any Leeds United board had ever come up with.

After turning the page on a few chapters of failure, the next part of the story saw Leeds become the best team in the land. The lives of Jack Charlton and his Leeds teammates were about to change beyond recognition. Success was just around the corner and it was going to be one hell of a lot more fun.

9

DON REVIE

1961–1974

"You get nowt for being second"

Born: 10 July 1927, Middlesbrough, Yorkshire
Died: 26 May 1989, Edinburgh, Scotland (aged 61)

Matches	Won	Drawn	Lost	Points	Pts/Match	Win %
743	396	197	150	1385	1.86	53.30%
				RANK	1st/36	1st/36

If you are reading this book you don't have to be a Leeds fan. To the non-believers, I can't share your views and I hope you didn't get a discount when you made your purchase! But there is one thing that unites us all as football fans — we recognise good football when we see it, even if the colour of the shirt playing might mean we can't always outwardly admire and admit it.

Whether you rant on about 'dirty Leeds', or you hold a more rational view, no one can deny that the Leeds United side that Don Revie assembled at Elland Road between 1961 and 1974 was one of the greatest teams English football has ever seen. It might even have been the best of them all.

Revie took a team of disparate individuals and made it an institution. A city not known for football became renowned for the style, determination and the beauty of its play. And Revie became a hero as big strong Yorkshiremen fell in love with men dressed in white.

"What Don did at Leeds was unbelievable," one of Revie's flair players Johnny Giles told *The Guardian* in 2010. "Don didn't revitalise a team. Leeds had no history. So, he had to create it from nothing. It was a rugby league area. For my first match, when we were in the Second Division, there were 15,000 people there."

Revie had ended a 19-year playing career with 76 appearances and 11 goals for Leeds United between 1958 and 1962. In March 1961, he had accepted the job of player-manager at Elland Road, but it could all have been very different had Leeds not priced him out of accepting the managerial position at Bournemouth. They decided he would be their man instead.

As Giles suggested, Leeds was a rugby league stronghold. 50,000 people turned out to watch the final Leeds Championship match of the 1960/61 rugby league season whilst short of 7,000 attended Leeds

United's final match that same season. And don't forget that the Yorkshire County Cricket Club side dominated the County Championship from the late 1950s throughout the 1960s. Football was some way down the pecking order.

"Leeds hadn't done anything," Revie remembered years later. "They'd been knocked out the FA Cup 11 years on the trot in the third round, which is the first round. And it was something that I really wanted to do even when I was a player. I set up this youth policy because we had no money, we were £250,000 in the red. And I just got stuck into it, good backroom staff, and off we went."

Revie had learned a lot as a player at the club and quickly implemented change.

"When I was a player, I played for five clubs and I think there was only the first club I played for, Leicester City, where I was made to feel part of the club," Revie acknowledged. "But with the clubs I played for you were only a number and nobody took a real interest in your family or what was happening to you. You just trained and you played. I tried to create a family spirit from the off."

He was meticulous in his preparation, players stayed in better hotels, a family culture was promoted at the club where everyone, from star player to cleaner, were recognised as vital cogs in a large wheel. He treated his players as adults, but didn't want big egos.

Revie was a very superstitious man. He changed the owl on the club badge as he believed birds brought bad luck. The club had been known as the 'Peacocks', but under Revie soon became the 'Whites'.

He gave his players freedom, although he was also quick to ensure they didn't take liberties. He kept tabs on their private lives and was not averse to telling players to finish with girlfriends if he felt they were unsuitable.

The meticulous nature of his planning led to lengthy dossiers compiled on oppositions which detailed weaknesses and threats. He routinely filled exercise books with handwritten notes on oppositions. He would split matches into 15-minute segments and gather data on every conceivable aspect, both defending and in attack.

"He would go through everything about the opposing team and we had to sit there, and we were so used to it we…," remembered Jack Charlton smiling. "That was the only time Don used to hail at you. 'Listen, somebody's gone and worked, and they've been travelling miles and miles to get this information for you, to make you, so that you know what's going to happen. Listen!'

"The attention to detail, to never leave a stone unturned," Charlton added. "To keep us occupied. If you make a promise to players, you always keep it. He'd move heaven and earth to keep a promise if he made you one."

Revie's concentration on Leeds United being one big family was legendary. "Well, I always place my family first. My wife and my boy Duncan, and Kim, are more important to me than anything in the world. But I'd say next to them is this club, Leeds United. I look on them all, every one of them in this club, as my own son. I'm not afraid to say that. I would do anything for them because they give me 150 per cent."

The manager's indoor bowling tournaments brought the squad together. They all wanted to win after they'd all put a few quid into the pot.

Revie was aware that Billy Bremner had become disillusioned under the previous regime and had considered returning north of the border. He once drove up to Scotland to meet Bremner's girlfriend and persuaded her to encourage Billy to remain in Leeds rather than return home to be closer to her.

Bremner and Jack Charlton had been teammates of Revie's, but the general standard in the squad was not high. Revie would become a legend, yet could easily have been sacked at the end of his first season in charge had Leeds not narrowly staved off relegation from Division Two. Revie played his final game for the club in March 1962.

Revie inherited Les Cocker, Maurice Lindley and Syd Owen onto his coaching staff, and they stayed with him for many seasons. The youth policy reaped rewards as Eddie Gray, Norman Hunter, Peter Lorimer and Paul Reaney were early graduates. He met young players personally to encourage them to join Leeds rather than the more established and glamorous clubs.

"People say 'why did you go to Leeds?'" recalled Peter Lorimer. "Because there were 30-odd teams trying to sign me — Manchester United, Chelsea, Rangers and Celtic in Scotland, and I came to Leeds who were a Second Division side. But I'd been down on several occasions and I'd worked with the young players and I'd seen how good they were, and Don had impressed himself on my family greatly.

"My mother was ill, and he got to hear about it. I got back from training and rung my mother up just to see how she was, and she said, 'I got a lovely basket of fruit and bunch of flowers from Mr. Revie'. He was looking after not only us, he was looking after our families and he was aware of your family and he realised how important it was that your family life, your home life and everything had to be right for you to be concentrating on your job in the field."

Eddie Gray told me about his first impressions of Revie: "The scout first approached my dad in Glasgow. I was playing a Glasgow schoolboy game and he asked my dad if I would be interested in going down and playing for Leeds and to be honest, at that time, I'd never heard of them. I'm serious.

"I had never heard of them because when I was growing up in Glasgow I was a Celtic fan and the big clubs in the fifties and early sixties were Wolverhampton Wanderers and obviously the Busby Babes at Manchester United," Gray continued. "I went down and I was so impressed with the manager and his ideas on the game.

"He had a chairman at the time called Harry Reynolds and he and Don had put a plan together. They knew they couldn't compete financially with the bigger clubs in the country so they decided they would use the money that Harry was going to put into the club to try and get the best young schoolboys.

"They got a tremendous amount of players who would come through the ranks. The year before I came down to Leeds, Peter Lorimer played. Peter was a sought-after schoolboy, a bit similar to myself, and we both ended up at Leeds on the groundstaff. With us we had Jimmy Greenhoff and loads of other players that would go on and make huge names for themselves.

"When I first came down Don impressed me so much with how he looked after me that I just went back home and told my Mum and Dad that I was going to Leeds, which my Dad couldn't really believe," Gray remembered. "When I first came down to Leeds I was only really coming down for a weekend to have a visit and a few days away. But Don met me himself at the station and took me to my hotel and then the first day I went to the club I was training with the 1st team. I was only 14 at the time.

"Don impressed me with how he was going about things and then he became all powerful at the club. It turned out to be a decent strategy with the success we had in the sixties and seventies. I made my debut on New Year's Day in 1966 against Sheffield Wednesday and I was fortunate enough to score.

"Don had a great knowledge of the game," enthused Gray. "I had never played outside left in my life before I came to Leeds. I was never a winger. When I made my debut, I was playing midfield as I had done all the way through my career as a schoolboy and for the Scottish schoolboys and Glasgow Schoolboys. I played the old left half position in midfield.

"Even in the early couple of years at Leeds I'd been playing in midfield or up front. Then Don said to me one day that he'd got Billy Bremner and Johnny Giles in midfield and would I mind having a go at outside left and that I'd find it easy. So that's why everybody thinks I was a winger when I was really a frustrated midfield player all my career," Gray laughed. "It was an easy transition for me to make because, as Don said, I could run, I was quick and I could get by people, so they are the attributes you need to be a winger. And being a midfield player, I could pass the ball as well. So it wasn't that difficult."

Revie was handed a healthy transfer kitty thanks to fresh board investment and Scottish international Bobby Collins was signed for £25,000 from Everton. Revie immediately installed Collins as captain and added Billy McAdams who he had played with at Manchester City. Ian Lawson arrived to play up front and at left-back Cliff Mason was recruited.

Club legend John Charles was brought back for a fee of £53,000 after five seasons at Juventus in Serie A. Revie had also signed Airdrie forward Jim Storrie for £15,650. The spending spree had created a degree of cautious optimism about the club.

The 1962/63 season was Revie's first as a full-time manager and the club made marked improvements. Sports teams experience many false dawns. Days come along when a performance generates hope that is never realised. The away match in Swansea in September 1962 was a day that Leeds fans look back on because the dawn was the real deal.

The two sides had nothing to shout about after mediocre starts to the 1962/63 season which saw the Swans in 10th and Leeds in 13th position in the Second Division table. Both teams had finished just above relegation in the previous season.

Charles had yet to relight the fires of his first magnificent incarnation as a Leeds player. He appeared overweight and more reluctant to fire at goal than before. That said, he had scored three goals in the first six games of the season.

A 2-1 home defeat to Bury had provoked Revie into changes ahead of the trip to Wales. Storrie (broken finger) and Charles (strained back) were out and captain Freddie Goodwin, Ian Lawson and Willie Bell were also on the injured list. With the physio already busy, Revie dropped experienced goalkeeper Tommy Younger and right-back Grenville Hair.

Revie and Syd Owen had been recruiting some of the best youngsters from around the country. Some of the names that had represented the reserves in the same week would become household names. The reserve team that played Liverpool at Anfield read as follows: Gary Sprake (aged 17), Paul Reaney (17), Barrie Wright (16), Mike Addy (19), Paul Madeley (17), Norman Hunter (18), Ronnie Blackburn (20), Rodney Johnson (17), Peter Lorimer (15), John Hawksby (20) and Terry Cooper (18).

Ahead of the trip to Swansea, Revie called together Sprake, Reaney,

Hunter and Johnson and informed them that they were to travel with the first team to Wales.

Sprake had already debuted after a late call-up in March 1962 when Younger was taken ill. Reaney was a Leeds lad who had been put to right-back by Revie after starting out as a centre-half. Hunter, a Geordie, had been offered a pro-contract earlier in Revie's rein.

Jack Taylor had previously balked at taking on Hunter full-time. Johnson had played at England youth level and would deputise for Charles. Irish international Noel Peyton came in too and Cliff Mason became Revie's third captain of the season in place of the dropped Hair.

"Mr Revie, I know, badly wanted a few more weeks at least for his crop of good 'young 'uns' to mature in men's football in the Central League, but events have overtaken him," wrote Phil Brown in the *Yorkshire Evening Post*. "He told me this afternoon: 'I didn't really want to play the lads yet — I wanted them to get a bit more experience — but I have to give them a chance now. We want to get cracking in the League.'"

Revie wanted leaders all over the park and Bobby Collins, the veteran Scottish international, was someone Revie placed a huge amount of trust in. Jack Charlton had matured into his leader at the back.

"There was a game against Swansea that marked a turning-point in my life," Charlton recalled later. "Don had left a lot of senior players out of the side. I said to Don, 'Well, I'm not going to play the way you've been playing with Fred, I don't want to play man-to-man marking, I want to play a zonal system where you pick up people in your area. I'll sort out the back four for you the way I want them to play' — and Don said OK. That, for me, was the moment when I stopped being one of the awkward squad and came on board the Leeds United ship. It was a sign that I would be one of the key players in the new team Don was building."

A 20-year-old Billy Bremner was tasked with steering the fresh crop through their new adventure. Brown described the changes as a "gamble", but Revie's thinking was clear. The rewards would be reaped later.

"We were a ball winning side and champing at the bit to go," Storrie would remark later. "We played a method game, high pressure football. Bobby Collins would get hold of the ball and spray passes all over the park for people to chase after. The forwards would hustle, cutting off the supply of back passes to the goalkeeper. I reckon we scored about 10 to 15 goals through forced errors that way."

After 20 minutes, Bremner played the ball through to Johnson who skipped past a couple of challenges before driving the ball into the Swansea net. Sprake had a cool, calm and collected game in goal as the side rapidly grew in confidence.

After the break South African Albert Johanneson passed to Collins who found Bremner speeding into the box. The Scottish youngster belted the ball home to make it 2-0 to the visitors.

The game, and the tremendous display by a flowing Leeds side, was the end of the absent Big John Charles. When the Welshman played, Leeds lumped the ball into him and trusted to hope. Charles was soon considered surplus to requirements by Revie and was sold to Roma for a £17,000 profit within months of his return.

Hunter played every game from then to April 1965 and Reaney all but one of the remaining games of the season. Revie had published the blueprint. When youngsters see other young talent at the club making it into the first team it provides them with inspiration and proof that, if they knuckle down, they can get through too. The youth would continue to come through and the team were in contention for promotion for much of the season, but were hindered by bad weather that led to many fixture postponements. Catching up on the backlog saw Leeds run out of steam and end in fifth place.

Positivity was growing at Elland Road as Revie spent big again ahead of the 1963/64 season. He signed striker Alan Peacock from Middlesbrough for £53,000. If seems the manager's bird superstition didn't stretch to player names, although it may have reinforced it as Peacock was often injured.

It was another trip to Swansea that saw Leeds promoted to the top tier of English football for the first time in four years. A victory from the third-last game of the season would guarantee promotion. They were top of the table and a point ahead of Sunderland, which meant winning all of their remaining matches would see Revie's team promoted as champions.

At the Vetch Field two years earlier, Bobby Collins had debuted as Leeds successfully staved off relegation. A year earlier Revie had successfully gambled on youth. Leeds had won both visits and Revie opted to hand a debut to 19-year-old Terry Cooper, in place of the injured Johanneson, on the wing as he bid to make it three-in-a-row.

The Leeds team was Gary Sprake in goal, Paul Reaney, Jack Charlton, Norman Hunter and Willie Bell at the back, Johnny Giles, Billy Bremner and Bobby Collins in midfield, with a forward line of Cooper, Don Weston and Alan Peacock.

Giles had been signed from Manchester United during the season and Peacock had joined from Middlesbrough. Both were internationals that had made significant contributions as Leeds moved up a level.

Leeds were 3-0 ahead inside the first half. Cooper crossed to Peacock who scored the opener after 15 minutes. Peacock added his second four minutes later and just after half-an-hour a Cooper corner was slammed home by Giles. Leeds sustained their 3-0 advantage to the final whistle.

Cooper's debut had been superb as Phil Brown reported in the *Yorkshire Evening Post*: "I've seen a few good League debuts since Mr Revie's nursery began to work, but Cooper's was among the best. This Pontefract lad had just astonishing composure and moves, admirable determination and enterprise, good control and judgement. You would have thought he had been in the team for months. One match can deceive, but I doubt it in Cooper's case. If ever a poor debut could have been forgiven it was in this match. But he was clearly United's best forward."

Brown added the Leeds performance was "just about the best of their 11 away successes in the League this season. I say, 'just about the best' only because their autumnal 4-1 win at Southampton was a really brilliant performance against a better side than Swansea."

Revie was full of praise for his side: "We have a family spirit at Elland Road, and everyone has been prepared to work that little bit harder and do that little bit extra. That has been shown on the field. The players have given 100 per cent effort in every game, and no team, win, lose or draw, can do more than that. Their obedience to orders, tactical and otherwise, has been most gratifying and I know they have repeatedly lost the chance to make flattering headlines by making sure of victory or a point with unspectacular methods."

Eric Stanger, in the *Yorkshire Post*, added: "Leeds United's return to the First Division is all the more remarkable when one considers that two years ago only a desperate late effort prevented them from slipping into the Third. Yet that was not the nadir of their fortunes in recent years. That followed their relegation from the First Division for the fourth time in their history at the end of season 1959/60. Muttered discontent became open revolt against the board after a moderate start to the following season and resulted in the moving of a vote of no confidence in the directors in the December of that year.

"The motion was easily defeated on a shareholders' vote, but the acrimony at the time helped not only to clear the air but eventually led to almost complete reorganisation. The hint was taken, new directors, with wealth to put into a club faced with liabilities of more than £100,000, were elected and generally there was a transfusion of both money and energy.

"A most significant step was taken the following March, when Don Revie, still an active player, was appointed team manager. He had no experience of management, only a wealth of football knowledge and ideas gathered from some 15 years as a player and he quickly showed himself a person of strong character. From the beginning he insisted on full control of the playing side. All he asked was five years in which to build up a really good side and that was not unreasonable considering the state of the club's playing register at the time.

"The gospel he preached in the boardroom and out of it was that no club could be successful in modern football unless it built from the bottom. By that he meant signing the best of schoolboy talent as junior professionals, coaching and teaching them so that as footballers they grew up with the club. That was long-term but it is a policy which has paid Revie and Leeds United much earlier dividends than they expected. How many miles Don Revie has travelled in search of young talent and how many hours he has put in only he knows. Few managers can have shown such an infinite capacity for hard work.

"One of the first things he did, and to my mind one of the most important, was to lay down with his coaches and training staff a club pattern and style of play. That was something which had been lacking in the 40 years or so I have known Leeds United.

"The benefit of an overall team plan is that players can step from the junior side to the reserves and to the first team knowing exactly what is required of them. The club's style and general tactics are ingrained in them. But in United's case, before it could be fully operative, there had to be a lot of improvisation, and a lot of make and mend in the first team if relegation to the Third Division were to be avoided. Of the signings in March 1962, none turned out to be more important than that of Bobby Collins, a bargain, so it proved, at £25,000 from Everton.

"Collins, whose best days were thought to be over at 30, not only led them to safety that season but his shrewd generalship and leadership have been decisive factors in taking them back into the First Division. Few inside-forwards work harder than Collins and generally they are a hard-working race — they have to be in the modern game. Few players can strike such a response from their colleagues. His influence both in the dressing room and on the field has been incalculable. It may be an overstatement to say that he has made Billy Bremner into one of the best wing-halves in the country, but not so much so. Bremner, I know, has such respect and affection for his fellow Scot and his football has improved so much under his lead that United, who could not get £25,000 for him a couple of seasons back, would now not take double that fee for him.

"Bremner and Collins have formed the hub round which the team has revolved — the midfield dynamo, as current football phraseology has it. They are responsible for the quick transformation from defence to attack, which is so essential if the modern blanket defence system is not to be completely stultifying.

"But Leeds United's success this season has not been due to any one or even two men. It stems really from a happy boardroom, a happy executive and happy players. Man-for-man, position-for-position, other Second Division clubs could point to a pull over United, but none can boast a better team in the full sense of the word.

"Every man has been prepared to pull every ounce of his weight, to shoulder extra burdens to help out a colleague in trouble. Individual glory has been readily sacrificed for the good of the whole, which is true team spirit and has enabled many a game to be won when victory has seemed unlikely. United may not always have been an attractive side to watch, in the sense of providing glittering spectacle, but they have been a mightily efficient one."

Revie had been too superstitious to purchase the celebratory champagne before the game. Swansea pubs saw the player find some celebratory bottles after the match and the train journey back to Yorkshire was a lively affair.

Chairman Harry Reynolds sent a telegram to Sunderland to congratulate them on their own promotion and promised to buy fish and chips on the journey home. He also offered Revie his third improved contract of his three-year tenure.

Leeds secured the tag of champions of Division Two with an Elland Road draw against Plymouth Argyle and a final day 2-0 defeat at Charlton Athletic.

"We wanted to get out of the Second Division, and we wanted to do well," remembered Revie. "I said that they were the most professional outfit in the business. That word, they didn't take the word right, because professionalism meant that they wanted to train hard, they wanted to live right, they wanted to improve themselves, they wanted to be the best side in the world. And everybody didn't realise all the things that the word professional covers. Everybody thought that word meant it was hard, we'd kick people and we'd push people to one side just through sheer power. Nobody gave them the credit for the tremendous abilities in the side."

Back in the top flight, Leeds began with a 2-1 away win at Villa Park. Then the champions of England came to town. On 26 August 1964, Liverpool arrived at Elland Road with Scot Bill Shankly, their larger-than-life manager and a team packed with quality like Ian St John, Roger Hunt, Ian Callaghan and Peter Thompson.

When he signed Ron Yeats, Shankly suggested that the press men should walk around him, stating, "With this man in defence we could play

Arthur Askey in goal." He also famously said: "People say football is a matter of life and death. I'm disappointed by that approach. I believe it is much more important than that." In short, Bill Shankly was one of the greatest football managers that ever lived. Revie developed a huge respect for 'Shanks'.

"Our sights were firmly set a lot higher than just survival," Bremner remembered. "Liverpool were a magnificent side. Bill Shankly had transformed them into a very special outfit and we knew they were coming to Elland Road intent on securing maximum points. We had also been made aware that a part of Shankly's psychology was to convince his players that they were playing against a bunch of nobodies, half of whom were limping. He was a canny guy and a brilliant manager and everyone respected him tremendously, but we also rated our own manager and we knew that he would have us prepared to take on and beat anybody."

Revie was without Alan Peacock (knee injury) and fielded the same side that had beaten Aston Villa: Gary Sprake, Paul Reaney, Jack Charlton, Norman Hunter, Willie Bell, Billy Bremner, Bobby Collins, Johnny Giles, Albert Johanneson, Don Weston and Jim Storrie. Few pundits expected what that team would do.

Revie assembled a thorough fact file on the red part of Liverpool. The Don became known for his intensely thorough preparation and his notes on Liverpool's Charity Shield encounter against West Ham was analysed as follows:

Liverpool took the field first and proceeded towards the Spion Kop end. This being the end they prefer to defend in the first half, an advantage may be gained by getting out first when we play there. Use the right-hand goal for warm-up and should we win the toss elect to stay as you are at K.O. Shankly has devised his team tactics to cover some deficiencies in his playing strength. Both full-backs lack pace and our wingers must seek the ball behind them. Liverpool depend a great deal on centre-half Yeats, who sticks like glue to the centre-forward and clears his lines decisively at all times. In this game both wing half-backs played a very stereotyped game, and should one go on attack, the other stays back, even when an opportunity may arise to move with ease into a position to change the point of attack. The majority of Milne's service goes towards outside-right, Callaghan, and usually consists of a short crisp pass.

The forward line missed the constructive ability of St John, and his deputy Arrowsmith was carried off the field after ten minutes, with a twisted knee. Hunt moved to centre-forward but was unable to free himself from the close attention of West Ham's Brown. Chisnall substituted for

Arrowsmith but on this display lacked the sharpness and guile to be creative. Wallace at I-R was aggressive and grafted throughout, always on the look out to shoot when half-chance arose.

The Liverpool defence play square with both full-backs endeavouring to keep close to the wingers even when a strike is made through the inside positions. It was noticeable that West Ham's inside-left, Hurst, was on to a number of balls behind the Liverpool right-back in the first fifteen minutes and I could not figure out why this approach was not sustained because it proved highly dangerous in the early period.

Balls into this area will probably be more productive because of the two wing half-backs. Right-half Milne tends to advance more than Stevenson. It was Yeats who was having to move out to challenge Hurst on most occasions.

After this early period, I consider West Ham played to Liverpool's advantage by building up attacks slowly, and neither Sissons nor Brabrook would seek the ball behind the full-backs or attempt to run without it to enable colleagues from behind to carry the ball into an attacking position. Once West Ham had gained possession Bobby Moore, playing in a position between C-H and L-B, was usually served with the ball by his colleagues, to distribute elsewhere.

Thompson at outside left has speed and ball control, and invariably takes on anybody in line with his striking runs. I feel there are times when he had the chance to cross balls from the wing but even so he elected to take on his opponent to get in on goal. Thompson tends to go inside or across the front of his full-back because he favours his right foot.

The cross-over was operated on the right wing a number of times. Callaghan already in the corner, coming out to take over the ball from the man carrying the ball in his direction. Callaghan then proceeds to strike through the I-R position towards goal, but he has difficulty in this situation because it demands using his left foot with the L-B running in close proximity.

It was in such a situation that left-back G. Byrne scored with a thirty-yard left-foot shot. Callaghan was forced to pull out of a run, turned the ball back in Byrne's direction, whose shot went across Standen inside the far post.

Wallace's goal was due to a mistake by Moore, who allowed a slow-moving ball to pass under his boot to Liverpool's I-R, whose first-time right-foot shot hit the far post before crossing the line.

West Ham's two goals resulted from practices we have done on numerous occasions, e.g. forward coming off for ball to feet, and laying it to R-H, who hits forty-yard ball through I-L position to advancing *forward running through defence, who helped ball into net as keeper advanced.*

Second goal: Hurst followed in a hard-driven ball from Brabrook who shot with his left foot from I-R position. Lawrence palms ball. Hurst nets from four yards. This incidentally was the only shot West Ham had at goal in the second half.

Yeats came into the area for corner kicks, taking up a very wide position to enable himself to have room to adjust in relation to the kick. At free kicks for them, Liverpool had players moving around in different directions seeking to lose defenders in an effort to enable the two players on the ball to select 'what's on'.

The level of detail was repeated match-after-match by Revie, who was not a man for assumptions or taking anything for granted. Preparation was everything. On the training ground, Revie rehearsed repeatedly tactics to cancel out perceived strengths in upcoming opposition. There was none of the 'we play to our strengths and they should worry about what we do' rhetoric so common in others. At times, Revie would be criticised for his cautious nature, but it worked against Liverpool as he strived to ensure Leeds would settle back into First Division life seamlessly.

Chairman Harry Reynolds was prone to his over-enthusiastic approach and believed he could make a killing at the turnstiles. There had not been a capacity crowd at Elland Road for 40 years, but Reynolds opted for premium prices with the visit of the defending champions and a mood of enthusiasm in the city. The crowd for the Liverpool game was a disappointing 19,000.

"Reynolds' misplaced optimism had potentially disastrous consequences for the fans that did bother to turn up," stated Rob Bagchi and Paul Rogerson. "His expectation of at least a 50,000-attendance led to the paddock stands being crammed full while vast swathes of terracing behind the goals were left vacant for all the non-existent latecomers. One fan complained that the crush was so intense he feared for his life; conditions, others claimed, were 'like the black hole of Calcutta'. Luckily for a penitent Reynolds, there were no major casualties."

Fancy a Leeds chairman getting his finances wrong!

Billy Bremner and Norman Hunter began well in midfield and Bobby Collins was brilliant as Leeds were up for the challenge. United took the lead in the 16th minute as Albert Johanneson shot from the edge of the area and glanced off Ron Yeats' shoulder into the net.

Liverpool were level within eight minutes as Sprake caught a Hunt header only to smash into Reaney and drop the ball into his own net. But

Leeds were 2-1 up at the half-time break when Weston headed home a Storrie cross.

Whatever Revie said at the break worked. Johnny Giles set up Bremner for Leeds's third and then Bremner rolled a free kick to Giles who thundered home a drive from 30 yards.

Elland Road was rocking with Leeds 4-1 ahead 10 minutes into the second half. The fans chanted *we want five* as their side made the champions look ordinary.

Gordon Milne made it 4-2 after Sprake saved his penalty and he converted the rebound, and that's how it ended.

"Don Revie told us to go out and prove that we were a match, and more, for them," said Bremner. "His words inspired us and put us in exactly the right frame of mind for the task ahead. It was quite a task, of course, but we settled quickly and played the way we had performed in the second half against Villa. Liverpool were excellent — as good as we had expected — but we were not going to pay them too much respect and I think they were uneasy long before we were because the unflappable Ron Yeats scored our first goal for us. I pulled his leg about that later. As a fellow Scot I got away with it."

Bobby Collins had become his manager's reflection on the pitch. He drove the team forward, was robust in a tackle and was desperate to win matches. It was sometime around then that the 'dirty Leeds' tag emanated. Leeds did not hold back.

"I think we were more cynical and applied gamesmanship in the early days when we were coming out of the Second Division and the first year in the First Division," Johnny Giles suggested. "I think that stuck with us and we never got credit for becoming a great side. And I believe we became a great side."

Bobby Collins too felt Leeds United were often miscast as the villains of the piece. "In those times I thought that was a bit unfair," he said. "I think a lot of people forgot about the brilliant football that we played then. And let's face it, if you're playing football when you've got the ball you play it and when they've got it, you don't let them play. And fortunately, or unfortunately, whatever you may think, we were like this.

"All we knew about was winning. And it's a man's game isn't it?"

Peter Lorimer added: "Yes, we were physical, we were a physical side. But the game was physical in those days. Every team had a 'Chopper Harris' at Chelsea [Ron Harris], Peter 'The Assassin' Storey at Arsenal, Tommy 'I'll Break Your Back' Smith at Liverpool, Norman 'Bite Yer Legs' [Hunter] was ours. And they didn't get names like that because they were nice guys. It was because that was the way they played the game, and these were the things they would say to you."

Such was Hunter's hard man image at Elland Road that when coach Les Cocker was informed that Hunter had broken a leg, he replied, "Whose is it?"

When Brian Clough had abrasively informed the defender, "Hunter, you're a dirty bastard and everyone hates you. I know everyone likes to be loved, and you'd like to be loved too, wouldn't you?" Hunter had fired back, "Actually, I couldn't give a fuck."

Tommy Smith was a ferocious Liverpool adversary, but there was a grudging respect there too: "You don't get a team who were as cynical as they said Leeds were with a gang of no hopers. They were all internationals, the same as Liverpool were."

United had feisty encounters with Sunderland the previous season. The referee had suspended play in a match against Preston North End on the hour to give both sides a chance to calm down. And then there was Collins's return to Goodison Park on 7 November 1964. The game against Everton descended into a brawl and the referee ordered the players off the field after 35 minutes to prevent further violence.

Revie's side had become synonymous with kicking itself to glory. Don deflected accusations anywhere other than towards his own players, but it has to have been a calculated tactic.

"We made a lot of enemies in that 1964/65 season," Jack Charlton wrote in his autobiography. "I remember lying on the treatment table in the Leeds dressing room with one of the young lads, Jimmy Lumsden. He was talking about a reserves match the night before, and he told me that he had gone in over the top of the ball to a guy who had then had to be taken off. 'I gave him a beauty,' Jimmy said. Don murmured something approvingly. 'Jimmy,' I told him, 'Jimmy, you live by the sword, you die by the sword. That guy might someday play against you again, he will remember you and he might just go over the top to you when you're not expecting it. You might finish up breaking your leg.'"

Irish playmaker Johnny Giles recalled: "You had to establish a reputation that would make people think twice about messing with you. I have certainly done things on the football field then that I am embarrassed about now, but one has to put them into the football climate that existed then. It was a different game then, much more physical than it is today — vicious even — and people like Bobby Collins and myself were targets.

"It's different today where if you look sideways at a player you get booked," Giles continued. "You had to be able to look after yourself to survive. And that was only to give you licence to play. I'm a small fella and I was regarded as a skilful player, but if you are regarded as a skilful player you are naturally a target for the opposition.

"I knew before they went out, they would say, 'First chance you get, get stuck into this fella and let him know you're playing, as they say in football, and try and put him out of the game.' My attitude to that was, well I'll give you as good as I get and then I'll go and play."

The Football Association sought to clean up the game and had published an article highlighting the disciplinary records of all clubs. Leeds United were shown to have had the most players carded, fined and suspended.

"We did not have a single first-team player sent off last season and we had only one suspended, Billy Bremner, after a series of cautions, which is a lot more than many clubs can say," Revie told the *Evening Post*. "The majority of our offences were committed by junior second team players or boys. For that I blame the tension which permeated the whole club in the long and hard drive for promotion in a very hot Second Division. It was a time of very great strain for us all, and the club spirit being as wholehearted as it is from top to bottom."

United wrote to the Football Association, concerned that, "the 'dirty team' tag, which was blown up by the press, could prejudice not only the general public but the officials controlling the game, and to put it mildly, could have an effect on the subconscious approach of both referee and linesmen, to say nothing of the minds of spectators, especially some types who are watching football today. It could lead to some very unsavoury incidents."

Opposition sides were geared for a battle when they faced Leeds and when Revie took his side to Goodison Park they were 4th in the table after winning four straight matches. Everton were 8th and experiencing a bad run and saw the visit of Leeds as a chance to reignite their season.

United had lost an FA Cup replay to Everton in the season before and the Toffees had memories of how hard Bobby Collins had played those games.

The game had barely started when Bremner fouled Everton's striker Fred Pickering. Charlton was clattered straight back. Giles jumped to challenge Sandy Brown after four minutes and left the Everton left-back complaining of studs to his chest. Brown threw a punch at Giles and was sent off. The match continued with fouls galore and the home crowd baying for blood.

Leeds took the lead after 15 minutes as Bobby Collins swung a free kick high into the heart of the Everton goal area and Willie Bell thundered a header into the Everton net. The goal only fuelled the rancour of the disgruntled home support. Missiles were thrown onto the pitch, Sprake was bombarded with coins and the event had ceased to be a game of football.

A high ball after 36 minutes saw Bell and Everton right-winger Derek Temple challenge each other at full throttle. Both followed the flight of the ball and, seemingly unaware of each other, collided at full speed, laying each other out. As both lay prone on the ground, Les Cocker and referee Ken Stokes were struck by coins. The referee had experienced enough and removed the teams from the field to allow the crowd to settle.

Before resuming, the crowd were told that the game would be abandoned if any more items were thrown onto the pitch. He also told both dressing rooms that he would report the teams to the Football Association if they didn't stop fouling each other.

The fans and players appeared to have paid little attention to the referee's warnings. Norman Hunter and Everton's Roy Vernon continued to tackle like men possessed. Hunter was given a yellow card and numerous players were spoken to. The referee could easily have dished out more red cards.

United ultimately maintained their 1-0 lead and withstood a barrage of Everton attacks late in the game.

"It was diabolical," Collins complained after the game. "They blamed us, yet some Everton players were going over the ball time and time again.

"When Sandy Brown got sent off, it was like a fuse on a bomb being lit," he continued. "It really got a bit nasty and brutal. There were a lot of hard challenges that day. But you can't turn the other cheek, or they'll kick you."

The crowd had to be dispersed by mounted police as the Leeds coach was pelted by angry Scousers. Their transport may have retreated back to the other side of the Pennines, but no inch was ever given on the pitch.

"For the first time in the history of the Football League both sides in a match on Saturday were ordered off the field for a space of five minutes to allow the tempers of both the crowd and the players to cool," reported *The Times*. "Such an event has occurred frequently enough abroad.

"It happened even here a year ago when the referee abandoned an international at Hampden Park as the Austrians got out of control against Scotland. It happened, too, lower down the supposed social football scale in 1959 when the teams of both Dartford and Gravesend were given communal marching orders. Those were isolated incidents within these isles, roundly condemned at the time. But for supposedly civilised senior British players now to follow suit against each other is something new and menacing. The image of the game, already damaged in other ways, cannot stand much more of this."

Revie's customary response was to defend his team: "After the incidents of this weekend I must defend my club and my players after all the bad things that had been said about them. I feel it started last season when we were in the Second Division when we were tagged as a hard, dirty side by the press.

"I am disgusted by these attacks on us and I ask that we be judged fairly and squarely on each match and not on this unfair tag that we have got.

"We were wrongly labelled by the press and then by the Football Association. The result has been that opposing teams have gone on to the field keyed up, expecting a hard match. I think the number of opposing players sent off in our matches proves it."

Ultimately, Everton were the only side to receive any punishment. Sandy Brown was suspended for two weeks for his red card and Everton were fined £250 for the behaviour of their supporters.

Leeds committed fewer fouls than Everton on that infamous day at Goodison Park, but the image of the club had changed. People saw Leeds as a side that wanted to win at all costs to the good image of the game. The likes of Brian Clough would criticise Revie and his team's disciplinary record on television.

Leeds appeared to love winning, but didn't care about being loved.

"Revie used to say, 'Anyone who beats you at home must know they've been in a game,'" recalled Jim Storrie. "I think we were over-exuberant more than anything. But Revie must take part of the blame because when we were getting all that bad publicity, he told us, 'Don't worry about the press, what matters is the fact that they are talking about you.' I am sure he later regretted this attitude."

The Whites though were far from the relegation fodder that some anticipated. They were battling at the very top of the First Division for the first time in their history.

Three straight wins to start the season had been followed by four losses, but form had been recovered and by the time they travelled to play league leaders Manchester United on 5 December 1964, they were 3rd in the table and four points off the top.

Only six years before, many of the Busby Babes had tragically died on a Munich runway and Matt Busby, Bobby Charlton and the survivors had been left to piece together their own health and Manchester United's future. They had won the 1963 FA Cup and were back to being one of the very best teams in the country.

Jack Charlton's brother, Bobby, was a world-class midfielder. George Best was ripping defences apart and Denis Law banging in the goals.

Revie had paid a lot of attention to Busby's work at Old Trafford and there was a degree of envy there too. Big Jack was seen as the second Charlton in the football world. Johnny Giles had been let go from Old Trafford and was the brother-in-law to Nobby Stiles.

Revie made Giles skipper against his former club and Bremner was tasked with marking Law, whilst Reaney took responsibility for Best. Revie had appreciated that the middle of the field would be where the battle was fought and that any attacking advantage would be gained down either flank.

Revie had his tactics right with Reaney and Bell enjoying plenty of possession on the wings. Sprake had an exceptional game in goal as Manchester United looked for goals. Collins ruled the roost in the centre of the park.

And then Leeds went ahead after 55 minutes. Bremner passed to Cooper, and Pat Dunne in the Manchester net could only parry his shot as Collins ran in to put away the rebound.

Leeds were almost denied a famous win with eight minutes remaining when referee Jim Finney suspended play due to thick fog.

"We went absolutely crazy and told him that he couldn't possibly abandon the game, that we could still see from the halfway line, that the spectators wouldn't mind because they had already seen the best part of the game, and so on and so on," Bremner said. "The poor man could not get a word in. A few of us were still young and impetuous in those days and we had a bit of a chip on our shoulders too. Referees were authority and we kicked against that at every opportunity — even if we were harming ourselves by doing it. When the referee finally got to have his say he explained that the fog had been made worse by a passing steam train and that he was only waiting for a couple of minutes for the smoke to clear. He was as good as his word and about four minutes later we returned to the game."

Leeds won 1-0 and narrowed the gap at the top to just two points. It had been their most famous win to date.

Leeds would beat Manchester United again in the FA Cup semi-final. A 0-0 Hillsborough draw, which had been more of a kick-fest than a football match, where "too many players on both sides behaved like a pack of dogs snapping and snarling at each other over a bone," according to the *Yorkshire Post*.

At the City Ground in Nottingham for the replay, it was hard fought, but a fairer contest.

"Terry Cooper played at number 11 but had to mark Crerand," Jim Storrie reflected. "Crerand was a great passer and could land the ball on a beer mat from 40 yards. So, we cut off his supply. It was like starving a deep-sea diver of oxygen and meant that Stiles and Foulkes, who were less gifted, had to put balls through. And instead of the goalkeeper being able to find Crerand, he had to kick it upfield where Jack Charlton would win it in the air. Best, Law and Charlton were locked in their own half of the field."

In the second half, still locked at 0-0, Sprake pulled off a miraculous save with a raised right hand when Denis Law bore down on him one-on-one. Leeds were pushed back and stuck to their task, long enough to weather the storm and gradually seize control, dominating the final period of the game.

Still goalless, two minutes of normal time to play, and Nobby Stiles caught Bremner late in the middle of the pitch. Giles sent the resulting free kick into the Manchester United penalty area.

Bremner watched the ball, moved in as it arced down into the box and contorted his body to dive away from goal and glance a header beyond Pat Dunne in the Manchester net. Bremner was off, jumping and bucking like a crazed new-born lamb towards the corner flag as teammates fought to catch and mob him. Leeds had booked their first ever Wembley final.

"My proudest moment in my career was when the whistle went," Revie would say. "And Leeds United were in the final. Manchester played some absolutely scintillating football. I thought we were going to crack, and we were certainly lucky not to go two down, but we came through it, and according to my instructions, if there was still no score, Jim Storrie switched to the right-wing and Bremner moved into the attack. It might not have come off, but it did. What pleased me most was that Leeds kept their heads."

Fans invaded the pitch and after the initial celebrations had died down a little, Revie needed to talk to Jack Charlton. Big Jack was on cloud nine after marshalling a defence that had kept a fearsome Manchester United attack at bay for three full matches that season. And, for the second time that season, he had got one over his more famous sibling.

Jack's performances that season had not gone unnoticed, as he explained in his autobiography.

"Right after the game Don told me that I had been selected to play for the national squad. I was so delighted that I didn't think, I just had to tell our kid. I went straight round to the Man United dressing room and said, 'Hey, I've been selected to play for England!'

"I'm smiling all over me face, and there's all the Manchester United team sitting round looking miserable. There was a bit of a pause, and then Bobby went, 'Ah, yeah, well, congratulations, great.' 'Now, f*** off out of here,' said someone else.

"And I suddenly realise what I'm doing, so I said, 'Excuse me,' and left. That's the tact I'm famous for."

Leeds entered the last few games of a superb 1964/65 season chasing the league and FA Cup double. Despite losing 1-0 at home to Manchester United on 17 April 1965, they were maintaining a strong title challenge. That Elland Road defeat ended an 18-match unbeaten run in the League.

A 3-0 away defeat against Sheffield Wednesday two days later appeared to have put paid to title dreams, but a 2-0 revenge win over Wednesday at Elland Road and a 3-0 victory away at Sheffield United had restored faith.

On 26 April 1965, Leeds had one more game of their league season to play, away to Birmingham City on a Monday evening. They were one point clear of Manchester United, but their rivals had two games left to play, against Arsenal that night and Aston Villa later in the week. Busby's side also had a far better goal difference.

Leeds felt they simply had to win. However, as things transpired, if they had beaten Birmingham City on the final day of the season, they would have claimed their first league title.

Birmingham were guaranteed to finish bottom and appeared easy win-fodder for Revie's side. Leeds found themselves 3-0 down and Manchester United were leading 2-0 against Arsenal.

"The boss told us to take it easy because of the Cup final and we took him at his word," Bremner said. "We went 3-0 down. Then I suddenly saw him on the touchline waving his arms about. You don't really hear what people are saying to you from off the pitch, but we got the message that he wanted us to get back into the game. We started to put the foot on the accelerator."

Leeds would salvage a 3-3 draw, but Manchester United had won 3-1 and were league champions. In their final match they lost to Villa.

Revie had achieved miracles. His side had been transformed, but second place felt like failure. And the season was not complete. The manager had to haul his team out of disappointment and prepare for the FA Cup final against Liverpool at Wembley on 1 May 1965 with both sides seeking their first FA Cup success.

Shankly's team had finished their league defence in a disappointing 7th, but were still chasing European Cup success, but would lose a semi-final to Inter Milan a few days after their FA Cup showdown.

Shankly turned to Collins as the teams walked from the tunnel and asked how he was. Collins responded, "I feel awful," capturing the mood of a nervous Leeds team.

Liverpool played classy, fast-paced, fluid football. Leeds were static, sluggish and not at the races in comparison. Revie had been outmanoeuvred by Shankly. Leeds were kept in the contest by the heroics of goalkeeper Gary Sprake who enjoyed arguably his best game in a Leeds shirt.

Described as "the worst final for years," it remained 0-0 at half-time as both sides remained resolute in defence. Hunter had injured his ankle in a strong tackle, whilst Collins had broken Byrne's collar bone in a crunching challenge. Byrne played on not knowing the severity of the injury and was classy enough to show no ill effects during the game.

Charlton and Bremner required early treatment, as did Storrie, who limped through the remainder of the game.

Liverpool controlled the second half as Sprake was kept busy, but 0-0 it stayed after 90 minutes and extra-time was required. If it had remained level it would have provoked the first replay since 1912, but it didn't.

Players were tired on a heavy rain-soaked pitch. Roger Hunt put Liverpool ahead from close range.

Leeds responded as Hunter fired the ball into the Liverpool penalty area, Charlton reached it with his head and Bremner stepped forward to drill a low volley inside the right-hand post and with 15 minutes of extra-time to go the teams were back level.

Leeds had little left in the tank as play resumed. Ian St John put Liverpool back in front as he headed the winning goal and Leeds ended a magnificent season trophy-less.

"Don't let it worry you, Billy," Revie consoled Bremner. "We will be back and next time you'll be skipper and we'll win."

Jack Charlton stated: "The disappointing thing about the final, I think, was not that we failed to win — but that we lost so dully. Every player, I believe, wants to be associated with a classic final and our display was so out of keeping with our ability that it really hurt."

When Revie entered his devastated dressing room, a player said, "We're sorry boss."

Revie responded: "You've run your guts out all season, have nothing to show for it, and you're sorry for ME? Don't be so bloody daft. Get dressed, we're going back to the hotel for a booze up."

Shankly was asked why he felt Leeds had failed. "Failed? Second in the Championship; FA Cup finalists; ninety per cent of the managers in the English League pray every night for 'failures' like this!"

Shankly was right, but a trend of finishing bridesmaids and not brides had begun. Revie's glittering trophy cabinet could have been so much bigger.

Revie chose to make no new signings ahead of the 1965/66 campaign and he continued to show his ingenuity. The success of the previous season had seen Leeds qualify for European competition for the first time. In the Inter-Cities Fairs Cup, the pre-cursor to the UEFA Cup, Revie sent his team out against Torino wearing unfamiliar numbers to confuse the Italian club's tight man-marking system.

"They are a hard, strong side and will be difficult to beat," Revie commented after flying to Italy to see Torino draw 0-0 with Cagliari. "Their defence is very tight, and they have several cracking good players. They will be hard to open out."

The first leg at Elland Road on 29 September saw United take the lead as Bremner scored their first European goal after 25 minutes as the Italian keeper fumbled his curling effort.

In the 48th minute, Peacock headed a second and was later controversially denied another when it appeared his shot had crossed the line. Torino decreased Leeds's advantage with a late strike by centre-forward Orlando.

"The team has never played better since I became manager at Elland Road," Revie enthused. "They were splendid in their skill and determination, and they gave the lot and a bit more in effort. They had not a thing left when they came in. How they maintained the pace on a poor night and soft pitch I do not know. I am the proudest manager in Britain today.

"Yet when I went with them into the dressing room after the game they were so grieved at having won only 2-1 that Bobby Collins said to me, 'Boss, just listen to them! You would think we had lost 3-1!'

"I would like respectfully to remind our critics and our doubters that seven of last night's United side were only 22 or under. The experience they gained last night against a very good team under a very good manager should be most valuable to them. But above all, my own feeling is of pride in them after this Continental football baptism."

Captain Bobby Collins had become a vital cog in Revie's machine since he had signed in 1962, but in the second leg in Turin he had his leg broken by a late challenge from left-back Fabrizio Poletti.

"Bobby was lying there, the referee wanted to move him off the park, and the Turin players were trying to bundle him off," remembered Jack Charlton. "I wouldn't let them move him; I knew that if Bobby Collins wouldn't get up, he must have something broken."

The referee had to work hard to keep tempers in check. Bremner chased after Poletti shouting, "I'll kill you for this."

Poletti later said: "It happened so quickly. He was going so fast. It has been a shock to me, and I am sincerely sorry."

With Collins stretchered away, Leeds had to see out 40 minutes with 10 men as substitutes were still not permitted in European competition. Revie's side dug deeper than it ever had before and it was in fact Bremner that came closest to adding to the scoreline as the home fans expressed their displeasure.

Collins' injury effectively ended his Leeds career and Revie had to rejig. He brought Johnny Giles into the centre of midfield to partner Bremner and Huddersfield Town's England winger Mike O'Grady was signed for £30,000 to fill in on the wing.

Incredibly, Collins was back for the end of the season as a draw against Manchester United saw Revie's team end as runners-up in the league for the second time. He would move in a free transfer to Bury in February 1967.

"They say that one man doesn't make a team, but Bobby Collins came nearer to doing it than anyone else I have ever seen on a football field," said Bremner.

Leeds progressed past SC Leipzig and drew 1962 and 1963 champions Valencia in the third round. If Leeds were forging a hard-man image, Valencia were in a different league.

Leeds were without a recognised striker with Alan Peacock injured and Revie, without any other senior striker available, opted to pick youngster Rod Belfitt.

The referee Leo Horn claimed: "Money was the cause of the trouble. You could almost smell it on the pitch." The referee suggested that the Leeds players were conscious of huge win bonuses and the finances of the game were ruining competitions. Revie later denied any such thing existed.

Jack Charlton, acting as captain with Collins injured, described it as, "One of the greatest storms in European football."

What happened led Revie to state: "If this is European football, I think we are better out of it."

Valencia had taken the lead after 16 minutes at Elland Road on 2 February 1966 after left-winger Munoz punished a mix-up between Hunter and Reaney. From thereon, Valencia coach Sabino Barinaga parked a large Spanish bus to frustrate the Leeds attack.

Horn's officiating was remarkably lax, and Valencia's tackling grew ever fiercer with Leeds, as they were accustomed, responding in kind.

"If Mr Horn had been firmer from the beginning the match might not have developed as it did," suggested Eric Stanger. "Leeds are no angels when it comes to rough house, but Valencia's tactics in the Fairs Cup-tie smacked more of the bullring than the football field. They were the roughest Continental side I have ever seen."

Bremner took serious punishment in midfield as Leeds began the second half with the majority of possession. They moved the ball quickly but were frustrated by Valencia's determined defence until Lorimer converted a cross from Giles. At 1-1, Leeds turned their attention to adding a second.

That was when the controversy erupted.

"I was at the centre of the row," Charlton recalled. "Three players, including myself, were ordered off. Both teams were also summoned from the field for a spell to allow heated tempers to cool.

"Fifteen minutes to go, and I raced upfield to add my weight to one of our attacks," Charlton explained. "As I challenged an opponent in the Valencia penalty area, I was kicked. This angered me, of course, but before I knew where I was, I found myself having to take much more. One of my opponents slung a punch which would have done credit to Cassius Clay.

"Right there and then my anger boiled over," he admitted. "I chased around that penalty area, intent upon only one thing — getting my own back. I had completely lost control of myself, after these diabolical fouls upon me, and neither the Spaniards nor the restraining hands of my teammates could prevent my pursuit for vengeance. Suddenly players seemed to be pushing and jostling each other everywhere. Police appeared on the field to stop this game of football from degenerating into a running battle. And Leo Horn walked off with his linesmen, signalling to club officials of both teams to get their players off, too.

"I was still breathing fire when I reached the dressing room," Charlton continued. "Then I got the word that I need not go back. For a moment I thought the referee had called off the match … then it sank home that it was only Jackie Charlton's presence which was not required any longer. For eleven minutes the teams remained off the field, to allow tempers on both sides to cool down. By that time, I was beginning to feel sorry for myself, and not a little ashamed of the way I had lost my temper. The only consolation I had was that a Valencia man — left-back Vidagany — had been told he need not return to the fray, either. So, it was ten against ten."

Billy Bremner remembered: "We all assumed it was the No 5 who had started the trouble which so enraged Big Jack. But when we returned to the pitch, there was No 5, as large as life. The man who was sent off was the left-back, and I reckon that it could be coincidence, but he had been pointed out by team mates as being the player involved in the first place, and it so happened that he had been given a right roasting by Jim Storrie, who had been having a blinder on the right wing. Certainly, the Spaniards risked very little by losing their left-back. Whichever way it was, this case of mistaken identity was a good thing for them."

The players returned to play out the final 15 minutes and played out the 1-1 draw.

The Fairs Cup Committee made it known they would meet after the second leg and conduct in the game in Spain would be taken into account. The referee came into criticism and his hopes of officiating in the upcoming World Cup were dashed. Othmar Huber replaced him for the second leg and took a much stronger stance.

Leeds were setup defensively and quick to break on the counter, which worked after 15 minutes when Paul Madeley slotted through Mike O'Grady to break the offside trap and put the Whites ahead in the tie. Valencia appealed in vain for offside. The keeper, who had stopped believing Leeds were offside, angrily confronted the linesman.

No action was taken against either side, other than a small fine to Charlton, as Leeds progressed to the quarter-finals.

"I am fast coming to the conclusion that there is just no end to their courage and fighting spirit," said Revie. "They were magnificent against a highly experienced club."

Leeds beat Ujpest Dozsa 4-1 at Elland Road, thanks to goals from Bell, Cooper, Bremner and Storrie and went through to the semi-final with a 1-1 draw in Hungary with Lorimer on the scoresheet.

A 1-0 defeat in Spain to Real Zaragoza in the semi-final first leg saw Leeds return to Elland Road and win 2-1 with goals from Charlton and Johanneson. Away goals were not applicable, and a replay took place on 11 May 1966.

Revie ordered the fire brigade to flood the pitch ahead of the replay to scupper the Spaniards, but his scheming did not work. Zaragoza won 3-1.

The partnership of Giles and Bremner flourished, but Leeds again finished second in the league, trailing Liverpool by six points.

Jack Charlton and Norman Hunter were members of Alf Ramsey's World Cup winning side, with Charlton playing an active part throughout and Hunter not featuring.

In 1966/67, Leeds won only three of their first 11 games, but rallied to finish fourth in the First Division. They reached the semi-finals of the FA Cup, losing 1–0 to Chelsea.

In the Inter Cities Fairs Cup second round, Leeds had progressed 8-2 on aggregate with Johanneson scoring a second leg hat-trick at Elland Road.

In the third-round draw, after the controversies of the previous season, Revie's side once again drew Valencia, but it didn't lead to a repeat of the aggressive affair of 12 months earlier.

Jimmy Greenhoff rocketed Leeds ahead from 15 yards after 12 minutes, but Claramunt levelled after 39 minutes and that was how the game remained.

Revie had to admit that a 1-1 score would give Leeds a tough task in Spain, particularly with a long injury list that included Paul Reaney, Jimmy Greenhoff, Mike O'Grady, Albert Johanneson, Terry Cooper, Alan Peacock and Rodney Johnson. Bobby Collins and Jim Storrie also missed out as they were on the verge of moving to other clubs.

Seven players in Revie's 13-man squad were aged 21 or under. David Harvey, Eddie Gray, Terry Hibbitt and Mick Bates were all 19. Peter Lorimer was 20 and Rod Belfitt and Gary Sprake were 21. The only players older than 27 were Willie Bell and Jack Charlton.

Johnny Giles shook off the challenges of three Valencia players to carve his way through from the halfway line and beat the keeper to open the scoring after just seven minutes. Giles had been told minutes before kick-off that his wife had given birth to a daughter.

Valencia threw everything they had at Revie's young side, as Sprake was kept occupied, Bremner inspired as the Spanish league's leading scorer Waldo had a night of missed opportunities. As Valencia pushed desperately forward, Leeds added their second three minutes from time as Lorimer nipped in to ensure Leeds progressed.

"The Boss really won it for us," suggested Bremner. He hammered it into us day after day and time after time that we would win — not that we might win or could win but that we would win. The result was we went on the field really believing that we were the better side and we proved it."

Revie added: "I am a great believer in the psychological approach and that if you are really convinced you are the better side, you will be.

"But if they ever make me any prouder, I'll burst. I don't know how they did it really. I didn't think a team, even a United team, could produce such a rate of work. And to win here with a forward line whose average age was hardly 20! It just shows that nothing is impossible in football."

Leeds lost 1-0 away at Bologna in the next round, bringing the Italians back to Elland Road where a Giles penalty levelled the tie 1-1 on aggregate. The referee blew the final whistle and invited United captain Bremner to join him and his Italian counterpart in the centre circle. The tie had come down to the toss of a coin.

The referee had Bremner on his right and the Italian on his left as he lofted the coin in the air. Bremner peered down, registered it had landed in his favour and raised his arms in the air before jumping into the arms of his manager.

In the semi-final against Kilmarnock, a Belfitt hat-trick and a penalty from Giles won the first leg in Scotland 4-2 and a 0-0 second leg put Leeds in their first European final where they would face Yugoslavian side Dinamo Zagreb. But due to fixture congestion they would have to wait until August for the first leg to be played in Zagreb.

For the first game, on 30 August 1967, Revie chose his team: Gary Sprake, Paul Reaney, Terry Cooper, Billy Bremner, Jack Charlton, Norman Hunter, Mick Bates, Peter Lorimer, Rod Belfitt, Eddie Gray and Michael O'Grady.

Leeds lost 2-0, a continuation to a poor start to the 1967/68 season where they had drawn 1-1 with Sunderland and then lost three games straight.

Revie made changes for the second leg: Gary Sprake, Willie Bell, Terry Cooper, Billy Bremner, Jack Charlton, Norman Hunter, Paul Reaney, Rod Belfitt, Jimmy Greenhoff, Johnny Giles, Michael O'Grady.

A crowd of 35,604 were at Elland Road on 6 September 1967, the vast majority hoping that Revie's team could overturn the two-goal deficit and they would witness Leeds United winning its first major trophy.

Revie's decision to play Reaney on the right-side of midfield drew criticism for its negativity. The manager knew that away goals now counted double in European competition and had the difficult balancing act of needing to score goals, but not being able to afford to concede.

"Revie was really defensive although we had been beaten away," commented Michael O'Grady. "He filled our heads with the opposition … He was really cautious, despite the away result. For one thing, he had Paul Reaney on the right wing but also, he filled our heads with the opposition. I was a winger, yet he was warning me about the other winger … expecting me to operate defensively as well as up front. It was hard work. You'd be sitting there thinking, 'God, just let us play!'"

Leeds could never forget about keeping a clean sheet and peppered the Zagreb goal, going close several times, but near misses were the feature of the night. Unfortunately, the tactics were one dimensional, route one style, but with attackers that lacked the strength in the air that the Zagreb defence possessed.

Zagreb won 2-0 over the two legs. Albert Morris, a United director, applauded as Sir Stanley Rous presented Zagreb with their trophy.

Revie's team were bridesmaids again.

Before the 1967/68 season got underway, Revie employed a gypsy to lift a curse he believed had been placed on the Elland Road ground. Whether you believe it or not, Leeds success snowballed after the gypsy worked her magic.

"Gypsies used to live at Elland Road before it was a football ground and I got this letter one day saying that there was a curse put on the ground by the gypsies when they were being moved off for it to become a football ground," Revie said. "The only way I could get the curse removed was getting a practising gypsy to come to the ground.

"I sent over to Blackpool a car to bring Gypsy Rose Lee to the ground. She shifted everybody out of the ground and she went out in the middle of the pitch, scratched the grass, threw some seeds down, went in each corner flag and did the same. She came off the pitch, came in my office for a cup of tea and said, 'Now you'll start winning things.' We did from that year on."

Revie's superstitions did not end there. He wore the same blue suit throughout the entire season, had a lucky tie, carried lucky charms in his pocket and walked the same route to his hotel every time.

"The suit he wore was a blue mohair and you could see his underpants through it, it was so worn at the backside," laughed Peter Lorimer. "But he wouldn't change it and it was quite embarrassing. I think he had to wear his coat even in the summer to cover it up. Obviously in the dressing room he would take his coat off and turn round and it was threadbare. But he wouldn't change that suit."

The match against Chelsea on 7 October 1967 was one of the finest performances from a Revie side during his time at Leeds United. That it came against Chelsea, a team that they had history with, a growing rivalry and been knocked out of the FA Cup at their hands in the previous two seasons, was pleasant symmetry.

Tommy Docherty had resigned as Chelsea boss the day before the game. Sometimes a managerial casualty galvanises a team and raises their performance. Not in this case.

After the disappointment of losing to Dinamo Zagreb, Leeds had conceded only five goals in nine league matches and were unbeaten. Four days before they faced Chelsea at Elland Road, they had beaten Spora of Luxembourg 9-0 in the Inter Cities Fairs Cup.

In stark contrast, managerless Chelsea were 19th in the First Division. They also were confronted by a Scotsman who was not happy. It was to be Billy Bremner's final game before he served a 28-day suspension for being sent off in a recent match against Fulham which had taken his disciplinary points to a harshly punitive level.

"Don Revie let me know, in no uncertain fashion, that I was letting myself down by such unseemly outbursts," Bremner recalled in his book. "Not only that, but even more important, I was letting my team mates down. And in his book, letting the side down in professional football is the cardinal sin. So, at long last, I realised that trouble and I MUST part company if I were to do myself and Leeds United full justice."

Bremner was determined to put on a show against Chelsea.

Revie smashed the club's transfer record, buying Mick Jones from Sheffield United for £100,000. He started up front.

Johanneson was making his first start of the season and opened the scoring after five minutes with a rare header. Six minutes later, Jimmy Greenhoff drove home the second and Jack Charlton headed home an Eddie Gray corner to make it 3-0 after 14 minutes. Lorimer added the fourth goal before the break and 15 minutes into the second half Gray hit a scorcher from the edge of the area. Lorimer's deflected effort and an outrageous bicycle kick from Bremner rounded off the 7-0 scoreline."

It had been an absolute battering and Bremner was the central player.

"The man of the match was unquestionably Bremner, who chose this final appearance to give a virtuoso performance," reported Eric Stanger. "To Chelsea's credit, however much Bremner teased and tormented them with his astonishing dexterity of foot and his remarkable sense of balance, so that he could turn and twist on the proverbial sixpence, they never tried to ruffle his temper. Nor, on his part was Bremner guilty of one foul tackle.

"It was a great demonstration of attacking wing-half play by any standards and, having made the first two goals (with considerable help from Reaney) and the fourth for Lorimer, Bremner bowed himself out of football for a time with a fine sense of the dramatic.

"Eight minutes from the end he got the last goal from Jones' forward header with a spectacular bicycle kick, so beloved by Continentals and South Americans. It brought down the house of 40,460 as it deserved to do."

A startling and memorable performance left Revie's Leeds breathing down the necks of those above them in the League, poised to launch a strong bid for the Championship.

On 9 December 1967, Leeds lost 2-0 to Liverpool. Roger Hunt had opened the scoring, but it was Liverpool's second that lives in the memory.

Leeds had stayed in the game as half-time approached when Charlton passed back to Sprake. Sprake was throwing out to his left-back Cooper, but balked when he saw Ian Callaghan closing in. He went to grab the ball against his chest and instead let go and watched it fly into his own net.

Bremner went straight to his keeper at the break in an effort to look after him. Sprake was shell-shocked. The Anfield music man had a sense of humour, playing 'Careless Hands' by Des O'Connor and 'Thank U Very Much' from The Scaffold. The Kop sang the lyrics through the second half. Sprake would make more mistakes, but in terms of gaffs, they don't get any bigger than Anfield 1967. Careless Hands would become his unwanted nickname.

Despite the progress, adventures and excitement, Revie's Leeds United had still not got their hands on a trophy. Two times second place in the league and two lost finals suggested that Leeds choked when it mattered most.

As Leeds approached the Football League Cup final against Arsenal on 2 March 1968, they were also still in the hunt for the League title, FA Cup and the Fairs Cup and on a run of 16 games unbeaten.

"It would be a nice reward if we could win this one following four years of hard toil and sweat," Revie said. "If we do succeed, I feel it will be a springboard for even bigger things."

Revie's team for the final: Gary Sprake, Paul Reaney, Terry Cooper, Billy Bremner, Jack Charlton, Norman Hunter, Jimmy Greenhoff, Peter Lorimer, Paul Madeley, Johnny Giles, Eddie Gray.

Leeds had beaten Luton, Bury, Sunderland, Stoke City and Derby County on their way to Wembley.

After 18 minutes, Gray's corner flew dangerously into a crowded area and broke for Cooper on the left-hand side of the area. His left-foot volley from 10 yards out smashed into the roof of the net.

Replays showed that Jack Charlton had gone in for Gray's corner and elbowed the advancing Arsenal keeper in the face. Regardless of whether it was intentional, it had definitely impeded Jim Furnell from claiming the cross.

A perturbed Gunners side dished out some retaliation as Frank McLintock charged into Sprake and punching and pushing ensued inside Leeds's six-yard box. The referee welcomed half-time as a chance to calm things down.

"The tension between the two teams was genuine and was similar to the hostility that had developed between us and Chelsea. The London press hated us, and this certainly created a north / south divide. Revie really stoked us up to put one over the London clubs every time we played them."

After the break, Revie had instructed his side to shut up shop. The defence registered its fifth clean sheet in nine games, and, after a tense showpiece, they were rewarded with their first taste of glory. Bremner hoisted the trophy aloft as he was lifted on to the shoulders of Sprake and Charlton. It hadn't been a classic, but getting a trophy was the priority of the day.

"The most important thing about that success was that it broke the ice as regards winning something," match-winner Cooper recalled. "Up until then we had been regarded as the bridesmaids, always coming runners-up in the League or losing cup semi-finals and finals. We didn't pick up as many trophies as we should have but after that win against Arsenal we went onto some big things. Our side wasn't far off its peak then. All the players were there, and it was just a pleasure to play in that team."

Any criticism aimed Leeds's way after a dour display was rejected by Revie in his *Evening Post* column: "Our pride in at last winning a major soccer honour has not been dented by fierce criticism about the way this was achieved. I make no apologies for the fact that Leeds United did not keep their vow to produce a more attractive display than on their last appearance at Wembley against Liverpool three years ago.

"Injuries and illness to forwards Jimmy Greenhoff and Johnny Giles forced us unfortunately to adopt a more cautious approach in the final. It was not our original aim to close up the game. I wrote here last week that we badly wanted to prove ourselves as a skilled and entertaining side in front of the millions who would be watching. I meant it.

"Now we have won this trophy, we feel that a great weight has been lifted off our shoulders. At last Leeds has cast away that champion runners-up tag — and are now in a good position to win more honours. I am positive we will take another title before the end of the season."

Leeds ended their league campaign in 4th place and were defeated by Everton in the semi-final of the FA Cup, but would land another major trophy before the season was technically over. I use the word technically because the two-legged final was delayed until the start of the next season due to fixture congestion.

A 16-0 aggregate thrashing over Spora was followed by wins against FK Partizan (Serbia), Hibernian, Rangers and Dundee (all from Scotland) to earn the right to play Ferencvarosi, of Hungary, in the final.

Both Sir Matt Busby and Bill Shankly felt the Hungarians were right up there with the best sides in Europe. Their star man was striker Florian Albert, whose six goals in the competition were only bettered by the eight from both Bobby Charlton and Denis Law.

Leeds warmed up with a friendly against Celtic where Giles and Lorimer scored for Leeds after Celtic had taken the lead after Sprake conceded a penalty.

The first leg of the final was played at Elland Road on Wednesday, 7 August 1968 and Revie made no secret of his disappointment that fans had stayed away, with only 25,268 turning out for a European final.

"One possible reason was that Leeds had an excellent Rugby League club and the area was a real hotbed of the game," suggested Sprake. "It took quite a while for the football club to win these fans around. Also,

Leeds was a very working-class area and so many people couldn't afford to take the family to both Elland Road and Headingley if fixtures clashed on the same weekend."

Revie's team to play the first leg: Gary Sprake, Paul Reaney, Terry Cooper, Billy Bremner, Jack Charlton, Norman Hunter, Peter Lorimer, Paul Madeley, Mick Jones, Johnny Giles, Eddie Gray.

Ferencvarosi set out to defend, more than comfortable with an away draw. The Hungarian keeper Geezi saved well from a brutal strike by Lorimer, but proved himself to be the weak link, particularly from high balls into the box. An early drop fell to Hunter who shot wide, but Geezi flapped at everything that came his way.

It was from a Lorimer corner that Geezi failed to claim in a congested area and Jones put Leeds ahead in the 41st minute with a sharply struck volley.

Giles was forced off after 65 minutes after a clash of heads and was replaced by Jimmy Greenhoff. Jones was stretchered off after being taken out by the keeper and Belfitt took his place. For a while Leeds had lost momentum. Charlton was a rock at the back and Sprake pulled off a brilliant save from a Rakosi shot.

Revie remained confident: "The fact that we kept a clean sheet was a good thing. If we get a goal over there, they have got to get three. They were body checking, deliberately handling and obstructing … Some of it was diabolically clever and screened. Mick Jones has been lucky. He was kicked in the groin and it is sore, but it could have been worse."

Ferencvarosi coach, Dr Karoly Lakat, had a contrary view: "It was more fighting than a real game of football. Leeds played the more vigorous and forceful football. I thought our team were the better technicians. I could not see clearly what happened when Leeds scored because I was too far away, but the goalkeeper says he was definitely pushed."

So, Leeds took a 1-0 advantage to the Nep Stadium Hungary on 11 September 1968, although they were nearly denied the opportunity to become the first English side to lift the trophy as political tensions in Eastern Europe almost saw the game's abandonment after the Soviet Union invaded Czechoslovakia.

"We will be condemned by many people for not refusing to play the Hungarian champions in view of what has happened recently in Czechoslovakia," Revie wrote in the *Evening Post*. "Much has been written and said about the ways in which the western world can show its disapproval. Sadly, soccer is being used as a weapon in the political arena.

"Celtic, who were due to meet Ferencvarosi in the first round of the European Cup this season, threatened to boycott the match because of the Czech crisis. They asked UEFA not to force clubs to meet sides from

Warsaw Pact countries, and as a result all Eastern and Western Europe countries, paired in the Champions Cup and Cup Winners Cup, have been separated in the draw.

"Politics? I prefer to leave this to the politicians. This does not mean I do not feel strongly about what has happened in Czechoslovakia — but I feel that political opinion should not be allowed to interfere in any way with sport. Boycotting matches against Communist countries is the easy way out. Surely trying to beat them on the soccer field is a better way to show one's distaste.

"I believe we have the ability to win, although I would have liked to go to Budapest with a bigger lead than the 1-0 margin we established in the first leg. The Hungarians did not set Elland Road alight with their attacking play, but I know from past experience that on their own ground some continental sides have the ability to let all hell loose.

"The Hungarians are probably the finest passers of a ball in the game. They have always been adept at playing one two football … their forwards have the ability to create chances with bouts of first time passing in confined areas. When up against this type of football, it is essential to stick to the man and avoid the temptation of following the ball. It is someone else's responsibility to pick up the player for whom the pass is intended.

"A very difficult match is ahead of us. We know how formidable the Ferencvarosi attackers are. We expect them to produce some fireworks. But Leeds has proved time and again that its defence can stand its ground in the hottest moments."

Revie was without Giles (knee) and Eddie Gray (ankle) unavailable through injury, and Jimmy Greenhoff had moved to Birmingham City. He picked the following starting XI: Gary Sprake, Paul Reaney, Terry Cooper, Billy Bremner, Jack Charlton, Norman Hunter, Mike O'Grady, Peter Lorimer, Mick Jones, Paul Madeley, Terry Hibbitt.

Revie's opposite number, Lakat, had to shed the defensive approach he had taken in Leeds and attack. The Leeds defence was in for a tough time as the Hungarian side possessed serious firepower up front.

"Although my recollection of some games is beginning to fade somewhat, the game at the Nep Stadium remains etched in my memory to this day," said Sprake. "I remember walking out of the tunnel to be greeted by a crescendo of noise and the atmosphere was unbelievably hostile.

"The political situation behind the Iron Curtain was very tense at that time and for the 76,000 Hungarian fans in Budapest it was one of the few chances they had to express and show their feelings in public. They certainly did that with their hostility focused directly towards us."

The game went as predicted with Ferencvarosi on the front foot in front of a 76,000-strong crowd and Leeds holding a defensive line. Rakosi's shot on 16 minutes was cleared by Cooper, and Cooper was again at hand to block an effort from Albert. A rare Leeds advance saw Jones's header clip the crossbar. Leeds were pressed deep, but survived until half-time with their lead still intact.

Sprake was forced into action early in the second half and the trend continued as Ferencvarosi camped in the final third. Nearly home, Leeds survived a scare in the 86th minute when the referee ruled out a Varga equaliser for offside.

"Our defence that night was amazing, and it was probably my greatest performance for Leeds," said Sprake. "Near the end of the game I made what I regard as my best ever save. With minutes to go the Hungarians were awarded a free kick outside the box in a very central position, to be taken by their dead ball ace Novak. I lined up the wall to my right-hand side and stood just behind it to cover my left-hand post. He hit the ball as hard as he could, and you could feel the crowd trying to suck the ball into the net behind me. After Novak hit the ball I had only a split second to see it as it dipped over the wall and I managed to dive full length to my left and slightly behind me. It was important that I got a full hand to it as it was hit so hard it rebounded off me and ended up halfway up the stand.

"I was still feeling the pain in my wrist when minutes later the referee blew for full time and we had won our first European trophy. Although I felt that I had more than helped us to win the cup it was a fantastic defensive effort from every player and Terry Cooper had a brilliant game. He was everywhere and even cleared one off the line. I think this game was the only really consistently good report I got off the national press."

Billy Bremner received the trophy from FIFA President Sir Stanley Rous before the players did a richly deserved lap of honour. It had been a truly heroic performance.

"After the disappointments over the past four years, when we got into those final few minutes, my heart nearly stopped beating," Revie said proudly. "Every minute as the final whistle drew near seemed like an hour. It was a real team effort here tonight. Ferencvarosi pressed very hard, particularly in the second half when they attacked all the time. The way the boys kept their heads and their cool play was really tremendous.

"We decided to keep it tight and play the game as it came. In the first half we had two chances to score in three minutes when a Mick Jones header struck the bar and a shot from Mike O'Grady hit the keeper. Everyone is in high spirits here, and we are proud to be the first British club to bring home the Fairs Cup."

Revie needed to order a trophy cabinet and leave space for the years ahead. After the cup success, Revie knew that winning the league title in 1968/69 would be the way to confirm Leeds United as the best team in the country.

And, after a 5-1 defeat to Burnley at Turf Moor on 19 October 1968, United went the rest of the season unbeaten in the league, including a revenge 5-1 whopping of Burnley on 21 December 1968.

The title decider against Liverpool had originally been scheduled for 22 March 1969, but a flu epidemic had swept through Elland Road. Leeds had lost to Ujpest Dozsa in the Fairs Cup on 19 March 1969 to go out 3-0 on aggregate. The Football League agreed to a request from Leeds for a postponement, much to the chagrin of Liverpool and their manager Bill Shankly.

By 28 April, Leeds led Liverpool by five points, with the Reds having one game in hand. As Leeds travelled to Anfield for their penultimate fixture of the season, a point was enough for Revie's side to claim their first ever league title. It was a tough trip. Liverpool were in equally good form but, if unsuccessful, Leeds could still lift the crown by earning at least a point at home to Nottingham Forest two days later.

Revie's team: Gary Sprake, Paul Reaney, Terry Cooper, Billy Bremner, Jack Charlton, Norman Hunter, Mike O'Grady, Paul Madeley, Mick Jones, Johnny Giles, Eddie Gray.

53,750 packed into Anfield and the Kop urged on their Liverpool heroes. The team in red started hard and Leeds were desperate to weather the early storm with so much at stake. Tackles flew in, free kicks were regularly given, and the trainers were on the pitch frequently.

Liverpool knew the importance of the game too and as Leeds settled, they found penetrating the Whites' defence an impossible task. Leeds simply were not going to give anything away.

"The match was a bit of a let-down," said Bremner. "I couldn't see Leeds scoring, but didn't think Liverpool would do so either. Generally, it was one of those frustrating games where the ball keeps running out of play every minute. After failing to get an early goal, Liverpool became over-anxious and made the mistake of hitting too many high crosses into our goal-mouth — Gary and Big Jack had no trouble gobbling these up."

The response of the disappointed Kop is one of the charming tales only sport can give.

"Beforehand, Revie had instructed Bremner, if they should get that decisive point, to lead the players after the game towards the Kop," wrote Bagchi and Rogerson. "Bremner took some persuading, but after they had celebrated before their own travelling support, Bremner duly marched his men forward. The ground fell silent, but instead of being lynched, the

Dick Ray became the first Leeds United manager in 1919. He had previously been the first captain of Leeds City and his footballing association with the city spanned 30 years.

Arthur Fairclough became manager in 1920 and took Leeds into the First Division for the first time with promotion in the 1923/24 season.

All photography:
Varley Picture Agency

Billy Hampson was Leeds United manager between 1935 and 1947 and had built an exciting young side until the Second World War intervened.

Willis Edwards had a 35-year association with the club, but was too soft a character to make his mark as a manager.

Major Frank Buckley was United's manager between 1948 and 1953. An authoritarian, war hero and strong character, he was the first manager appointed by the club that had previous success elsewhere. The Major couldn't restore United's Division One status but, across his managerial career, he revolutionised the sport.

Raich Carter managed Leeds between 1953 and 1958 and had been an immensely talented player. He took Leeds back to the First Division, but his arrogant air meant some players did not warm to him. He was shocked to be sacked before he could establish the club in the top flight.

Bill Lambton's inexperience showed. He quickly lost the dressing room. He did bring Don Revie and Billy Bremner to Leeds though.

Jack Taylor was manager between 1959 and 1961. Billy Bremner described the club as "unprofessional" during his tenure and he left Leeds struggling in the Second Division.

Don Revie (far right) is remembered as the most successful manager in Leeds United's history. Between 1961 and 1974, when he left to manage England, he won two league titles and turned Leeds into the best team in England and one of the best in Europe. He brought trophies to a dressing room packed with talent.

Revie developed a youth policy that transformed the club and created some of the best players Leeds fans have ever seen. He created a family atmosphere and the players travelled in style.

Revie collected numerous Manager of the Month Awards, pictured here with comedian Eric Morecambe. He was also Manager of the Year in 1969, 1970 and 1972.

Don Revie is pictured on his last visit to Elland Road on 11 May 1988. In a wheelchair due to suffering from motor neurone disease, the club held a charity match to raise funds to battle the disease. Many of his former players were in attendance.

Brian Clough (far left) may have stayed in position for a mere 44 days in 1974, but his period as Leeds United manager is remembered disproportionately to his achievements. Movies have been made about it.

Jimmy Armfield
restored calmness
to the club after
Clough's departure
and took Leeds to
the European Cup
final in Paris where
his side were
"robbed".

Jock Stein was a great Celtic manager who had won everything north of the border, but he was made Scotland boss in 1978 before his office chair at Elland Road had become remotely warm.

Jimmy Adamson left behind a club in freefall and the recollections of his managerial tenure are mixed at best.

Allan Clarke (pictured bringing England winger Peter Barnes to Leeds) was the first of Revie's players to take charge as manager in 1980.

Eddie Gray was another Don Revie great who struggled to meet his aspirations as club manager. Gray was in charge between 1982 and 1985 and returned to the dugout as caretaker boss and coach on numerous occasions in the decades that followed.

Billy Bremner was captain fantastic as a player under Don Revie, but his time as Leeds United manager never hit the same heady heights. He came very close to promotion, but left with no cigar in 1988.

Leeds team were surprised to find themselves being loudly hailed as 'Champions' by the 27,000 Koppites massed in front of them.

"The players stayed put for 20 minutes, soaking it all in, larking around, jumping on one another and paying their tributes to both sets of fans. They had been derided and despised for such a long time that one could not blame them for basking in the adulation."

Eddie Gray remembered: "Being cheered by a rival crowd, any rival crowd, was a new experience for us. This in itself was as much of a turning point for Leeds as the Championship achievement."

Back in the dressing room, where Shankly had provided a crate of champagne, Revie clearly felt flattered by the two extraordinary events of the evening: "The reception given us by the sporting Liverpool crowd was truly magnificent," he said, "and so, for that matter, was our defence tonight. It was superb in everything."

Shankly simply said: "Leeds United are worthy champions. They are a great side."

For Revie, that tribute meant a great deal. He had looked up to Shanks from the start and the pair were friends, often in communication throughout the season.

"That wonderful night at Anfield saw our burning faith in ourselves justified," Billy Bremner remembered. "At last we were well and truly vindicated."

Revie's champions had set a number of records during the 1968/69 season: the most points (67), most wins (27), fewest defeats (2), and most home points (39); a still-unbroken club record is their 34-match unbeaten run that extended into the following season.

Allan Clarke was purchased for the 1969/70 season for a British transfer high of £165,000 from Leicester City. Clarke would form a partnership with Mick Jones up front and Peter Lorimer was allowed to play in a more advanced position after O'Grady was moved on to Wolves for £80,000.

Revie received an OBE in the New Year's Honours List and travelled to Buckingham Palace with his family to collect the award from the Queen. "My award should be recognised as a club rather than personal achievement," he said.

The 1969/70 season was a case of so near, yet so far. Revie wanted the treble but would fall narrowly short on all fronts.

The season started in great style. Revie added another trophy when Leeds beat Manchester City 2-1 at Wembley, thanks to goals from Jack Charlton and Eddie Gray to claim the Charity Shield.

Then on their European Cup bow they met Lyn Oslo of Norway in the first round. The first leg ended a club record 10-0, which included a Mick Jones hat-trick, a brace apiece for Johnny Giles, Allan Clarke and Billy Bremner and a goal for Mick O'Grady. The second leg in Norway ended goalless, but Revie's side were through at a canter.

A 6-0 aggregate win over Ferencvarosi in November, was followed by a third-round win over Standard Liege in March with Leeds winning both legs 1-0.

Leeds finished second in the league behind Everton and lost the FA Cup final to Chelsea after a replay. Celtic accounted for Revie's team at the semi-final stage of the European Cup. That set up a mouthwatering 'Battle of Britain' in the semi-finals against Scottish giants Celtic. The disappointment was that the teams could not meet in the final.

English pundits didn't give the Scots a chance. Celtic were out to prove everyone wrong. The press was full of jingoistic vitriol.

Jock Stein, who would go on to briefly manage Leeds United, had led Celtic to become the first British side to lift the European Cup in 1967.

Stein responded to the draw: "I honestly felt that we were destined to meet in Milan. But now I have adjusted to the fact that we are drawn together in the semi-final and I can assure you that I can scarcely wait for the games to begin. We know Leeds and we respect them too, but we are not frightened of them. I think these will be great, great games."

"We had already comfortably won our fifth successive League title and had once again reached the final of the European Cup, having eliminated Basle, Benfica and Fiorentina — the last two being top quality sides," Bobby Lennox said, as he summed up the mood in Scotland in his autobiography. "That had taken us into a semi-final with Leeds United and there, it was widely predicted in the English press, our little sortie in the 1969/70 European Cup was destined to end.

"The English press and television people, with supreme arrogance, claimed that Leeds United were unstoppable that season and were champions of Europe in all but name. Those media people failed to consider whether some other teams in the competition might rival the talents of the club they were championing.

"A lot was said about the Scottish League being inferior to the English League but at Celtic we were forced by Jock Stein to maintain a set of specific standards. If Leeds had thought they were coming up against an amateurish mob from an unprofessional League, they were wrong."

Don Revie said: "It's going to be a tough task in Scotland if we don't take a lead, for on their own territory, they are great. We have not found any cracks in their side in the matches we have played against them or in the three we've seen them recently."

And Leeds's assistant manager, Maurice Lindley, saw Celtic's 3-0 win over Ayr United and said, "I saw enough to realise that this match with Celtic will be the toughest we have ever had to play in almost 10 years of European competition."

And so it proved. Leeds were in the middle of a run of fixtures that defied belief. They needed two replays to get past Manchester United in the FA Cup, which meant they had to play eight matches in 15 days. Revie was resting players for league matches so he could concentrate his efforts on the one trophy he coveted above all others.

"Leeds have shown us so much respect that it has cost them the League," crowed Stein. "But they must chase the game because supporters expect victory at home, and they won't allow them too long to score."

On 1 April 1970, it took 90 seconds for Revie to be wiping Scotch egg off his face after a long, high ball into the Whites' area wasn't cleared and dropped for Connelly whose deflected shot found its way past Sprake.

There's no question that Leeds's tired legs were playing their part and immediately after half-time Connelly thought he'd added a second goal for Celtic, with the offside verdict hotly contested.

Leeds improved after the let off and Clarke forced Celtic keeper Williams into action, but them Bremner was substituted after receiving a knock to the head and only a 72nd minute shot on the crossbar from Eddie Gray gave the Scots any real problems. Jimmy Johnstone was superb for Celtic on the wing as his team had certainly not rested on their lead.

"Celtic were the better side and deserved their victory," Revie conceded after the game. "Every one of them was magnificent. It makes it very hard for us at Hampden, but we are still not out of it. Anything can happen when we play the return game."

Jock Stein was unsurprisingly jubilant to have got one over the English: "They have laughed at our football long enough down here. I'm not talking about Leeds United or Don Revie, they have respect for us. I'm talking about the critics and commentators who have rarely given credit to Scottish football. Maybe tonight's result will stop them laughing."

But even Stein had to remember that there was a second leg to play, but for Leeds's trip north of the border, Revie's men were going to have to raise their game.

"Whoever it was in Leeds United jerseys that Celtic beat 1-0 at Elland Road in the European Cup semi-final, it was not Leeds United. With the exception of Sprake, the men who have dominated the English season for months were unrecognisable," suggested the *Yorkshire Evening Post*.

Celtic had announced their decision to play the home leg at the massive national stadium in order to accommodate the huge crowd that was expected. Their own stadium had a 60,000 capacity, while Hampden could accommodate a crowd of 136,000 in those days. In 1937, it had housed 149,415 for a Scotland-England contest. 136,505 turned out on 15 April to see which British club would reach the final. The suggestion was the crowd was far bigger with many more locked outside desperate to see the game of the season. Of the crowd inside the stadium, only 4,500 were officially Leeds supporters. Even Leeds fans couldn't out-sing their rivals that night.

Between the European legs, Leeds lost their League title after Everton's win over West Brom meant they couldn't finish higher than second. Paul Reaney broke his leg against West Ham, an injury that would see him miss England's 1970 World Cup defence.

And then Chelsea's FA Cup final equaliser to end a magnificent encounter 2-2 condemned Revie to yet another match to shoehorn into the season. Leeds had gone ahead at Wembley, but a long-range shot had crept under Gary Sprake's body to level the final at 1-1.

"We are keener than ever to win the FA Cup and the European Cup now for Paul's sake," Revie told the media. "I would give a year's wages to beat Celtic."

The players suggested their manager put his money where his mouth was, and Revie agreed to their challenge. We will never know whether Don would have handed across his salary to the players' pool as Leeds lost 2-1 to the Scottish champions.

Revie highlighted the need to nullify the threat of Jimmy Johnstone ahead of the game and brought back Norman Hunter, who had been missing prior to the Cup final with an injured knee, in place of Reaney.

The Leeds boss again drew criticism for his negative mindset and Stein's encouraged his Celtic side not to fear the Yorkshire team and emphasised that their manager was incredibly nervous, and the Leeds team would take his heed.

"Jimmy had everything you could wish for in a winger," Terry Cooper reflected after the Scottish winger had once again run rings around Leeds. "He had such a low centre of gravity and it was so difficult to stop him. Unless you took him by unfair means it simply wasn't going to happen. Jimmy was a bit like George Best. That's the best compliment I can give him. But at Elland Road and Hampden, especially the game in Glasgow, I wasn't looking to pay him any compliments.

"I would love to have kicked Jinky, but I couldn't get near him! I still have nightmares. I reckon I had good anticipation, but I could do nothing to take the ball off Johnstone."

Bremner described Johnstone's performance at Hampden as "one of the greatest exhibitions I have ever seen", and he'd not had a bad game himself, scoring with a stunning 25-yard shot into the top corner to level the tie at 1-1 midway through the first half. It stunned the home support and was a goal of such venom and quality it was fit to win any game. Unfortunately for Revie's Leeds, it wasn't going to win this one.

Celtic roared back, but couldn't make the breakthrough before half-time, but two minutes into the second half an Auld cross was headed into the Leeds goal by the diving Hughes. Celtic were back in front. And then a few minutes later, Sprake had to be carried from the pitch after being caught overly late by the unrelenting Hughes.

And then Celtic sealed it in the 53rd minute when Johnstone pushed the ball to Bobby Murdoch who shot low under the substitute keeper David Harvey. And despite Leeds's best efforts to come back, 2-1 is how it remained and Celtic progressed to the European Cup final 3-1 on aggregate

"We lost our chance at Leeds," confessed Revie. "When we scored, I thought we could do something, but Celtic are a very, very good side. I sincerely hope they win the European Cup again."

They didn't. Celtic lost 2-1 to Feyenoord in the San Siro final.

"How one can feel sorry for Leeds," wrote Albert Barham in *The Guardian*. "The challenge of 60 matches this season has been too great, and after living for the past month on a razor's edge of hope, they have failed to win two of the three major honours they sought. It has all been too much for them."

United's season, that had promised so much, ended in defeat to Chelsea in their 64th match as the FA Cup eluded them too. The Old Trafford replay saw Leeds without the injured Sprake in a physical encounter where Leeds took the lead in the 35th minute when Mick Jones scored a tremendous solo goal. Peter Osgood's diving header levelled the occasion and extra-time was required to separate the sides. David Webb's header proved the difference as a late Leeds onslaught came to nought.

There was no love lost between the two sides and the replay was a hugely physical encounter.

Chelsea's Peter Osgood summed up the relationship between the sides: "I've got to say that over 90 minutes, we hated them, and they hated us, and we knew we were in for a battle. We knew they were going to come over the top, they were going to do you, they were going to kick you off the ball when the referee's not looking, they'd moan, they'd whinge and they would do everything to try and win. They got to the referee.

"They were a great side," Osgood continued. "I played all over the world and I've got to say that the Leeds side was the best club side I ever played against."

Peter Lorimer insisted: "They knew they couldn't beat us. They came out there to have a kick at us and that's just what they did. In the modern-day rules, there'd have only been two players left on the park at the end of the game."

After the late season disappointment, Revie simply promised, "We'll be back."

Don Revie remained at Leeds United for the new season after turning down a lucrative £100,000 four-year contract offer to manage Birmingham City and chose not to add to his Elland Road squad.

United began their quest for the league title with a trip to Old Trafford. Mick Jones headed Leeds ahead and Revie's boys took the points. That form continued as Leeds and Arsenal pulled away at the top.

Ray Tinkler was the referee for Leeds's game against West Brom at Elland Road on 17 April 1971. His decision to over-rule his linesman who had flagged for offside as the Baggies broke clear led to a goal that would be one of the most contentious Leeds have ever conceded and one of the costliest. Brown had picked up the ball near the halfway line with teammate Suggett clearly offside. The flag was raised and with Leeds players committed in attack and halting when they saw the flag, Brown went through on goal before passing to Astle, who was also offside as he scored.

The game had been held up by a pitch invasion as many United fans showed their own displeasure. Leeds lost the game 2-1 and handed the title to Arsenal, who won by one point, with Don Revie saying: "I have never been so sick at heart. The ref's decision on Suggett, the worst I have seen man and boy, was wrong and it wrecked nine months of hard work at our club. I regret the crowd scenes like anybody else but, by heaven, I can understand why they cut loose. Astle was also offside, in my opinion, when he took the pass from Brown to score."

Tinkler never refereed at Elland Road again and, after the pitch invasion and Revie's comments, Leeds were forced by the Football Association to play their first four home fixtures of the following season on neutral grounds.

Fourth Division Colchester United performed a giant killing to eliminate a humiliated Leeds from the FA Cup, but Revies's team again enjoyed European success by winning the Inter-Cities Fairs Cup, beating Sarpsborg FK (Norway), Dynamo Dresden (East Germany), AC Sparta Prague (Czechoslovakia), Vitória (Portugal) and Liverpool before playing Juventus in the final.

A 2–2 draw at the Stadio Olimpico di Torino was followed by a 1-1 draw at Elland Road as Leeds took the UEFA Fairs Cup trophy on away goals.

Leeds played their first four games of the 1971/72 season at Huddersfield's Leeds Road and took four wins and two draws from the opening seven matches. Revie had his side ticking, playing great football, particularly winning praise for their 7–0 and 6–1 wins over Southampton and Nottingham Forest.

The Southampton victory on 4 March 1972 is one of the most famous of Revie's tenure as the BBC *Match of the Day* cameras recorded their flowing play. The dour, stubborn and cautious image of many of The Don's sides was banished as the press described "Super Leeds" and the crowd shouted "Ole" at every completed pass.

Allan Clarke and Peter Lorimer had put Leeds 2-0 ahead by half-time and a scintillating 18 minutes of second-half football saw five goals scored. Clarke notched his second after 60 minutes, Lorimer made it 4-0 four minutes later and completed his hat-trick on 68 minutes. Jack Charlton headed the sixth before Mick Jones made it 7-0.

Despite the brilliance, Leeds ended their campaign poorly and a 2-1 final day defeat to Wolverhampton Wanderers saw them gift the league title to Brian Clough's Derby County by a single point.

An FA Cup run that involved wins against Bristol Rovers, Liverpool, Cardiff City, Tottenham and Birmingham saw Leeds contest the 1972 Cup final against Arsenal on 6 May 1972.

The Leeds team picked by Revie: David Harvey, Paul Reaney, Paul Madeley, Billy Bremner, Jack Charlton, Norman Hunter, Peter Lorimer, Allan Clarke, Mick Jones, Johnny Giles and Eddie Gray.

Clarke had struck the crossbar with a first-half header as Revie's team was more attacking than in their previous Cup final efforts. In the 53rd minute, Clarke propelled himself forward to meet a Lorimer cross. Clarke's dive met the ball and powered it from beyond the penalty spot into the corner of the net.

Arsenal's chances were rare. Alan Ball had a shot cleared off the line by Reaney and Harvey saved well from a Frank McLintock effort, but Leeds's defence was rock solid. Lorimer hit the post and Gray almost scored towards the end as Leeds won their first FA Cup.

Mick Bates had dislocated an elbow in a challenge just before the final whistle and as Bremner led his team to collect the trophy, he was still receiving treatment. Hunter had collected his medal and returned to the pitch to lead his teammate up the famous Wembley steps as the striker collected his medal.

Revie had won the FA Cup as a player, with Manchester City in 1956, and now claimed it as manager.

"I've waited and sweated years for this day," the Leeds boss said. But he'd be denied the league and cup double two days later with the defeat against Wolves.

Scottish defender Gordon McQueen was signed from St Mirren for £30,000 ahead of the 1972/73 season as Revie's replacement for Jack Charlton. £100,000 was also spent on defender Trevor Cherry and £35,000 on central defender Roy Ellam. Striker Joe Jordan began to get more games, but once again the league season fell away and the team finished third.

Brian Clough, acting as a TV pundit, commented that "there is no way Sunderland can beat Leeds" in the FA Cup final, but they did as the 1973 showpiece went to the Second Division side 1-0. Ian Porterfield had pounced when the Leeds defence had failed to clear a corner. The Sunderland manager, Bob Stokoe, wearing red trousers and a beige overcoat, charged on to the pitch in one of the most famous FA Cup victory celebrations.

Then came the most frustrating European night in the club's history. In the final of the European Cup Winners' Cup in Salonika, Greece, they met Italian giants AC Milan at the Kaftanzoglio Stadium.

Leeds were beaten 1–0 following some controversial refereeing decisions by Christos Michas, which eventually saw Norman Hunter, frustrated at being constantly fouled, push Gianni Rivera to the floor and be sent-off.

"It hasn't been a good week," Revie said a couple of days after the game. "I always feel it takes tremendous characters to start on Monday morning again after disappointments. But it is one of the hazards of the job, it spoils your steak, you don't enjoy your weekend, it takes me until Monday morning to get over it, but when I see all the lads' faces and we start off again then I can lift myself as well as they can."

Peter Lorimer recalled: "It was quite obvious on the field that we couldn't win the match. In fact, it was so obvious that at the end of the game during the celebrations and the trophy presentation in Greece, there was this word being shouted by the Greek people. We didn't have a clue what it was. One of the Greek press guys who spoke English told is that what they were chanting was 'shame' at the referee.

"It was so obvious that they knew straight away what had gone on. I think Milan got banned for four years from Europe and the referee got banned for life. The reason we didn't get awarded the trophy was because they said something happened, but they couldn't prove it was Milan who had done it."

Yorkshire and Humber MEP, Richard Corbett, unsuccessfully petitioned the European Parliament in 2009 to have the result of the final reversed after allegations had been made that referee Michas had taken a bribe from the Italians.

Revie could have moved on in the summer that followed after Everton offered him a five-year £100,000 contract, plus a £50,000 signing-on fee, but he remained at Elland Road after the move broke down due to a new law preventing wage rises in order to curb inflation.

Revie challenged his side ahead of the 1973/74 season to go unbeaten throughout the entire league campaign and at one stage put together a record run of 29 games unbeaten. Three straight defeats in February and March put paid to the team's efforts to comply, but they did secure Leeds's second league title when they finished five points clear of second-placed Liverpool.

Leeds had their second league title under Revie, who had played a weakened side in the UEFA Cup to secure an early exit and maximise his team's league chances.

Revie made no secret of his desire to win the European Cup and he considered turning down the Football Association's offer to him to manage the England international side. He chose England, knowing that he faced a tough challenge of building a new Leeds side with the majority of the squad ageing. Fresh legs were required.

Fans loved him, but the Leeds United board not so much. They ignored Revie's recommendation that Johnny Giles should be his replacement to copy Liverpool's successful strategy of promoting from within. Revie firmly believed that Giles knew the club, the system and methods and could therefore pick up the baton.

Peter Lorimer, however, indicated that the decision to appoint Giles may have upset one of the star players.

"To all the players Johnny should have taken over," Lorimer said. "Unfortunately, I don't think Billy thought that. I think Billy, to a degree, had thought that he was being brought forward to do the job and I think it came as a great shock to Billy when Don recommended John. Now Billy, I believe, had said that he was interested in the job himself. I think that created some doubt in the chairman's mind, thinking how will the team react to Johnny, and this is Billy Bremner, the captain."

Instead, the hierarchy appointed Brian Clough, a fierce critic of Revie, as his successor. It was a move that surprised everyone.

Despite lasting just 44 days in the job, Clough spent more in transfer fees than Revie had in his 13 years at the club.

Revie was the man who made people think football when they heard the name Leeds. He will take some beating as the greatest Leeds manager of all time.

Gary Sprake, the keeper that Revie trusted between the sticks for much of his success, died in October 2016, aged 71. From a team of brothers, tied together by a common bond of winning trophies, Sprake became the outcast after accusing Revie of match-fixing and attempting to bribe opposition clubs.

Sprake had not attended reunions of the great Revie side, despite playing 508 times for Leeds United. He made some mistakes, but mainly pulled off stunning saves and was a huge component of the era of success. The Welshman had moved to Birmingham City for £100,000 in 1973, the highest fee ever paid for a keeper to date, after losing his place to David Harvey.

The *Daily Mirror* paid Sprake £7000 in 1978 to spill the beans about Revie fixing matches and bribing opposition players. No criminal or Football Association charges ever arose from the accusations.

"I said something wrong about the great man, even though I still think he was a great manager," he told the BBC in 2012. "I broke ranks and I've lived with it for more than 30 years now. It doesn't really bother me."

It bothered his former teammates and a lot of Leeds supporters. However, Sprake was not the only former player to query Revie's impropriety. Wolves midfielder, Danny Hegan, claimed that Billy Bremner had attempted to arrange a bribe. Bremner won £100,000 in libel damages when neither Sprake nor Hegan would give evidence in court.

The manager of Bury in 1962, Bob Stokoe, alleged Revie had offered him £500 to "go easy" on Leeds who were fighting relegation. When Stokoe refused, he said that Revie had asked, "In that case, may I speak to your players?"

England World Cup winner, Alan Ball, told of how Revie had given him £300 to sign for Leeds, but he'd taken the cash and signed for Everton. Both men were charged with bringing the game into disrepute.

As England manager, he failed to qualify for the 1978 World Cup and the nation finished third in the 1976/77 British Home Championship. He missed the trip to Brazil for a scouting assignment to Italy, which was really a trip to Dubai to negotiate a deal to take over as manager of the United Arab Emirates. Revie asked to be released from his contract with England and on 12 July 1977 the *Daily Mail* announced he was quitting his country to manage the UAE.

"I sat down with my wife, Elsie, one night and we agreed that the England job was no longer worth the aggravation," Revie told the *Daily Mail*. "It was bringing too much heartache to those nearest to us. Nearly everyone in the country wants me out. So, I am giving them what they want. I know people will accuse me of running away, and it does sicken me that I cannot finish the job by taking England to the World Cup finals in Argentina next year, but the situation has become impossible."

'Don Readies', as he was christened by the media, received a Football Association ban of 10 years for bringing the game into disrepute, but that was later overturned in the courts who stated the FA had overreached its remit.

Revie earned a £340,000 four-year deal in the UAE, where there was no football history, and also received £20,000 from the *Daily Mail* for his story.

Revie left the UAE role in May 1980 and managed Al Nasr in the Arabian Gulf League before being sacked in 1983. His last job in football was a brief stint as manager in the Egyptian Premier League. The UAE national team qualified for the 1990 World Cup, in part because of Revie's work in building football in that part of the world.

That he bowed out with a whimper and not a roar, with controversy and not celebrations, was not befitting a man who had given Leeds United so much.

The Don made his last ever appearance at Elland Road on 11 May 1988, a few weeks before Bremner was sacked as manager. He had been diagnosed with motor neurone disease in May 1987 and entered from the tunnel in a wheelchair. The crowd stood and applauded the man who had turned their dreams into reality. The players who had worked wonders on the pitch for him assembled for photographs ahead of a charity match played in his honour and to raise money for research into motor neurone disease.

Don Revie died in his sleep in Edinburgh on 26 May 1989, aged 61. At the end of the 2011/12 season, a statue was unveiled in his honour outside Elland Road. The North Stand, or the Kop, was made all-seater in 1994 and renamed the Revie Stand. It was opened in the October by the President, Lord Harewood, and Elsie Revie, the Don's widow.

10

BRIAN CLOUGH

1974

"Is it only seven weeks? I thought it was seven years!"

Born: 21 March 1935, Middlesbrough, Yorkshire
Died: 20 September 2004, Derby (aged 69)

Matches	Won	Drawn	Lost	Points	Pts/Match	Win %
7	1	3	3	6	0.86	14.29%
				RANK	34th/36	35th/36

It was one of the shortest, but also one of the most famous tenures in the Leeds United dugout. As the credits rolled and the upbeat, punchy theme music filled Yorkshire's living rooms on the 12 September 1974, Brian Clough shifted uneasily in his chair. But he was determined to go out with a bang.

The brash, confident Clough was not far away, but, in his position, one could excuse a slightly flummoxed feel within Leeds United's recently sacked manager. He'd been in charge for six matches and won only one.

Yet it was his previous outspoken criticism of Don Revie's Leeds that had made friends and allies in West Yorkshire hard to come by.

It would never happen now. Managers depart and don't resurface until the next job offer comes along. Or they might be snapped at a charity golf day. But for Clough to walk into the ITV studios to face questions from the presenter, and future Member of Parliament, Austin Mitchell, was, even then, quite extraordinary.

Perhaps it was a complete belief in his own virtues that made him agree to be cross-examined. It could have been a wish to set the record straight and assert that he had not been given a fair crack of the whip at Elland Road. Maybe he just couldn't say no to hearing the sound of his own voice coming out of television sets, whatever the circumstances. It was probably a combination of all of those factors. Clough and the word 'arrogant' have been included in the same sentence many times. But there was far more to him than often met the eye.

The reason was definitely not a willingness to confront Revie in front of the television cameras. For Clough, as he drove through Leeds, still smarting from being handed his P45, had no idea that Revie, by then the England manager, was making his own way to sit in a seat alongside him.

Clough could have said no when he saw Revie was there. Most would have run a mile at the thought of publicly facing their keenest adversary at such a sensitive moment.

Clough was ahead of his time. He thought about things differently. The term 'closure' hadn't been coined by psychiatrists yet, but possibly that was what Clough sought.

These days, Clough is generally derided by Leeds fans, but I have to admit to feeling a little sorry for him as he was metaphorically kicked and punched from the left and right once the red light appeared on the cameras.

No one can argue that Clough was not a great manager. He cut a Marmite figure at times and Leeds fans gave the taste test a thumbs down, but his record elsewhere more than stands the test of time.

The television viewers were about to witness one of the most bizarre, brutal and brilliant live sports interviews ever broadcast.

The 'GOODBYE MR CLOUGH' title leaves the screen and Austin Mitchell begins to speak…

"Good evening. Tonight the football world was stunned by the shock news that after only seven weeks in the job, Brian Clough has been sacked as manager of Leeds United," Mitchell shot down the lens. "It's been claimed that the footballers passed a vote of no confidence in him and, certainly today, the Board took the shock decision that Clough must go."

The picture flips to a view of Clough, dressed smartly in a grey suit, attempting a half-smile. The frame pans out to include Revie, in a smart blue blazer, legs crossed and stern of face.

"Tonight, on this live *Calendar Special*, we're talking, not only to Brian Clough himself, but also to the man that he succeeded as manager of Britain's most successful football team, to Don Revie, the England manager," Mitchell continues. "But Brian Clough first-of-all. Brian, what's your reaction to being booted out in this fashion?"

And we are up and running. Ten three-minute rounds. No low punches. Touch gloves please, we want a good clean fight.

Yeah, right! That was never going to happen.

"Oh. It's a very sad reaction," responds Clough. "Obviously, to be sacked, as you profoundly put it — and the only way you could put it — it's a very sad one. It's a very sad one for me personally. And I also think it's a very sad one from Leeds Football Club's angle and from the Leeds city."

"Do you think you were given a chance in the job?"

"Well, seven weeks is hardly a long time to be given a chance in any job. I would hope that Mr Revie would get a lot longer time in his job."

"Well, you began with very high hopes. We talked on a programme on here only a few weeks back. When did you first realise that it wasn't going to work out?"

"Oh, I didn't realise it at all. I was always convinced right up to tonight that it was going to work out. It was inevitable. To replace the best manager by record in the Football League, Leeds had to get somebody that was slightly special. I don't want to be blasé or conceited, but I'm not sure who they could have got to have improved on his record."

"You were the best man for the job you thought?"

"I believed I was and obviously the Leeds Board did," Clough retorts.

"Why didn't it work out? What was the main single thing that went wrong?"

"Results. In seven weeks there is not a lot of time to become established." Clough is warming to the task ahead. "When you've taken over a job of a man that has been there 10 or 15 years and he's been regarded as the kingpin, as the father figure, as the man that made everything tick, and then within seven weeks it is impossible, utterly impossible, to replace that type of thing. If the results had gone a bit better then obviously it would have been easier, but due to circumstances, due to the fact that there were inherited suspensions and little Billy was sent off and banned for a long time and Paul Madeley's injury and that type of thing, the results weren't as good as they should have been."

"Okay then, let's turn to Don Revie," Mitchell interjects. "Do you consider that it was in fact possible to step into your shoes to replace you?"

"Being very, very honest, I think it would have been a very difficult job for anybody to do, but I do feel that they had the players at Leeds United that won the Championship last year to possibly go on and do things this year—"

"Was Brian Clough the man that you would have picked to—"

"Well let me, Ooorstin," Revie responds as he addresses the presenter throughout the 30-minute show. "Ooorstin, you asked me a question and I'm going to answer it. I think the players were there to do the job. Now whether, after six matches, they are going to be judged on six matches, I don't know. But all I can say is I was with these players, most of them for 10 and 11 years, I was manager for thirteen-and-a-half and I basically think that they are good enough to win a trophy this season. Last season we had an awful lot of injuries and suspensions and we played without four and five and six players from the very first match. I knew the players. Clough, because he calls me Revie, didn't know them."

The camera cuts to Clough who removes his hand from his chin and smiles broadly at Revie's first jab to his ribs.

"And he didn't have time to do that," Revie concedes. "But the players are there, and they are dedicated professionals and I had no trouble with them for thirteen-and-a-half years."

"In saying that the team was good enough you are making an implied criticism of Brian Clough. Do you think Brian Clough was the man for the job?"

"That is entirely Leeds United directors' opinion."

"What's your personal opinion?" Mitchell appears a man with fish on his hook and who is not going to let them go.

"My personal opinion, as I stated at the time before Brian took the job — I won't call him Clough as I wouldn't take him down like that as I think it's a sad night for anybody to get the sack in any job — nobody likes to see this happen at all," Revie concedes. "I openly stated before anybody took the job, when I took the England job, that I thought Johnny Giles was the man for the job. Only because he knew our system, he knew how I worked, he knew how the staff worked, he knew how the players reacted to things. He knew everything because he'd travelled all over Europe with us, he'd played in matches, a great player, a great thinker of the game and I recommended him to Leeds—"

"If I can interrupt there," Mitchell dives in. "Does that mean that he was going to carry on in the Revie tradition, that he was going to be a manager much as you've been?"

"No, well Tottenham must feel that, they've taken Terry Neill, but he was in the last three for interviews for the job at Tottenham," Revie fires back. "I've never talked to Bill Nich about him, but Johnny Giles I've felt he's proved it with Eire, he went to Brazil with them and did well, he's done well in South America, he's done well with the Eire team. I only passed a personal opinion. Whether Leeds United directors want to take it or not is entirely up to Leeds United directors. I could only recommend him for the job — they didn't take him; they went for Brian. So, I can't do any more than that."

"What, in effect, I read from that is that you weren't the right man to step into this legacy that Don Revie had left at Leeds," interjects Mitchell, directing the point to Clough.

"No, no, no, Ooorstin," Revie fires back quickly. "You are totally out of order there. What you take out of that is totally untrue. What I said, that I recommended Johnny Giles for the job before anyone else was recommended at all. Before anyone else was mentioned I recommended Johnny Giles for Leeds United's job."

"Well, apart from your own respect for your own abilities, Brian Clough, would you say you were the right man to step into the kind of legacy Don Revie had left?" Mitchell turns to Clough.

"Errr, that's a very difficult question. It's like saying, 'If religion goes out of our way of life, who takes over from religion?'"

"Your style is very different from his style." Mitchell wants blood. "For players used to Don Revie's style, it might have been upsetting."

"My style's not different at all in the sense that I wanted success and I believed I could deliver it," Clough replies in his measured tone. "And my methods — 99%, or 90%, are the same as Mr Revie's. My style was exactly the same. Management is 90% right throughout the country, irrespective of who the manager is. It's the extra 10% that's the special bit." And in the last few words we get the first gleam in Clough's eyes.

"But look, over the years, Leeds United have been run almost like a family," responds Mitchell. "Like sons of Don Revie. Now, didn't you go in and upset them, unsettle them by going for a big buying policy?"

"Well, a big buying policy, I'm not sure," counters Clough. "What I did was, I bought a wing-half to replace Eddie Gray, who, there is grave doubts about his future. I was informed when I took over Leeds that Mick Jones could possibly not be fit for the rest of the season, at the very earliest February or March. So, I bought a reserve centre-forward in John O'Hare and all of Leeds know he is a very talented player. Now, what I also did was, I tried to provide a little striking power added to the Leeds machine, as I once called Don's team. He wasn't very happy with it, but it was a machine, a superbly oiled one, but it was a machine. And I added Duncan McKenzie to it because I knew up front we were a little bit thin with Peter Lorimer, Joe Jordan and Allan Clarke. So, the fact of big buying wasn't big buying in the sense—"

"You don't think it was unsettling for the players?"

"Oh, it could have been slightly unsettling because they'd been there so long and one or two of them are getting on to 32, 33, possibly even 34."

"Well, Don Revie, would you have gone in for this kind of buying, or would you have worked it in more cautiously?" Mitchell faces Revie as he continues to stir the pot.

"First of all, let me answer Brian's question" responds Revie, in no mood to have his agenda dictated by someone else. "About them getting old and about injuries and one thing and another. Erm, as I said already, we had this all last season. But what you must remember is this: that team was written off by the press in '70, when we won three tournaments, in '71, in '72 and in '73, when we lost against Sunderland and AC Milan. They all said, 'That's it, they're finished, they're over the hill, they're too old,' and this, that and the other. Then last season, with all these injuries and all these suspensions to Allan Clarke and Norman Hunter and all these people, we only lost four matches out of 42 and won the Championship. They went 29 matches from the beginning of the season without defeat—"

"Are you saying from that, that Brian Clough's buying was not necessary?"

"No, Ooorstin, will you please just give me a chance—"

"That was incredible — what the man is saying was incredible," Clough tries to interject, but not for the first time finds it futile.

"Let him finish," Mitchell cuts off Clough, after being the one to interrupt Revie in the first place.

"Now then, if Brian felt after three months — I would have given them personally three months to settle down and play as they're capable of playing," Revie concludes.

"Don, even with Billy's eight match suspension?" Clough asks softly.

"Yes, I'd have had Terry Yorath, I'd have had Mick Bates, I'd have had Joe Jordan, I'd have had Frankie Gray. You had four very world-class players in the making who I juggled about last year. Frankie, whether you think Frankie is a good player, or not—"

"Well, world-class, you said," Clough responds.

"Well, I think if he got the chance, Brian, he could be world-class," Revie counters.

"Yes," Clough answers.

"And I'd have played Terry Yorath up front," Revie suggests. "This is what I'm saying, you didn't get the chance to see them. I knew them. I'd have played Terry Yorath up front alongside Joe Jordan. I'd have played Terry Yorath, I played him at full-back, I played him at sweeper. I played Mick Bates up front, I played Frankie Gray up front and outside left. Now these players I felt should have had a chance."

"Don, why didn't they get a chance?" Clough remains calm despite the attack he is undergoing. "Terry had a tummy bug. Enteritis, I think they call it, and he was in bed for 10 days."

"Yeah, but you still had Mick Bates and Joe Jordan and Frankie Gray, who didn't play at all, Brian," Revie continues to probe. "And the thing is Mick Bates, Terry Yorath and Frankie Gray — and I feel the unsettling part came when you didn't give these lads a chance and, quite rightly a manager has got to stand and fall by his decisions, every time, whether he's going to buy, his team selection, or whatever he's going to have, he's got to stand and fall by what he says and what he does. And Brian decided to go in the market. Whether it was unsettling to the players, I don't know."

"The question then arises," Mitchell jumps back in as Revie pauses. "Was Brian Clough allowed to stand and fall by his decisions? Was he given time to carry through his policies? Was he given the backing that he needed from the team to do what he wanted?"

Clough turns his head from waiting for Revie's answer and responds himself. "I would prefer you to say 'the board of directors' to that, because 'the team' don't dictate that much. The team can have a vote of confidence and that type of thing. The team are the be-all and end-all regarding the results on the field, but regarding the confidence? It's essential to have the confidence, but the men who make the decisions are the directors in football."

Clough's correction of Mitchell riles the interviewer who comes back on the attack. "Let's talk team first of all. Are you sure that team was playing it's best for you?"

"Oh, I'm absolutely certain," Clough smiles back.

"With results like that?"

"Oh, results like that, of course they were playing their best," Clough goes up a notch. "They couldn't do anything else; it was second nature to them."

"Austin," Revie jumps back in. "Let me ask you a question. How long have you been living in Leeds?"

"Five years," Mitchell states. "And I have never seen such a disastrous start to the season."

"But have you ever seen a Leeds United team ever, and the present team starting off this season, ever not try?" For the first time, Revie appears to be defending Clough. "They might have bad times, they might miss open goals, but never can you accuse, or insinuate, that a Leeds United side never tried. Because there's never been a player in a white shirt gone out on that pitch and never tried. He might have a bad game, they might miss open goals, they might do bad things, but never not try."

"Okay, well I accept that," Mitchell responds. "But there have been claims that there was in fact a vote of no confidence, or something amounting to that, passed by the players. Is that correct?"

"That is absolutely correct," Clough confirms.

"Well, how did you react to that?"

"Oh, I wanted to be sick," Clough grins back as Mitchell returns with a smile, but the former manager isn't joking. "If you had a vote of no confidence with the people that you work with, I would assume you would react exactly the same. I felt sick."

"What was the main reason for it, do you think?"

"I don't know what the main reason was," Clough admits. "I think the fact that I didn't have time to get to know them and this type of thing. I do believe, honestly, that whoever would have walked in would have had the same thing. Plus, the fact that all the other incidentals went against us, i.e. results and that type of thing, which as I have already pointed out are the main thing."

"Let's stay with this thing about a vote of no confidence." Mitchell turns to Revie. "How do you react to the players, in effect, passing a vote of no confidence in a manager. After such a short period?"

"I honestly feel, knowing Leeds United players as long as I have known them, they must have had a very good reason to do that," Revie comments. "No disrespect to Brian, I must feel and say what I feel about Leeds United players. They must have had a very good reason to do that. Why? I don't know. I had enough problems on my hands with the England job."

"Whatever the reason, do you condone players acting in that kind of fashion," Mitchell asks Revie. "It must make a manager's job impossible?"

"No, I do not condone players at all doing that in any club, because I think it is totally wrong and I think directors are wrong to listen to it." Revie again gives Clough a modicum of support. "But I can't understand why the Leeds United players, if Brian is true in what he is saying, if they voted a no confidence vote in you, Brian—"

"Not exactly a vote, but the feeling was there, yes." Clough climbs down a little. "Vote is a very strong word, but the feeling was definitely there."

"How far was that kind of feeling there, because you've been critical of Don Revie himself," Mitchell probe. "We had a programme a few weeks back where you were implicitly critical of Don Revie, you said there were contracts unsigned—"

"Implicitly critical?" Clough laughs.

"Is that the right kind of line to take for a man stepping into the shoes of a revered manager?"

"Ahh, you are asking me now, 'Did I make mistakes?' The answer is 'yes'. I am not infallible, I definitely made mistakes. Erm, having said that, when you say I criticised Don Revie about unsigned contracts, I stated a fact that there were, when I took over, 11 contracts not signed. Now if it was Don's fault, if it was the chairman's fault, if it was the players' fault, that's immaterial for this particular argument." Clough takes a breath to emphasise the point. "There were 11 contracts not signed. That is fact."

Mitchell turns to his right. "Well, Don Revie, you saw that programme and the accusation. What was your reaction to it?"

"Yes, and Ooorstin, I phoned up that night and asked you if I could face Brian the following night and I got no reply." Revie looks down as he plays with the bottom of his tie. "Talking about the 11 contracts that were unsigned, all contracts were basically agreed in the minutes with the directors of what each player was going to get. Brian is possibly right, the contracts weren't signed, not by 11, I'd say about five or six. And all these things were agreed in the minutes that these contracts were agreed, and I'd agreed with the players. And all players have signed blank contracts for me for thirteen-and-a-half years and I have never had one scrap of trouble ever with one player throughout thirteen-and-a-half years with contracts. And why they weren't carried out and signed and sent off by the secretary I will never know."

Clough tries to jump back in, but Revie isn't interested in being stopped, "On that same programme, Brian said that there was no warmth in the club. Now that really shook me."

"Did I say no warmth?" Clough queries.

"You said no warmth in Leeds United," Revie reiterates. "Now that was the closest thing that any relationship between players and manager and staff I've ever had."

"Did I say no warmth between me and them, or no warmth in the club?"

"You said no warmth in the club, Brian."

"I don't remember," Clough says defensively. "If I did say it then obviously the warmth you generated between you and the players, that can't be taken away."

"No, never, ever," Revie insists.

"That's ridiculous. It can't be taken away," Clough confirms.

"What was wrong with Brian Clough's approach to Leeds as a manager?" Mitchell attempts to get things back onto his agenda.

"Now that's asking for me to do something that I know nothing at all about," Revie suggests. "I've known Brian a long time. What his approach is as a manager, I've never played under him, I've never worked under him. That is impossible for me to answer."

Mitchell opts to prod Clough with his next question. "You say you have different styles as managers and it's generally believed, I don't know with what accuracy, that you don't get on particularly well. Now, why is that, Brian Clough?"

"Well, when I was a manager at Derby County I was in direct conflict with Don Revie and his Leeds side," Clough is back in ground her feels more comfortable with. "It's natural. I didn't get on with him because invariably they were above us. That's the flippant answer. Having said that, I believe in a different concept of football to Don, I think. I believe that it can be played slightly different to the way Don plays it and get the same result. Now that might be aiming for Utopia and it might mean being a little bit stupid, but that is the way I am. I'm a little bit stupid regarding this type of thing and I'm a little bit of an idealist and I do believe in fairies and that is my, you know, outlook. Now Don's slightly different and his record proves over results that he perhaps is right but having said that I want to be like me, and Don obviously wants to be like him."

"Is this question of style the reason why the two of you don't get on?"

"Well, I don't know." Revie sets himself as Clough looks down and rests his mouth on his knuckles. "I think, truthfully, Brian is a fool to himself. I must be very, very honest here. I honestly feel that he's criticised Matt Busby, Bertie Mee, me personally, Norman Hunter, Peter Lorimer, Billy Bremner, Peter Storey. He's criticised so many people within the game whose records stand to be seen. He's criticised so many people, this is his style and if he wants to be that style, fair enough. But I think that is totally, totally wrong for the game of professional football. He says about honesty and things like this, but when you talk about honesty, if honesty is going to destroy the game, then you are in all kinds of trouble. I think you're doing the game a great disservice."

"Yes, I would—" Clough gets cut off and repeats, "Hang on, hang on," as Mitchell stops his response.

"The accusation is that you are too eager to shoot your mouth off," Mitchell pounces on Revie's accusation.

"I would agree completely—" Clough gets cut off again.

"Let me ask this question first," Revie says, determined to assume control.

"I'm sorry," Clough climbs down.

"You talked about winning the Championships better," Revie recalls. "Or differently. Our record is there to be seen for 11 years."

"Yes," Clough agrees.

"The first four or five years, I've always said this, we played for results," Revie continues. "The last four or five years we've been the most entertaining side by crowd entertainment and topping charts with national newspapers and television."

"Also, Don, the disciplinary chart," Clough introduces an issue he has discussed many time before as a TV football pundit.

"The disciplinary chart—"

"You topped that."

"We topped that once," Revie admits.

"Well, you topped it for the last two or three years."

"No, no, no, that's not true," Revie refutes Clough's suggestion. "It wasn't one hundred per cent right, I will agree, and last year we straightened it out."

"You were at the top."

"Yeah, yeah," Revie moves the conversation on. "When you, you see Brian, when you talk about coming to take the Leeds job and you had all these things and all these worries about stepping in my shoes and one thing and another—"

"Which I had."

"Yes, you had." Revie is getting to his main point: "But why, why did you come from Brighton to Leeds to take it up when you'd criticised them so much and said we should be in the Second Division for this and we should do that. Why did you take the job?"

"Well, because I thought it was the best job in the country," Clough says.

"Of course it was the best job—"

"I was taking over the League champions," Clough adds.

"Yes, and you were taking over the best bunch of players that you've ever seen and you'll ever—"

"I didn't know about the players, Don." Clough finally manages to shoehorn himself back into the chat as Revie looks quizzically at him. "I didn't know them intimately like you do. But I know that you were the League champions and I was taking over the League champions. I wanted to have a crack at the European Cup this year and I think that was near and dear to your heart also. I wanted to win it. I wanted to do something you hadn't done. Now, when I said it — I think I said it to Trevor Cherry, actually — he said to me, 'What can you do that the boss hadn't done?' You are the boss; he was referring to you. And I said, 'I want to win the League and I want to win it better.' Now, there is no other reply to that question. Because you had won the League."

"Yeah, but there's no way you can win it better," states Revie, visibly annoyed.

"Why not?" Clough slaps his palm on his knee. "But that's the only hope I'd got!"

"We'd only lost four matches—"

"Well, I can only lose three. I couldn't give any other answer. And I wanted to win the European Cup. I believe that it was just a fraction, Don, a fraction — I don't know this because I've not spoken to you — but I believe it was a fraction that you took the England job or had another shot at the European Cup."

"That is totally true, because I was so involved with the players and everyone at Elland Road," Revie agrees.

"Good lad." Clough is warmed up now. "And I wanted to do that, and I wanted to do it better than you. You can understand that, can't you?"

"Yes," confesses Revie. "And I think if you had said that to our players then you would have got the message across."

"I couldn't say that to our players, as you say, I couldn't say that to our players just as a bald statement. You see, when I went in there, there was friction. There was unhappiness."

"What do you mean friction?" Revie's hackles rise again.

"There was unhappiness because you had gone and unsigned contracts."

"No, no, no, when you walked in, tell me honest, when you walked in, did you have a meeting the first day with them?"

"No."

"Why?"

"Because I didn't think it was necessary to have a meeting the very first day."

"So, you were taking over as manager of a new club and you don't call all your new players and you don't get the coaching staff and office staff together and introduce yourself and meet them and tell them exactly what you feel and what you want to try and do?"

"Don! The first day I walked in, I came back from holiday and I did two hours training with them!"

"Irrespective," Revie dismissed. "What you do—"

"I went out on the field with them."

"You went out on the field. My immediate reaction to any job, the same at the Football Association, I got 70 people together and we had a cocktail party to introduce myself to them."

"That is your way!"

"Yeah. I talked about Ramsey's record. I talked about how great Ramsey was. His record as a professional man. I never got close to Ramsey. He was a cold man—"

"I think you are—"

"But as a professional ... a cold man?"

"Yes."

"Ah. Don't ask our players that," Revie feigns amusement "They'd have laughed their socks down."

"That's opinion."

"No, but Alf Ramsey, I felt, did a good job." Revie tries to move on. "I thought it was important to me to introduce myself to everybody in the Football Association offices. And I thought it was your duty, when you walked into Leeds United's ground, everyone saying, 'Well, Brian Clough's arriving today, we'd love to meet him—'"

"You didn't have a training session?"

"How long did you wait then? Irrespective of training sessions, Brian — training sessions didn't mean anything — how can training sessions overcome meeting everyone at the club? It would have taken you 10 minutes to get everybody together as a group and say, 'I'm pleased to meet you—'"

"I walked into the dressing room and shook hands with Billy Bremner the very first second—"

"No, Brian, don't hedge."

"I'm not hedging."

"Why didn't you get everyone together?"

"Because I didn't think it was necessary."

"Why?"

"Because I thought I would do it more subtly and different, instead of having everybody bang, bang, bang. They were all on edge. I was on edge."

"So, you could have put them at ease," Revie seems to be enjoying himself now.

"Hang on, how?"

"By going in and talking to them."

"Oh, talk to them! I took their shirts off their backs after they finished training."

"I used to do that and massage them when I first came in."

"Of course, that was my approach. Of course."

"But you didn't meet everybody the first day," Revie is a dog with a bone.

"I shook hands and said, 'Hello'. Met them."

"Everybody? The laundry ladies and the office staff?"

"No, oh no. No, I'm sorry—"

"Did you go to the groundsmen?"

"I didn't have time to do that, Don. It was players."

"You must have had time; it only takes 10 minutes."

The ding-dong was doing Austin Mitchell's job for him, but the presenter, conscious of time, intervenes.

"We're getting towards the end now. I've got to ask, what's your reaction to a Board that doesn't back you up and sacks you after seven weeks?"

"I haven't had time to know them either," Clough laughs. "Just as I believe I haven't had time to do the job."

"What's your reaction to the Board?" Mitchell perseveres.

"My reaction to the Board is very, very mixed. My reaction to the Board is oh so mixed up. I don't believe they've done Leeds Football Club a service. I don't care whether it's me or whoever it was. I'm talking about a manager. I don't believe they've done football a service. I think they struck a blow to send us back in the dark ages. And I think if the Football Association, who employ Mr Revie, sack him if he loses his first match, I think they will set football back 30 years, or 50 years. In turn, I believe that Leeds perhaps have done that a little bit also. Manny Cussins was under a lot of pressure. He was my chairman. If he didn't stand up to it as much as he should have done, that's a matter of debate. But he was under a lot of pressure and he, today, when the final decision was made, and it was a Board decision, he then made it right with me regarding a lot of things, as he made it right with this guy for 15 years."

"What's going to happen now to Brian Clough?"

"Oh, many things are going to happen to Brian Clough. I'm going to have 48 hours, or three days, or I don't know. I think, and please don't think I'm being flippant, I've had many ambitions in life and one of those ambitions is, and I wanted this when I was manager of Leeds, and manager of Derby, I wanted to coach the England Youth. I just might apply to this guy," Clough nods to the new England manager and there is not a flicker in return.

"Well, aren't you going to be in a very difficult situation?" Mitchell doesn't respond to Clough's bait. "Because after the argument with Derby, you left Brighton under a cloud and now this with Leeds, who's going to touch you with a barge pole, as it were?"

"Well, I think many, many people will touch me with a barge pole, because the whole country now, including Leeds, and you've heard it in Don's own mouth tonight, I do not think — SEVEN WEEKS — seven weeks is not even enough time to find out where the local butcher's shop is."

"Okay, well what do you see for Leeds United now?" Mitchell asks. "What do you see as their future?"

"Well, obviously they will prosper, well I hope they prosper," Clough states. "Despite the fact that I've only been involved with them seven weeks, you've got to hope they prosper. I hope everybody in football prospers. I hope they go on to win the European Cup—"

"Don Revie, what's your feeling about Brian Clough's personal—"

"You are a terrible man for interrupting that," Clough cuts in. "I hope that Leeds win the European Cup."

Mitchell asks Revie: "What's your feeling personally about Brian Clough's personal situation?"

"Well, naturally, anyone sacked in football, you feel a little bit sad for, but whether Brian has gone about it the right way I don't know, because I wasn't there," Revie insists. "But if Leeds United players have had a meeting with Brian and the chairman, there must have been something totally wrong."

"Okay gentlemen, there we must leave it on what's been a tragic day for Leeds United supporters of which I number myself one. Gentlemen, thank you very much and goodnight."

Austin Mitchell predictably giving Revie the final word in a one-sided interview, which Eddie Gray believes Clough would have been better avoiding altogether.

"I don't think that should have happened," Gray told me. "I don't think that was fair on Brian because he was turning up to do an interview and didn't know Don was there. When Don suddenly walked onto the stage he was taken aback, and it belittled him a bit. Obviously, Don knew what he was going to say and had all of his questions and ammunition ready. Brian hadn't had the chance to sit down and think about how he was going to answer. I don't think that was the right thing to do.

"I know it was good television at the time, but I don't think it was fair to Brian. If it had been the other way around, I don't think Don would have liked it. Brian should have got up and walked out of the studio. That would have been the best thing for him to do, because that interview never did him any good whatsoever.

"You can understand why Don went there because the two of them didn't get on — simple as that," Gray added. "It was tit-for-tat. Brian was criticising Don's players, and what they'd done in the past. I wouldn't have minded the debate if Brian had been given the opportunity to sit and think what he was going to say. It was probably, at the time, one of the most iconic sports interviews, just how it happened, because Brian didn't even know Don was in the studio. He just wasn't able to prepare himself."

I'd called Eddie to have a chat about his time at the club and his own managerial tenure that, in terms of Leeds United's history, is still to come. I think that's what they call a teaser.

But, inevitably, Clough and Revie dominated the early parts of our discussion. I have to admit to feeling quite sorry for Clough throughout that ITV interview. As I watched it more than once before transcribing it for this chapter, there was no doubt Eddie was right. It did make great television, but as Clough was manhandled by Mitchell he was never going to get a knockout punch in against Revie, a colossus. It was obvious which man a Leeds supporter would side with.

The section where Clough wishes Leeds well and says that he hopes they win the European Cup is magnanimous talk from a man that has been sacked by the club just hours before. But Mitchell cuts him off and is desperate to engineer Revie gets the last kick before the credits roll.

I met Brian Clough once at a book signing in Nottingham in 2002. He was exactly what I expected. A little brusque, a twinkle in his eyes, an innocent flirt with some older ladies who loved it, a playful clip for a couple of young lads and a bit of time for every one of the many people that had turned out to see him. If I was to sum up Brian Clough as a football person, I would suggest he was bordering on genius. He loved the game and had a way of getting the best out of his players.

Not everyone that played for Clough saw eye-to-eye with their gaffer, leading to one of his most famous quotes: "I ask him which way he thinks it should be done, we get down to it and then we talk about it for twenty minutes and then we decide I was right."

Unfortunately for Clough, it would have taken longer than his time span at Leeds to get such agreement from the United players. Eddie Gray gave me a refreshingly honest assessment on Clough's time at Elland Road.

"I don't think anybody really got to know the man," Gray suggested. "I think Brian's biggest problem, when he came to Leeds, was that he was on his own. He brought little Jimmy Gordon who was, more or less, a PT instructor. But Peter Taylor wasn't well, and I think that was his downfall at Leeds.

"When you look back at Brian's career, Peter Taylor would probably be the only man who could pull the reins on him and say, 'Just slow it up there, hold back a bit,' and he didn't have that at Leeds.

"I think he found it lonely," Gray suggested to me. "I think he thought he'd be able to come in with his normal manner, which was Brian Clough — brash and this is it. But what I don't think he really understood was that he wasn't coming into a club where the players hadn't done anything. He was coming into a club with World Cup winners and players that had won everything. To treat them in the way that he would have treated players with less talent, or at lesser clubs, didn't really work at our club.

"There were just one or two little things that he did that set him off on a bad foot. In saying all that, I would still have given him longer. I know a few of the boys wouldn't have, but I would have done."

And it seems to be Clough's attitude from his very start at Leeds that put people's backs up. It's why Revie quizzes him so much on how he conducted himself on his first day in charge.

"He said to me, 'If you'd have been a horse, they'd have shot you,' because I had a bad thigh injury," Gray laughs. "He did say that, and I thought it was quite funny, but a lot of the boys took exception to that.

"Just little things like, 'Throw your medals in a bin,' and all that stuff. I think Brian was just a complex character. There is no doubt he will go down as one of the greatest managers that ever managed in this country."

And if you consider what Clough achieved before and after his time at Leeds, one has to wonder how things could have been very different had Clough chosen wiser words and had the players been a little more patient.

Also, Gray's suggestion that the absence of Peter Taylor, a constant assistant at all of his other clubs, was a key factor is borne out by Clough's tribute upon Taylor's death in 1990. "I've missed him," Clough said. "He used to make me laugh. He was the best diffuser of a situation I have ever known; I hope he's alright."

Clough had an excellent playing career ended prematurely through injury aged only 29 after sustaining anterior cruciate ligament damage. He had scored 251 goals in 274 appearances for Middlesbrough and Sunderland between 1955 and 1964 and also played for England twice in 1959.

He embarked on a managerial career with Hartlepool United in 1965, but it was with Derby County that he first made a name for himself as he took them from a decade in the Second Division to the title and promotion in 1968/69 and the First Division's top prize three seasons later.

But with the customary glory came the controversy as he fell out with the Derby directors, most notably Sam Longson. Clough refused to go on a pre-season tour of the Netherlands unless he could take his family, he signed David Nish for a club record £225,000 without getting board approval and criticised the home support as a "disgraceful lot" for not cheering his team enough.

On these issues and others, Longson was often found publicly disassociating himself from Clough's antics. Clough's work in the media and high profile meant the world was listening as he criticised all and sundry, most notably Revie's Leeds United, who he claimed in a *Sunday Express* article should be relegated for their poor disciplinary record. In October 1973, Longson recommended to the Derby board that both Clough and Taylor should be sacked, but his proposal was rejected.

Longson told Clough that he must refrain from writing newspaper articles, stop appearing on television and he shut the club bar where Clough and Taylor drank. Both men resigned in October 1973 to mass despair from the club's support. They had resigned briefly before, but Longson had negotiated their stay. 13,000 supporters signed a petition demanding that Longson reinstated their manager, but their pleas fell on deaf ears. This time, Longson was happy to see them go and what might have been another Clough bluff backfired. Derby County haven't competed at the top end of English football since.

Clough won 12 of 32 games played with his next club Brighton in Division Three, but then Leeds came calling.

Eddie Gray remembers how Clough treated his teammate and brother, Frank, at Elland Road.

"He didn't play Frank a lot, but when he went to Nottingham Forest, he signed Frank," Gray recalled. "Frank won the European Cup with him. Years later, I said to Frank, 'What is it that makes him a great manager?'

Frank said, 'I don't really know.'

"That was it. He was a one off, but like I say, one of the greatest managers. If you win the league with Derby County and European trophies with Nottingham Forest, that takes some doing."

As Derby manager, Clough had made no secret of his dislike of Don Revie's methods. He famously said, "I think they have sold themselves short as men and as players," when asked about Leeds United's success. He had also said, "Leeds have always sold themselves short. They've been champions, but not good champions."

Johnny Giles remembered: "Brian Clough's attitude towards the Leeds thing was that we were dishonest. I don't think Leeds ever got the credit for playing the type of football that they played. I mean I played in a Leeds team that played as good a football as any Brazilian team or any team have ever done. Brian Clough's attitude to football was the complete opposite to the attitude that was there at Leeds at the time and I think it was a clash that neither of us could understand."

Former Derby player Roy McFarland said, "It would be like Arsene Wenger taking on the job at Manchester United," in a parallel that possibly isn't extreme enough.

"Oh crikey, I mean there'd be no equivalent today I'm afraid," suggested Gordon McQueen, a young defender at Leeds when Clough arrived. "You couldn't get a more controversial appointment at all than Brian Clough going to Leeds at that moment in time. It really was major. We were waiting for him to be controversial and outspoken and we certainly weren't let down, that's for sure. He came in and basically ripped into everybody: 'You've won your medals with cheating.' The lads were totally shocked. We knew he'd be outspoken, but we didn't think he'd be anything like what he was. And you've got to remember, these players had won the league in style the previous season. If he had any hope of getting a relationship going with players like that and influential players within the dressing room, it was gone in a day or so. It was bedlam for the first couple of weeks, there's no doubt about that. There was nearly anarchy at the football club."

It was not an obvious match made in heaven, given the bad words and acrimony that had gone before, but there was no doubt Clough viewed the Leeds role as a chance to win things and to be successful playing what he considered proper football. It's hard to subscribe to the view that he went to Elland Road to put the nail in the Leeds coffin. Clough was too professional to take that kamikaze mission.

Gray told me that it was always going to be tough for anyone to follow Revie, but admits that Clough was his own worst enemy in that regard.

"The most disappointing thing when Don left was that Brian never hid the fact to the players that he didn't like him," Gray barbed. "And it's got to be said that the feeling was mutual. I don't think they got on at all, but he never hid that fact and that would have turned the boys against him.

"You've got to remember that we played as a group of 15 or 16 players for 10 years and all had the highest regard for Don. For someone to come in and on his first day throw all the furniture out into the car park and bring new furniture into the office. Don had left behind a new car and Brian said he wouldn't drive that car. I don't think that got him off on the right foot and then telling the boys they'd cheated for their medals. It was all because there was a mutual dislike between the two men."

Johnny Giles stated, "I'm not so sure he had as much confidence in himself as he sometimes portrayed, but I think he was a genius."

Clough was back in football management less than three months after he left Leeds. On 6 January 1975 he was unveiled as the new boss at Nottingham Forest. Peter Taylor was reunited with him 18 months later and the duo went on their most successful adventure yet, as those 44 days in West Yorkshire were long forgotten.

Forest won back-to-back European Cup successes in 1978/79 and 1979/80, lifted the European Super Cup in 1979, the First Division in 1977/78 and also four League Cups, two Full Members Cups and a Charity Shield.

Forest lived and then relived the dream and it was down to a magical chemical reaction that Clough and Taylor found in their dugout.

Taylor was managing Derby County in May 1983 when he signed John Robertson from Forest without telling his former colleague. Their friendship had already become strained and they never spoke to each other again. Rifts between mates are often healed, but Taylor died in October 1990 and Clough was "deeply upset" and dedicated his 1994 autobiography to his former right-hand man.

Upon Clough's death from stomach cancer on 20 September 2004, the fierce rivalry between the cities of Nottingham and Derby was temporarily forgotten, as they grieved and celebrated the life of a man who had given them all the realisation of hope.

In Leeds, I wondered what might have been if Brian Clough had lasted a little bit longer than 44 days. Sometimes two wonderful people don't make the perfect couple.

11

JIMMY ARMFIELD

1974–1978

Gentleman Jim

Born: 21 September 1935, Denton, Lancashire
Died: 22 January 2018, Blackpool, Lancashire (aged 82)

Matches	Won	Drawn	Lost	Points	Pts/Match	Win %
196	88	49	59	313	1.60	44.90%
				RANK	8th/36	8th/36

I was very sad to hear of the passing of Jimmy Armfield. The news came as I began to write this book. Not only had football lost a genuine football man, I had missed the opportunity to speak to him about his time as Leeds United manager.

Don Revie had passed on an ageing squad to Armfield, via Brian Clough. I would have loved the chance to ask Armfield what it had been like to follow on from that infamous Damned United period. Was it the poisoned chalice and thankless task it seemed, taking Leeds United forward after all of those years of success?

Forget the glowing eulogies after his death in Blackpool on 22 January 2018, aged 82, after a battle against non-Hodgkin-lymphoma. Most people get a glowing report after they have left us. Armfield genuinely seemed worthy of the heartfelt tributes.

Armfield managed the club through a predictable period of decline. Clough had alienated the players with his anti-Revie approach. Armfield chose a softer style. Eddie Gray's tribute in the *Yorkshire Post* illustrated Armfield's selfless side.

"With Jimmy it wasn't about him," Gray said of the man who had encouraged him to start thinking about coaching the youth team when he was recovering from injury. "Managing Leeds, as far as I could see, was about the club and the people there. You never got any ego with Jimmy. He was a proper gentleman."

Armfield had stepped into football management shortly after hanging up his playing boots. He took charge of Bolton Wanderers in 1971 and made them Third Division champions in 1972/73. He was offered the Everton manager's post, but he couldn't turn down Leeds United.

Taking over from Clough after his infamous 44-day reign, Armfield walked into a dressing room full of high achievers, embittered by recent events and a poor start to the season. Many of the legs in the squad that had served the team brilliantly were reaching their best before date.

When appointed, Armfield said: "This is one of the hardest things, to follow the 60s period when Leeds were one of the top teams in Europe. To reach that sort of peak again will take time and I think people realise that. But on the other hand, I'm quietly confident really."

Armfield retained the best of the old squad to keep a core of experience to bring in new recruits alongside. He took Leeds to the European Cup final and sought to rebuild the team by bringing in Joe Jordan and Tony Currie, but the high expectations weighed heavily.

"The challenge for any manager coming to Leeds back then was that the players compared you to Don," Gray added. "None of us took to Brian Clough, but Jimmy's way was different. He steadied the ship which, no matter how good some of the players still were, wasn't an easy job. Unlike Brian, he tried not to make too much of the fact that Don's team was reaching the end. That season could have gone either way. When Brian left, we were struggling to win a game.

"The players were very experienced, and they knew their way around England and Europe. After a while it started to go well again."

Armfield remembered his first few days in Leeds: "I let Maurice Lindley, the assistant manager, pick the team for the first match after my appointment as Leeds boss. We sat down somewhere near Roundhay Park and he said his words.

"I watched the players and I could tell they were looking at me," he continued. "Eventually, I said, 'I'll just say one thing to you. I will not make my mind up about you all until I've been here a bit of time. I'm the total opposite of Brian. Just answer me one question — why is this title-winning team full of internationals next to the bottom of the table?'"

Armfield described it as "a difficult job" and one he started by throwing a selection of his players into the pantomime season in Christmas 1974 at the City Varieties Music Hall in a bid to regain squad harmony. He took charge of the script for the production of *Cinderella*, as Duncan McKenzie took the lead and Billy Bremner gave a performance that Armfield would describe as the "best Buttons I have ever seen."

There was still fight within the squad and they were not finished yet. They were the reigning English champions and eager to live up to that billing. They would finish 9th in the First Division after the atrocious start and Armfield took them to a replay defeat in the quarter-finals of the FA Cup against Ipswich Town.

But it was the European Cup, the one trophy that had eluded Revie, and the one he had coveted above all others, that gave Armfield the biggest opportunity to stamp his own mark on the club's history.

Leeds advanced to the semi-final after wins against Zurich, Ujpest Dozsa and Anderlecht. In the last four they travelled to play in front of 110,000 in the Camp Nou in April 1975 after winning the first leg 2-1 at Elland Road.

Peter Lorimer secured a precious away goal, headed in on goal by Joe Jordan, before making no mistake as he put a customary right-foot rocket past the keeper. The striker's 30th European goal broke the British record. Half an hour left, Barcelona piled forward, with United giving all they had to cling on to their two-goal cushion.

But on 69 minutes it was all square on the night as Manuel Clares headed Barcelona back into the tie. Gordon McQueen saw red for retaliating for punching a Barca player who pulled his shirt. McQueen would miss the final, if United could survive the final 20 minutes.

The key man in ensuring Leeds would become only the second English side to reach the European Cup Final, after Manchester United seven years before, was goalkeeper David Stewart. He saved brilliantly from a Juan Carlos Heredia header before miraculously getting a hand to a deflected strike from Johan Cruyff.

"This must be the high spot of my football life and I include in that some great experiences as a player," Armfield told reporters.

Armfield selected the following team for the final: David Stewart; Paul Reaney, Frank Gray, Billy Bremner, Paul Madeley, Norman Hunter, Peter Lorimer, Allan Clarke, Joe Jordan, Johnny Giles, Terry Yorath.

Anyone watching the final, other than the most passionate Bayern Munich support, would agree with the claim that Leeds were robbed of the trophy. It was a hostile evening in Paris, Bayern were negative in their play and a referee stamped on United's dreams in what Peter Lorimer has described as "the disappointment of our lives."

World Cup-winning German captain Franz Beckenbauer appeared to handle the ball as he knelt in the area as Lorimer tried to pass him. Just before the break, Beckenbauer brought down Clarke. As the Leeds players appealed for spot kicks, Kitabdjian waved them away.

Peter Lorimer's volleyed goal was cancelled when Billy Bremner was adjudged offside as he ran out of the box and away from play. Leeds were left frustrated because the referee had awarded the goal only to change his mind after conferring with his linesman. There was no way that Bremner had been interfering with play.

"Although they were favourites, we dominated the first half and the least we deserved was a penalty when Beckenbauer brought me down just before half-time," Clarke remembered. "I picked the ball up and went on a run; Beckenbauer came over, I dropped my shoulder and went past him and was about to bend the ball round Maier, when he wrapped his legs round me and pulled me down. It was a blatant penalty. When I got to my feet, I couldn't believe the referee had given a goal kick. We all appealed, but the referee, who was less than ten yards away from the incident, didn't want to know."

To rub salt in fresh wounds, Bayern took the lead as Franz Roth raced through to finish and doubled their lead after 81 minutes when striker Gerd Muller stole in to finish from close range.

Leeds had lost a second controversial final in three years. 8,000 supporters rioted and Leeds received a four-year ban from European competition.

Armfield, recalling the 2-0 defeat to Bayern, said. "I've always felt we were robbed. What should have been a great day wasn't a great day in the end.

"In the European Cup final, I could not have asked more of the players," he said. "I turned at one point to our physio Bob English and said that I hope we finish with a draw. When he asked why, I said, 'I don't think we are going to win this one.'

"Afterwards, I was livid. I was upset for the players. They left their medals in the dressing room. I picked them all up and gave them to them when it all settled down.

"I didn't want to believe that — all the talk about the referee. I'll never know if he was got at.

"I went to the board and said we should appeal against our ban. They told me I was wasting my time. Nobody wanted to do it. So, I got my air ticket and went off to Geneva. A journalist went with me. Everyone thought I had no chance, but I got it reduced to two years. At least the secretary paid my air fare back."

He had come so close to becoming the first English manager to win the European Cup, but the Parc des Princes experience signposted the end of a glorious era. It was the final game for Johnny Giles, Bremner would soon move on, Norman Hunter left, Paul Reaney went and Clarke eventually left for Barnsley. Lorimer would go and then return to Leeds after relegation in 1982.

"I think it was always going to be a night tinged with sadness," admitted Bremner. "We realised that this was the split-up of that side. We knew Johnny was going into management and that others would go. We went to Norway for a friendly straight afterwards and then to Spain to play golf. It was sad because we knew it was over."

Armfield moved to replenish the squad with the signing of Tony Currie and Brian Flynn and Leeds finished 5th in the 1975/76 season. It was 10th a year later and 9th in 1977/78.

John Hawley joined from Hull City in the summer of 1978, but Armfield never got to write his name on a team sheet.

Armfield did a solid enough job for four years and almost 200 games and had galvanised the squad enough to mount another serious bid for the European Cup.

United finished consistently inside the top 10, reached the last four of the FA Cup in 1977 and the same stage of the League Cup the following year. In Armfield's mind, all was going well, but United's directors were less enthused. He was sacked in 1978 after a series of disappointing results and then turned down offers from Chelsea, Leicester City and Blackburn Rovers. He had devoted his playing career to Blackpool and his heart always remained there. He didn't want to move his family away from the town he loved.

"After one defeat when we'd dropped to around seventh in the division, the chairman called a board meeting for the Monday morning," he recalled. "The gist of the discussion was him asking what was going on and whether the team had had it. I was slightly amazed and said, 'You do lose in football, you know.' After four years there, my contract wasn't extended."

That was the end of Armfield as a football manager. He received offers from Chelsea, Athletic Bilbao and Newcastle, but opted for a career in the media instead.

Armfield was a juxtaposition of a normal, down-to-earth bloke and an extraordinary man who was exceptional at all he tried. He was a man who didn't care for glamour and riches, he concentrated on family and the pursuit of happiness.

He had prepared for a life in the media when a player at Blackpool, where he worked late shifts on a local newspaper, the *Evening Gazette*. As he developed that string to his bow, he was in demand as a former England player, but celebrity can only take a journalist and pundit so far. He took a job with the *Daily Express* and anyone hearing Armfield chipping into Radio 5 Live football commentaries knew they were in safe and knowledgeable hands.

He was also employed by the Football Association as a consultant from 1994 and played a key role in the appointments of Terry Venables and Glenn Hoddle as England managers.

During the Second World War, a young Jimmy Armfield had been evacuated from his native Manchester to Blackpool. It was the start of a lifelong love of the seaside town. He began watching the town's football team, which at the time was one of the best in the country and featured the great Stanley Matthews.

He joined Blackpool when he was 17 and made his debut in a 3-0 defeat to Portsmouth on 27 December 1954. Blackpool had won the FA Cup the year before Armfield arrived and the 1955/56 season remains the best Blackpool have ever experienced. Armfield was ever-present in the team that finished First Division runners-up. He was voted the Football League's Young Player of the Year 1959.

A one-club man, despite attempts by Sir Matt Busby to take him to Manchester United, and also interest from Arsenal and Tottenham Hotspur, Armfield captained the Seasiders for over a decade. He would make a club record 627 appearances over a 17-year career. He was still their when Blackpool won promotion back to the First Division in 1969/70. He played his final game on 1 May 1971 as 30,000 fans said their goodbyes, not only to Armfield, but also to top-tier football for 40 years as Blackpool were relegated.

He was inducted into the club's Hall of Fame in April 2006. The South Stand at the Bloomfield Road ground, opened in March 2010, is known as the 'Jimmy Armfield South Stand' and a nine-foot statue, with Armfield standing with one foot resting on a football, was commissioned by the Blackpool Supporters' Association in 2009 and unveiled in May 2011.

"I feel quite humble about it," Armfield said about the Bloomfield Road tributes to him. "I must be honest, I will be very proud to see it. Blackpool is my team and my town; it is nice to think that anything I have done has been appreciated."

Along the way he was capped 43 times for England between 1959 and 1966 and captained his country 15 times. He had debuted against Brazil on 13 May in front of 120,000 spectators at the Maracana Stadium and was named the 'best right-back in the world' at the 1962 World Cup in Chile.

A groin injury sustained in Blackpool's final game of the 1963/64 season allowed George Cohen the opportunity to step in and claim his England shirt. He made the 1966 World Cup squad, but did not feature in Alf Ramsey's winning sides and his cap against Finland in Helsinki during the pre-World Cup tour would be his last.

In those days, indeed prior to the 1974 World Cup, only the players that took the field in the final received a medal. In 2009, after a campaign led by the Football Association, FIFA announced that an additional 14 medals would be made for each winning side between 1930 and 1970.

"It's nice to get it, but I can't say it's something that's been bothering me all these years," he said, after finally receiving his medal from Prime Minister Gordon Brown at a ceremony held at 10 Downing Street on 10 June 2009. "We just didn't expect it and I wasn't bitter about it at all."

"His time at Leeds is too easily forgotten," Gray said. "It's sad he didn't end up with the European Cup."

He showed his forward-thinking nature by earning coaching qualifications in the 1960s, a time when, as he said, "coaching badges weren't really in vogue."

Armfield told BBC Radio Lancashire, on 11 May 2007, that he had been undergoing chemotherapy treatment for non-Hodgkin lymphoma in his throat. He had been told by doctors to rest and the cancer was removed. Sadly, it returned in November 2016 and Armfield died in his beloved Blackpool on 22 January 2018, aged 82. His reputation as a gentleman whose natural enthusiasm for football was infectious was well deserved.

12

JOCK STEIN

1978

Big Jock

Born: 5 October 1922, Burnbank, Lanarkshire, Scotland
Died: 10 September 1985, Cardiff, Wales (aged 62)

Matches	Won	Drawn	Lost	Points	Pts/Match	Win %
10	4	3	3	15	1.50	40.00%
				RANK	11th/36	15th/36

Jock Stein was appointed Leeds United manager in August 1978. The former Celtic boss was only in charge at Elland Road for 44 days before he was offered the Scotland position and moved on.

Stein fell in love with Leeds United very quickly, but he loved Scotland more.

Leeds players welcomed a man of Stein's proven pedigree. He had earned a huge reputation in Scotland, but the players also questioned his motivation in coming to work in England when he had never previously expressed a desire to come south.

As Celtic manager, Stein had taken on Don Revie's Leeds in the 1970 European Cup semi-final. Ahead of the first leg, the referee ordered Celtic to change their socks to avoid both teams wearing white. Leeds offered Stein the choice of red or blue. Blue was never an option as it was the colour of Glasgow Rangers, Celtic's great rivals, so Stein chose red. He believed that they would look orange under the floodlights and Celtic supporters would think their team were wearing the colours of the Irish tricolour.

Stein then revelled in the fact that Revie had been unsettled by the tactic. Stein is alleged to have said something along the lines of: "He's shitting himself. I've never seen that man as nervous in all my life. He's as white as a sheet. If he's like that, what do you think his players are like? They're there for the taking."

Celtic won that first leg 1-0 and qualified for the final with a 2-1 victory at Hampden Park in the second leg.

As a former centre-back, who had played for Celtic 106 times between 1951 and 1957, Stein had been forced into retirement at the age of 34 by a persistent ankle problem which had blighted his 1955/56 season. The injury needed an operation, after which the ankle had become septic which meant he had lost flexibility in the joint and officially retired on 29 January 1957.

Leeds chairman Manny Cussins had wanted Lawrie McMenemy to replace the outgoing Jimmy Armfield, but had failed to get the name past the United board. Cussins then suggested former player Johnny Giles, only to be rebuffed again.

Cussins then met Stein in Newcastle and then, on 17 August 1978, offered the Scot £30,000 a week to take over at Elland Road. Stein told Cussins that the money was not important. Whether Leeds United was important, probably only Stein knew. He moved south without his wife, Jean.

Stein had an enviable track record north of the border. He had begun his coaching career with Celtic Reserves upon retirement and followed that by starting his managerial career proper at Dunfermline Athletic in 1960, winning the Scottish cup in 1960/61. After four seasons there, he had short spells at Hibernian and Scotland before taking charge of Celtic in March 1965.

During 13 seasons at Celtic Park, Stein's greatest achievement was winning the European Cup in 1967. He also added 10 League titles, eight Scottish FA Cups and six Scottish League Cups.

Stein had been demoted at Celtic to the position of general manager. It was a job with no clout and taken as an insult. Selling lottery tickets was not what Stein had got into football to do.

The Leeds board viewed what Stein had done at Celtic as the equivalent in Scotland of their own Revie era. If Stein could replicate that success in West Yorkshire, he was worth every penny. Leeds United were prepared to give Big Jock the respect that Celtic had removed.

"Jock Stein is the finest man in the business," Cussins told the media. "We need him here."

When Stein first met the Leeds players, he took a completely different approach to the one Brian Clough had employed four years earlier.

Peter Lorimer recalled how Stein had addressed the players on his first day at the club. "He's come in and said, 'Right boys, only a few seasons ago this was the best club in England, and we will be again.' We loved hearing that. He filled us with confidence, absolutely got us floating on air.

"Jock got us together and said we'd been successful by using our own methods and we should continue in that manner. I went home thinking that was all I wanted to hear.

"Clough insisted on players doing as he said at all times," Lorimer stated. "Stein knew it was possible for there to be two sides to a story, so you could actually have a conversation with him.

"He came down to Leeds because of the Scots colony there and there's no saying what he could have achieved if he'd stayed," Lorimer added. "I was excited when he arrived, but I knew the Scotland job was more up his street when it was offered to him.

"I regret his decision to go to this day. We had the likes of Joe Jordan and big Gordon McQueen breaking through at that time and the partnership of Leeds and Stein could have been spectacular. You can't leave an influential mark on a club if you've only been there for 44 days."

Manny Cussins believed the team were shaping up better under Stein, who was known for his attacking style of play. By this time, Leeds fans were growing increasingly disillusioned at the club's fall from the highest echelons and were staying away.

Leeds played their first game of the Stein era on Wednesday, 23 August 1978. Huge excitement existed for the new manager, the home fixture against Manchester United and anger expressed against returning players, Joe Jordan and Gordon McQueen, by then in the red of Manchester.

McQueen scored as Manchester United won 3-2. The following weekend, Leeds beat Wolverhampton Wanderers 3-0 and then put three past Chelsea.

"He had Don's quiet authority," Lorimer remembered. "Didn't need to shout and roar. All he needed to do was say something once and you bloody well did it. You did it out of respect."

Results worsened, however, with back-to-back goalless draws in the League Cup against West Brom, a 3-0 league defeat at Manchester City and a 2-1 home loss to Tottenham.

Stein moved to reinforce his midfield with a £300,000 bid for Derby's Gerry Daly. Tommy Docherty countered with a demand for £400,000 and neither party would budge. Stein withdrew interest in a public sulk.

Leeds drew 0-0 with Coventry and there was a feeling that Stein missed the big European nights he had experienced so often with Celtic. Although Leeds were becoming more organised, they were struggling. Stein was cutting a solitary figure. Some thought he had become more introverted.

It would seem that the lure of the Scottish managerial job was on Stein's mind from the start. His family never moved to Yorkshire and Stein was living from a hotel. He missed his wife. The sparse crowds and lack of big pressure European competition was missing for Stein and he was already growing hungry for a fresh challenge when the Scotland job became available.

Ally MacLeod had vocally proclaimed that Scotland were heading to the 1978 World Cup in Argentina to return with "at least a medal", but they lost 3-1 to Peru, could only muster a 1-1 draw against minnows Iran and were finally sent home with a 3-2 defeat to Netherlands. MacLeod had become something of a laughingstock, leading Scottish comedian Billy Connolly to say: "Ally MacLeod thinks that tactics are a new kind of mint."

It was no surprise when, after one more game in charge, MacLeod resigned on 26 September 1978.

Leeds beat Birmingham City 3-0, but the crowd was small in comparison to previous seasons. Fewer than 24,000 were at Elland Road. They finally edged past West Brom in the League Cup as 8,000 turned out to see it.

Stein asked commentator Archie Macpherson to spread the word publicly that he would be interested in the national job. Macpherson would write Stein's biography and described the voice he heard at the other end of the phone as 'morose, slowly spoken, husky', as he suggested that the journalist should phone London and tell his bosses that he had a story for them.

"Tell London that you can say something about the Scotland job and me," Stein suggested. "You could go on to say something to the effect that you believe I would be interested in going back to Scotland. You can't say you've been talking to me. Just play it like you're confident I would take the job. Make it sound like the SFA are being a bit slow on this."

Macpherson's story sparked huge interest as the campaign for Stein to become the new Scotland manager gathered pace.

Cussins was not happy. He refused initial requests from the Scottish Football Association to talk to Stein. He met Stein at his Leeds hotel, offered him more money, to buy him a house, but struggled in vain to convince his manager that the grass was greener at Elland Road than Hampden Park. Cussins had seen Clough go and now Stein was deserting him too.

Stein resigned and was full of guilt for letting Cussins down. "It's the hardest decision I've ever had to make in my football life," he admitted. "This is one of the worst moments of my life. I feel I have let people down here."

It was not a partnership broken in the same way that Cussins and Clough had parted. Stein and Cussins shook hands and wished each other well as the offer from the SFA for the Scotland job was accepted. Stein's ego had been drained. He needed to be back in his homeland living up to his billing of Big Jock again.

In his brief spell at Elland Road, Leeds played 10 matches, winning four, drawing three and losing three.

"In my deepest subconscious I felt Big Jock was trying to force the SFA's hand," Eddie Gray told the *Daily Record* in 2012. "The big man wanted to be the full-time manager of Scotland and when he moved to Leeds, he made the SFA change their way of working and made him the most powerful manager they'd ever had.

"People forget Jock was there [at Leeds] for the same length of time as Brian, but there the similarities end," added Gray. "I'd always fancied the idea of working under Stein. I was a Scot and I leaned towards Celtic. He was the man for me, and he had Revie's charisma into the bargain. When he spoke, people listened.

"There was no scepticism about a Scot taking over a club like Leeds. Mick Jones was our centre-forward when we lost the European semi-final in 1970 and he recently told me he thought Celtic were the best team he'd ever played against.

"That's why I'll always be left wondering how far Stein would have taken us if he'd stayed at Elland Road.

"Clough arrived with the wrong attitude," Gray continued. "Stein came saying all the right things and I had absolutely no doubt he would have been an outstanding success in England. But he wanted to be in charge of his country."

"I am heartbroken," Chairman Cussins said on 3 October 1978. "Nothing in my life has worried me more than Jock Stein leaving Elland Road, not even the Brian Clough affair."

Leeds officials were back to the drawing board. Where to next to return Leeds to the top tier of English football? Their choice was Jimmy Adamson.

13

JIMMY ADAMSON

1978–1980

Adamson Out!

Born: 4 April 1929, Ashington, Northumberland
Died: 8 November 2011, Nelson, Lancashire (aged 82)

Matches	Won	Drawn	Lost	Points	Pts/Match	Win %
96	35	30	31	135	1.41	36.46%
				RANK	20th/36	23rd/36

Maurice Lindley had been put in temporary charge after Jock Stein's departure until a full-time replacement could be found. Chairman Manny Cussins had lost the manager he had put his faith in and had to find a replacement, big enough to take control, strong enough to restore former glories and captivating enough to reignite interest and win back the shrinking crowds.

In stark contrast to that brief, Leeds appointed Jimmy Adamson. His time at Leeds saw them exit the UEFA Cup early in 1979 in front of a sparsely populated Elland Road ground as banners were lofted with 'Adamson Out' the common theme.

During his two-year tenure at Elland Road, his last job in football, he barely caused a ripple.

History could have been written very differently had Adamson accepted the England manager's job when it was offered to him in 1962. The Football Association turned in his direction to offer him the role after Walter Winterbottom resigned his 16-year run as national boss.

Adamson had been acting as Winterbottom's assistant and turned the job down as he felt he lacked sufficient experience. To follow a man of Winterbottom's stature in the game was certainly a daunting one.

Alf Ramsey took the England job instead and the rest is history. As Bobby Moore raised the World Cup trophy at Wembley in 1966, Adamson could have been forgiven for thinking what might have been.

Upon his death on 8 November 2011, the tributes poured in, but the contrast in feeling between those from Burnley and those from Leeds was marked. Leeds fan site, *To Ell And Back*, wrote: 'Former Leeds, Burnley and Sunderland manager Jimmy Adamson has died at the age of 82. He is fondly remembered in Lancashire as the captain of Burnley's 1960 League Championship-winning team, but we don't look back at his time at Elland Road quite so favourably!'

In Burnley, he was a bona fide legend. Adamson had been a success as a player of superb skill and elegance. He had captained Burnley to their 1960 league title and was named the Footballer of the Year in 1962 as Burnley lost the FA Cup final to Tottenham.

During a 17-year playing career, he played 486 games for Burnley. He became a coach when his playing days were over and took the managerial hot seat in February 1970 and began with relegation in the 1970/71 season, his first full season in charge. Promotion back to the top flight came in 1972/73 and then a 6th place finish in the First Division in 1973/74 and a run to the FA Cup semi-finals. A superb start to the 1974/75 season had them challenging for the title, but pressure from above forced Adamson to sell some of his better players. Burnley were experiencing a period of financial decline and were seeking to expand the stadium, whereas naturally Adamson wanted to create a team.

That conflict forced Adamson away from Turf Moor for the first time in his career when he quit in 1976. He sought brief refuge as the boss at Sparta Rotterdam, but realised quickly that he wanted to live in England.

Sunderland approached him to recover a bad first quarter of the 1976/77 season. Sunderland were in serious decline and Adamson lost his first seven matches and, although results improved, relegation was inevitable. A 6th placed finish the following season was a failure and he was sacked in October 1978.

Sunderland fanzine, *A Love Supreme*, wrote: 'When he wasn't driving around Whitley Bay full of drink, was trying to sign the entire Burnley team.'

It wasn't a managerial CV that you'd have expected Mr Cussins to put his trust in to restore Leeds United's fortunes.

Adamson had issues with drink. Leeds players would refer to him as Howard Hughes as he was rarely seen at the training ground. He was often found asleep in his office and for one home game assistant manager Dave Merrington took the team after Adamson disappeared around lunchtime.

The 1978/79 season saw Leeds finish 5th and qualify for the UEFA Cup. It had been the club's best return since Don Revie had left. Adamson had taken the helm with the club in the bottom half of the First Division. One defeat in 20 games restored the season and a run in the League Cup saw Leeds in the League Cup semi-final.

Tony Currie's wife was missing London and he left for QPR. Frank Gray moved to Nottingham Forest. David Harvey, Peter Lorimer and Ray Hankin were let go. Adamson failed to replace the star names adequately. Alex Sabella, Gary Hamson and Derek Parlane were recruited and were not a success.

John Hawley, signed by Jimmy Armfield, was the most likely goalscorer, but Adamson let him go. He replaced Currie with Brian Greenhoff, a player of considerable talent, but it was not like-for-like. Currie was an advanced playmaker, Greenhoff more functional. Kevin Hird was effectively signed as Gray's replacement and was not in the same class.

Whether it was desperation, Adamson bravely injected youth into the side in the shape of Carl Harris, Byron Stevenson, John Lukic, Terry Connor and Martin Dickinson with varying degrees of success. Decent signings on paper, Adamson didn't get the best out of them.

Fans were quickly losing faith in his management when the UEFA Cup run was ended in the second round by Universitatea Craiova of Romania.

One bright spot, a League Cup semi-final appearance, which ended in further fan frustration. Leeds were leading the first leg at Elland Road against Lawrie McMenemy's Southampton, only to lose 3-2 on aggregate.

The anti-Adamson movement gathered pace as Leeds lost to Bristol City at Elland Road and played out a dire goalless draw against Coventry. It wasn't pretty, exciting or going anywhere and an 11th placed finish was their worst since being promoted in the 1963/64 season. Survival was not enough and couldn't mask a plethora of inadequacies.

Adamson was rapidly falling out of love with Leeds United and football.

The 1980/81 season saw no improvement. In fact, the mood, tone and results had worsened further. The side had lost any semblance of creativity and relegation was a genuine possibility after losing four of the first five games. Ugly rioting with police occurred after a demonstration was held following a home defeat to Aston Villa.

Adamson, questioned about his future, stated: "As far as I'm concerned, I've got a job to do here at Leeds. The Leeds directors have not interfered at all and if they don't interfere with my job and I get on with it and I'm a failure, then I expect to be kicked out the door."

The opinion of fans was that his time was up, and the Northumberland-born manager was left with no choice but to tender his resignation. Leeds were one place from the bottom of the First Division table after six games.

He retreated into the shadows, living a quiet and private life in Burnley.

When I spoke to Eddie Gray, we discussed Adamson and Gray had a far more positive recall than I expected.

"You pick up things from all the managers and I liked Jimmy Adamson because he had a good knowledge of the game, but I don't think he came out to the training pitch enough," Gray said. "So, we were consequently doing things on the training pitch only for him to change things in his team talk on a Saturday.

"If you're the manager of a football club you are the governor and need to know exactly how you want your team to play and how it should be run.

"But everybody in football has different ideas on how the game should be played," Gray explained. "Your other coaches might be telling you that you should be doing something one way and then Jimmy might say something completely different. But if he's at the training pitch and been through things with you and told you how he as manager wants to see the team play then that's great.

"I don't think he did that enough. It would have been beneficial to him and the players if he had done that, but maybe that was how Jimmy did things."

Brian Flynn had followed Adamson from Turf Moor to Elland Road and also held Adamson in high regard.

"Firstly, he was a top-drawer, first-class coach," said Flynn. "England wanted him for the top job after the World Cup in South America in '62. He was only in his early thirties then. He's also probably the best man-manager I've had in terms of getting the best out of people. He was one step ahead, always."

And Dave Merrington, Adamson's assistant at Leeds, who would move on to manage Southampton, also held his former boss in high regard.

"It was a transitional period when we took over," Merrington recalled. "The team really needed altering and Jim was in the process of doing that, but unfortunately didn't get the time to do that.

"I think what cost Jimmy his job was not the fact he wasn't doing the job, but the fact the gates were falling.

"I think the board had budgeted for more than was going through the gates. Sometimes, it's the financial aspect that costs a manager as well, which was unfortunate really.

"But Jimmy was an excellent guy to work for. I learnt a great deal under Jim and developed my coaching ideas around him and eventually put my own ideas into my portfolio.

"He was one of the old school in that he believed in balancing the books. He didn't believe in leaving a job for the next man to come in and struggle. He wanted the next man to have a chance. Today, I don't think they (managers) give a monkey's.

"We had some good players and got into Europe. Personally, I'll always be grateful for Jimmy when I was coming through the ranks at

Burnley and developing as a coach under him because he was probably one of the best in his field."

Merrington believed that Adamson was not given long enough, yet there were thousands of stay away fans and 'Adamson out' demonstrators at games who would suggest he had far too long.

Was Adamson the worst Leeds United manager to have held the job for a season or more? It's hard to compare as every manager has different personnel, budgets and challenges to confront. A couple may run him close, but I would suggest it would be difficult to argue against that assertion.

Merrington's assertion that Adamson would leave the club in a healthy state for the next man in is also difficult to support. The fallout from Adamson's regime hampered Leeds for several seasons. Allan Clarke, Leeds's next manager, was certainly in for a rude awakening.

14

ALLAN CLARKE

1980–1982

Sniffer

Born: 31 July 1946, Willenhall, Staffordshire

Matches	Won	Drawn	Lost	Points	Pts/Match	Win %
84	27	21	36	102	1.21	32.14%
				RANK	27th/36	30th/36

Allan Clarke became the first to have played under Don Revie to take charge of a Leeds side, but the gloss was fast peeling off the walls.

When Allan Clarke took over he was shocked at the poor physical state of the playing squad he inherited. Jimmy Adamson had completely neglected to supervise any proper pre-season training and there was a huge amount of rebuilding to do to get the club anywhere near former glories.

At 34 years old, Clarke was the youngest manager in the First Division when he took charge. Unsurprisingly, he was a very popular appointment, which was much needed to regain the goodwill of the supporters. He inherited a Leeds that were second from bottom in the league and initially results gradually improved.

Clarke had begun his playing career with Walsall as a 16-year-old in 1963 where he scored 41 goals in 72 appearances. In March 1966, he was bought by Fulham just ahead of the transfer deadline and again showed his immense promise with 45 goals in 86 games. Leicester City took a £150,000 punt on the then 21-year-old and, although bagging the winning goal in the 1969 FA Cup semi-final against West Bromwich Albion, his 12 goals in 36 appearances, which included the FA Cup Final defeat to Manchester City, didn't quite deliver.

But it was enough to spark the interest of Don Revie. Clarke signed on at Elland Road on 24 June 1969 as a £165,000 purchase and was soon dubbed 'Sniffer' for his innate ability to smell out a goal. Clarke was the ultimate predator with 26 goals in his first Leeds season. It would, however, be a season of disappointment with the club coming close to the League Championship, FA Cup and European Cup, but ultimately ending up with nothing to show for their efforts.

That talent to strike a football was in the blood. He was one of five brothers to all play professional football. The oldest of the Clarke boys was Frank who played for Shrewsbury Town, Queens Park Rangers, Ipswich Town and Carlisle United over a 17-year career. Allan was the second of the boys, followed by Derek (Walsall, Oxford and Orient), Kelvin (Walsall) and Wayne (Wolverhampton Wanderers, Birmingham City, Everton and Walsall).

In all, Allan scored 151 goals in 348 appearances for Leeds and picked up winners' medals for the 1973/74 First Division, 1972 FA Cup, Inter-Cities Fairs Cup in 1971 and of course a runners-up medal in the 1975 European Cup. He also played 19 times for England with 10 goals.

"The reason we packed in, we were absolutely shattered, but we didn't make enough money, because you'd still got a mortgage to pay off, so you had to look for work elsewhere," Clarke told Leeds Fans United, for whom he became an ambassador.

"Whereas these days it's completely different. I think the day came when I was going to hang my boots up. I always fancied having a go at management and I can remember I went on a coaching course. So, I got my coaching badges and I went into management in 1978 with Barnsley when they were in the Fourth Division."

Clarke left Leeds as a legend in 1978 when a knee injury restricted his capacity to operate at the highest level. At Barnsley, he had played the last of his 47 matches in 1980 as player-coach.

Maurice Lindley had once again taken temporary charge of Leeds after Adamson had resigned, but the Leeds officials opted for tried, trusted and someone that had been part of the Revie years. Clarke had gone into management at Barnsley and had earned the South Yorkshire side promotion to Division Two.

Leeds were not doing well when Clarke was installed. Clarke established consistency and lifted them to 9th position, but the sparkle was missing and supporters staying away. The team mustered just 39 goals all season and fans struggled to correlate 'Sniffer' the attacking flair player to Clarke the defensively-minded tactician.

In a bid to reignite his side, Clarke signed winger Peter Barnes from West Bromwich Albion for a club record £930,000. Barnes flopped and Clarke had almost emptied the coffers for one player.

Leeds won only one of their first 10 matches in 1981/82 and Clarke rolled the dice once more by bringing in Frank Worthington up front and Kenny Burns to add some defensive stability.

It didn't work. Leeds were relegated to end a period of 18 years in England's top tier and Clarke was sacked before the start of the next season.

Eddie Gray was still playing under his former teammate in the relegation season. He said: "There were a lot of players in the dressing room that felt they were too good to go down, but that is never the case if you don't work hard enough."

Clarke still felt he had something to give in football and was manager of Scunthorpe, Barnsley again and finally Lincoln City before he opted to become a travelling salesman for MTS Nationwide in 1983.

"I had 12 years in management when I'd had enough really, fighting directors and whatever," Clarke stated. "I then went into repping until I retired."

Clarke lives in Scunthorpe, Lincolnshire. A regular visitor to Elland Road, he still gets a very warm reception as a genuine legend of the most memorable era in Leeds United's history.

EDDIE GRAY

1982–1985

"When he plays on snow, he doesn't leave any footprints"

Born: 17 January 1948, Glasgow, Scotland

Matches	Won	Drawn	Lost	Points	Pts/Match	Win %
157 (26)	57 (6)	55 (7)	45 (13)	226 (25)	1.44 (0.93)	36.30% (22.22%)
				RANK	19th/36	24th/36

(BRACKETED FIGURE IS CARETAKER SPELL IN 2003/04)

When people think of Leeds United they think of Don Revie as manager. Billy Bremner, Peter Lorimer and Big John Charles head the players. And there is Eddie Gray, right up there in that legendary company.

Not only was Gray a superb player over 19 years at Leeds, initially under Don Revie through the glory years, but also beyond. He is a Scotsman that came down to Leeds and, in all but accent, became a Yorkshireman.

Revie left no stone unturned in his quest to ensure his young targets had only positive first impressions of Elland Road.

Rather than fitting square pegs in round holes, Revie had purchased multi-dimensional hexagons who could slot in almost anywhere in the honeycomb.

"Don was building a team," Gray agreed. "It was similar with Peter Lorimer, as when he came down he was playing as a striker, but he was outside right and still scored a hell of a lot of goals, but at that time Don had bought Allan Clarke and Mick Jones in to be strikers.

"When I first came to the club, Terry Cooper was an outside left and Don turned him into a left-back. We developed a great understanding on the left side, especially with Norman Hunter, who was a midfield player, playing in the old defensive left half as well.

"Don could see something in players and knew he could transform them into playing in certain positions," Gray continued. "When Johnny Giles had played in the 1963 FA Cup final for Manchester United, he was an outside right, but Don bought him to play in midfield.

"It was Don's great knowledge of the game that was what first impressed me," Gray admitted. "Even though I was young I had been to a few clubs and Don, as a manager, was the man that impressed me most with his knowledge and how he looked after people. And his thoughts and philosophy on the game."

"You'd have to say he was a bit like Matt Busby, Jock Stein, Sir Alex — they were all-powerful. They ran the football club. There weren't any sports directors back then — the one man ran the football club and his word was law."

Revie's career as a player made him a rare breed of an exceptional footballer that would become a superb manager. Many great players don't have the empathy to tirelessly work with a training ground struggler that can't master the arts that had come to him naturally. And even as a player, Revie had developed a head for tactics and strategy.

"What people tend to forget about Don was that he was a terrific player as well," Gray recalled. "Manchester City had the Revie Plan with Don playing as a deep lying centre-forward. And I think it was Don that introduced that to City when he played there.

"The great Hungarian team of 1953 came to Wembley and they had a number nine called Nandor Hidegkuti who never played like a centre-forward. The English players didn't know how to mark him because he wasn't playing like a number nine. It had always been that number five picked up number nine and number two would pick up number eleven. Hidegkuti sat deep and that's what Don introduced to Manchester City. He wore number nine but was basically a midfield schemer and therefore had plenty of room for himself. That gives you a glimpse on his thoughts on the game."

Gray had learned from one of the very best. Revie had a rapport with his players, a steely drive to be the very best, and with the football vision to achieve miracles. It may be that it was right man, place and time, and Revie operating the same way somewhere else would not have brought the same level of accomplishment.

Nobody would have foreseen the young Eddie Gray moving down to Yorkshire and still being there over 50 years later. A player, a coach, a manager and a media pundit. There will be few who have seen more of Leeds United's ups and downs than Eddie.

Gray's achievements as a player are documented elsewhere in this book and he was central to the success the club achieved. No defender was safe as he scored 68 goals for the Whites. It's nigh on impossible to compare players from different eras, but what price Eddie Gray on today's transfer market? He'd add value to any of the current great European club sides. He was a player that in modern Premier League transfer markets would break records as the best players today profit from £1million-a-month-plus.

If you have never seen it, search YouTube for the brace he bagged against Burnley on 4 April 1970 at Elland Road. In the first half, he picked the ball up in the centre of the park and lobbed the keeper with glorious disdain. In the second half, he went even better. Picking the ball up on the left-hand side of the area, he showed superb tight control as he swivelled from the by-line to beat seven tackles before burying the ball in the bottom corner. It left the crowd speechless, stunned by brilliance, until they realised that Gray, trotting modestly back to his own half, had delivered something they'd never forget.

When I asked Eddie about the famous Revie quote suggesting that if he played on snow he would have left no footprints, he confessed that he took it as a great compliment.

"It's not true," Eddie laughed. "I tried it and it doesn't work! That quote hangs up at Elland Road in the Don Revie Lounge and of course it fills you with confidence.

"The game has changed now with academies and the way players are looked after," Gray continued. "But when I first came down, I was an amateur because Scottish schoolboys couldn't sign for English clubs as apprentice professionals when they were fifteen. I had to sign as an amateur.

"The way Don got around that was I was supposed to be a motor mechanic; Peter Lorimer was a printer. We were amateurs and that was how it had to be. We became professionals when we were seventeen.

"When we were youngsters, we had to do jobs around the ground, sweep the terraces, clean the toilets, clean up the ground basically. Even when we had a lunch break, Don would take us out and join us and play. And he could play. You could tell he'd been a top player. For the manager to do that, it filled all the young boys with that sense that they really wanted to be a player. He would always speak to you about the great players of the past — Tom Finney, Stanley Matthews, Duncan Edwards — he'd always try and impress upon you what it was like to be a top player.

"He took me off the ground-staff when I was sixteen and I didn't have to do the jobs the young boys did anymore, which a few of them didn't like, but that was Don's way of trying to impress upon me that he thought I was going to be a player. And I was then training with the 1st team from a young age."

And the rest is there in the Leeds United trophy cabinet. Under Revie, Gray won two First Division titles (1968/69, 1973/74), a Second Division crown (1963/64), one FA Cup (1972), a Football League Cup (1968), one Charity Shield (1969) and two Inter-Cities Fairs Cups (1968, 1973). It's one hell of a trophy haul and, but for a series of second places, could have been even bigger.

When the legendary Scot took over from his former teammate Allan Clarke, he was still a player, defying the Clough jibe that, "If he was a horse he'd have been shot."

Leeds, however, missed out on promotion for three successive seasons under Gray. Critics suggested that the side he had assembled was too lightweight.

"When I took over in '82, the club didn't have a lot of money and I was told that in no uncertain terms that some of the big earners would have to go," Gray remembered. "We had a few decent young players at the club. And we took the decision that we were just going to go with them but that probably cost me the job at the end of the day."

Gray had played under all of the managers from Revie to Allan Clarke.

"They all had their good points, but for me no-one could better Don in basically any point-of-view," Gray asserted. "Jimmy (Armfield) came in and he steadied the ship, got results, wasn't as powerful a character as Don.

"The only man that seemed to have the same power of character as Don, other than Cloughie, was Jock Stein. He had the same aura about him as well. If Don, or Jock Stein, Matt Busby or Sir Alex walked into a room they would immediately be the centre of attraction.

"Managers have changed over the years," he added. "The game has changed a lot. You get directors of football, sports scientists and all sorts. Although Alex Ferguson would embrace all the changes that happened at the football club, there would only be one final say and that would be Alex's.

"There are a lot of people in football that know exactly how the game should be played. Well if you feel like that then go and stand on the white line and be prepared to take the flak if it doesn't work.

"Allan Clarke had a terrific knowledge of the game. I enjoyed playing with Allan as manager. It was him that put me to left-back and I found that quite easy.

"Football goes in cycles. It always has done and always will do. You only need to look at Man City now and years ago. Look at Man Utd years ago before Alex took over.

"We were losing players," Gray recalled. "All our players had moved on and Allan was working with a new bunch and that's not easy. I found that when I took over from Allan. We had to sell a lot of players and had to play a lot of young boys."

All of those years as an exemplary player, was Gray ready to step up to the task of becoming player-manager at Leeds United? And was it an easier transition still being one of the team? Or did that make it even more complicated?

"I think one of the biggest mistakes I made was not playing long enough," Gray responded. "I thought I could have played on a little bit more. It's a hard thing to do as player-manager to cut back your schedule, and I mean the office schedule and going to games. It becomes tiring because you are out watching games after being at the club all day dealing with different things, but I still wish I had played on a little longer. But to do that you have got to be training all the time and keeping yourself up to a certain level of fitness. Although I was fit.

"The mentality that comes into it as well, it can get to you. Not physically tired, but mentally tired, because you are trying to juggle two things, your own performance and the performance of your players. And you are trying to tell them things.

"I wanted to be playing. If I hadn't have taken over as player-manager, I think I would have played the game until I was forty.

"It wasn't an easy decision to make, to take the job, but I felt like it was an opportunity," Gray revealed. "Anybody young, I don't think you are automatically ready for it.

"When Don Revie came to Leeds, he was a player. He then became manager. When are you ever going to be ready? You have to start somewhere.

"It wasn't as if Leeds were a top team in Europe or anything," Gray said, suggesting the pressure was off a little. "We'd been relegated, we were in the Second Division, we knew the financial situation at the football club, so we didn't have a lot of money to spend and had to try and introduce some young boys.

"I enjoyed that time even though I got the sack at the end of the day. But when I got sacked, I felt I left the club with good players and a lot of them went on to do terrific things. Andy Linighan, Terry Phelan, John Sheridan, Tommy Wright, Scott Sellars — a lot of players that went on to have good careers in the game.

"The people that run the club are in charge and they do things how they see fit and they felt we were not progressing enough. When I got the sack, I think we'd been unbeaten in seven games. You accept the decision because that's the nature of football. If you get into the game, you know it's going to happen."

The Leeds board turned to another former legend to try and resurrect their status amongst the big boys of English football. And it didn't get more legendary than Billy Bremmer.

16

BILLY BREMNER

1985–1988

"Side before self every time"

Born: 9 December 1942, Stirling, Scotland
Died: 7 December 1997, Clifton, Doncaster, Yorkshire

Matches	Won	Drawn	Lost	Points	Pts/Match	Win %
143	59	32	52	209	1.46	41.26%
				RANK	16th/36	14th/36

"If every manager were given the choice of one player to add to their squad, some would toy with the idea of George Best," said John Arlott. "But realists would have Billy Bremner."

Don Revie said of his captain: "No manager could wish for a greater leader or a greater player. If I was in the trenches at the front line, the man I would want on my right side is Billy Bremner."

Teammate Allan Clarke said: "When Billy Bremner took us across the white line, whether it was at Elland Road or Anfield or Old Trafford, Stamford Bridge, those players, my team, we died for Leeds United, we died for that club. Billy was the best player who ever played, they don't make players like him today."

And of course there is the song that fills the stadium on match days as the crowd sing 'Glory Glory Leeds United': "Little Billy Bremner is the captain of the crew, for the sake of Leeds United he would break himself in two, his hair is red and fuzzy and his body's black and blue, but Leeds go marching on."

Bremner was a 5-foot 5-inch giant of Leeds's midfield. The captain during the glory years was the poster boy for a generation. A former boss of mine had just one thing hanging on his office wall. When he left it was the only item he took home with him.

A product of Gowanhill Juniors in Stirling, Scotland, Bremner came down to Leeds as a teenager and joined a squad where Don Revie was still a player, about to become player-manager.

Little Billy had debuted for Leeds in 1960, aged 17, and went on to play 585 times for the club over the 16 years that followed. If this book documented the players that had added most value to Leeds teams down the years, Bremner's entry would have been the longest.

He may have been a passionate adopted Yorkshireman, but he was certainly a true Scot who took pride in his 54 international caps, his country's win over world champion neighbours England at Wembley in 1967, and their journey to the 1974 World Cup finals, where they finished level on points with Brazil and Yugoslavia and only failed to progress to the next round on goal difference.

The 1974 Charity Shield against Liverpool became an infamous record of the unruly side of Bremner. The tension had been building in a game ridden with fouls. Bremner had just been the victim, then Johnny Giles clashed with Kevin Keegan on the left-side of defence. Keegan appeared to go down easily, but the referee booked Giles and play resumed. But attention soon returned to the edge of the Leeds box where punches had been exchanged between Bremner and Keegan.

Tempers spilled over as both men were dismissed. Keegan ripped off his red shirt and stormed angrily toward the tunnel before hurling it down on the touchline. Bremner trudged off behind him. Both men were suspended for 11 games

Bremner played his last Scotland game in 1975 after he and four teammates were banned for life for unruly behaviour in a Copenhagen nightclub and in the team hotel. A year later, he left Leeds to play for Hull City.

He became manager of Doncaster Rovers in 1978 and spent seven years in South Yorkshire before replacing Eddie Gray at Elland Road.

"We'll give it our best shot," Bremner told Yorkshire Television after his appointment. "We will work extremely hard. We want to bring success to the club and I'm sure the players are hungry for success. People keep talking about 20 years ago and the good old days, but they've gone."

Eddie Gray told me: "When Billy came in he was probably a little bit unfortunate that he never got the team back into the big league, the First Division as it was then."

The fans had not been happy to see Gray go as the board were split about what the club's approach should be. The chairman, Leslie Silver, had to win people around and chose a replacement who was universally loved.

Bremner had very little money to spend as the Elland Road ground was sold to the Leeds City Council with Leeds retaining a 125-year lease. He also lost some of the young talent that Gray had been blooding. Ian Snodin, who had played under Bremner at Doncaster, was sold to Everton for £800,000.

Leeds finished a disappointing 14th in the 1985/86 season, but in the following season went all the way to the FA Cup semi-finals.

In the league, Bremner took the team to the Second Division play-off final where they were beaten by Charlton.

But Bremner couldn't sustain a level that would see him take Leeds back to the top division and a seventh-place finish in 1987/88 did not meet the requirements of the board. They kept faith, but after collecting just one win in the first six games of the 1988/89 campaign, Silver fired the former star in September 1988. Bremner's active association with Leeds United was over.

He returned to Doncaster Rovers where he was manager between July 1989 and November 1991, after which he became a fixture on the after-dinner speaking circuit.

Of course, he remained a fans' favourite and you can't escape his stamp on Elland Road with the Frances Segelman statue of Bremner standing proudly outside the stadium since 1999. It's the mark that sets Elland Road apart from the stadia around the country. In times of grief it becomes the shrine and in times of joy it is where everyone wants their photo taken. Bremner continues to make the difference even now.

Bremner went too soon. In December 1997, he was rushed to hospital after suffering an attack of pneumonia and, soon after, the heart that had encapsulated the most successful period of Leeds United's history gave out. He suffered a heart attack when at his home in Clifton, near Doncaster, and died aged only 54.

He was named on the list of 100 League Legends by the Football League in 1988 and has been included in both the English and Scottish Halls of Fame.

And Leeds fans voted Bremner the Greatest Leeds Player of All Time in 2006. In 2013, he was voted the greatest ever captain in the history of the Football League.

He will not be remembered for his tenure as manager, but Billy Bremner the player will never be forgotten.

17

HOWARD WILKINSON

1988–1996

"I think we've just won the Championship, Dad!"

Born: 13 November 1953, Sheffield, Yorkshire

Matches	Won	Drawn	Lost	Points	Pts/Match	Win %
400	173	115	112	634	1.58	43.25%
				RANK	9th/36	10th/36

Howard Wilkinson will always be remembered as the last manager to win the old First Division title when he saw his Leeds side crowned Champions at the end of the 1991/92 season.

Wilkinson took charge with Leeds a million miles from former glories. The two previous title-winning seasons had come under Don Revie in 1969 and 1974 and some time had passed, most of it filled with frustration and disappointment, when Wilkinson took charge on 10 October 1988.

"My main job now is to get Leeds United away from the foot of the Second Division and eventually get them into the First Division," Wilkinson told the media at his unveiling.

I'd never spoken to Wilkinson before we chatted about his eight-year period as Leeds manager. He was exactly what I expected. Forthright, friendly and with few frills around the edges, he gave me his time. I began at the start, asking why, when others, including his wife, suggested he might need his head testing for leaving First Division Sheffield Wednesday for Leeds, who were loitering fourth from bottom of the second tier.

"They offered me the chance to win the First Division," Wilkinson recalled. It had taken chairman Leslie Silver two weeks to woo his man. Wilkinson had initially driven up to meet Silver at his paint company when dark so he wouldn't be spotted after his friend and journalist David Walker had told him of Leeds's interest.

Wilkinson set out his timescale for achieving success at the club before Silver asked how much money would be needed to finance the plan.

"I said the difference was about £2million, which I knew from a look at the finances would have to be Leslie's money. I liked Leslie from the start and knew I could work with him and where necessary, in the early stages, he was prepared to put his own money in.

"I told him that supporters of the football club would never be happy unless it had aspirations to win the First Division Championship. If it had not got aspirations like that then people were going to get disenchanted and you are going to have an unhappy club. No matter how long we say we are going to take to get there, we have to tell them, and we have to mean it.

"I had always had a great relationship with the chairman at Wednesday (Bert McGee)," he continued, but requests Wilkinson had made to increase the transfer budget at Hillsborough were met with resistance by a board who had been scarred by previous financial problems. "The day I made the decision, I went to see the Wednesday chairman at his home and discussed it and I gave him my reasons. We'd always had a great relationship and he understood. He understood reluctantly and with some sadness, but he understood and said, 'Good luck, wish you all the best.'"

I told Howard that when I had worked at Yorkshire County Cricket Club, just prior to the side winning the County Championship in 2014 and 2015, Martyn Moxon and Jason Gillespie had put photographs of previous greats on the walls. They had told the current crop to write their own history and make sure their own photographs would adorn the walls in the future.

Wilkinson's approach at Elland Road was different. He had inherited a club still operating in the image of Don Revie, but without Revie's players.

"The club had lived in the past and from the outside I saw Leeds as a city dominated by Don Revie," Wilkinson told me. "I got the feeling they tried to create a Don Revie club and my view was that Don took that club over when they were in the Second Division and the club he created was based on him gradually acquiring more and better players. What had been happening at Leeds was a bit unrealistic.

"The driving force was that I was looking at ways to say to people 'we need to change.' That decision didn't come lightly because I knew it would possibly be seen as insulting. I hope I deferred the insults by saying they will go back up when we have a team that's worthy of those pictures that have been on the walls up to now. I think the Revie era pictures went back up after we secured promotion.

"My firm belief is that my job when I go to a football club is to look at what's there and find a way for them to win," Wilkinson continued. "It was different at Notts County, to what it was at Sheffield Wednesday, to what it was at Leeds. I started off with a blank piece of paper and on it were the players I was inheriting and it's great to have a long-term picture, but Leeds were fourth bottom and in the shit.

"When I went to Notts County they were in the shit and Sheffield

Wednesday were starting to go into decline after Jack had got them promoted. So, I'm not going there saying 'this is my philosophy'. I'm not Socrates.

"I went in there saying to the players what we have and what we are going to have and what we are going to do, I think this is the way that we can win football matches."

Wilkinson embarked on a managerial career with Boston United when only 27-years-old.

"It's good that I was at Boston United," he told BBC *Look North* in 1992. "Training two nights a week, driving a clapped-out Cortina down through Newark and looking out the side window because it was so foggy you couldn't see, three of you in it, picking people up at motorway restaurants and laybys. When the power strike was on, winning the Championship playing something like four games a week for three weeks running.

"The thing I like about non-league football is that generally the people involved in it love football," he continued. "They have to because what they get out of it in terms of finance nowhere near compensates for the trouble they have to go through to play."

After three seasons at Boston, Wilkinson spent a year with Mossley before his coaching ability was recognised when he took charge of England C.

His first full-time managerial role was with Notts County. He had joined as a coach under Jimmy Sirrel's management, but became manager when Sirrell moved upstairs as the club's General Manager. County finished in 15th position in the First Division in the 1982/83 season and Wilkinson went down a tier to become Sheffield Wednesday boss.

He oversaw Wednesday's promotion from the Second Division in his first season and kept them in the First Division for four seasons. It was Wilkinson's ability to take a side to promotion and solidify their position in the higher level that appealed to the Leeds board. In fact, Wilkinson did more than keep a team clinging on after promotion. He'd led Wednesday to a 5th place finish in 1985/86 and would do even better at Elland Road.

Wilkinson's first words to his new players were: "There's a plane sitting on the runway. It's going to take off and it's going to fly. You have three weeks to decide whether you want to get on it or not."

Many climbed on board and they began to win matches as success came ahead of the schedule Wilkinson had originally pitched to chairman Silver.

"In reality, it happened a lot quicker than we all thought," Wilkinson remembered. "I said we should be looking realistically at a target of winning the big prize after five years in that top division. I felt we needed that timescale in order for everything to come to fruition. We wanted a newly reorganised academy and a new training ground, all of which were necessary."

Affectionately dubbed 'Sergeant Wilko' for his disciplined style, much needed in a side that many felt was going through the motions, success was achieved by design rather than good fortune.

Wilkinson's approach was one of professionalism. He prepared thoroughly and the players' diets and fitness improved. He also needed a group of players that bought into the vision he had for the side and in order to assist that process he signed Gordon Strachan from Manchester United for £300,000, pipping his former club Wednesday to the Scotsman's signature.

Strachan had been a part of Sir Alex Ferguson's title-winning side in Aberdeen, but when Ferguson had also moved to Manchester United the midfielder had mixed feelings.

"He'd not had a good time at Manchester United, due to him and Alex (Ferguson) not having the best of relationships following his departure from Aberdeen," Wilkinson stated. "I needed a captain to whom I could relate very closely, who was ambitious, who could play, who was inspirational and willing to take responsibility.

"I was lucky, and it was an opportunity that cropped up for me again to say to people, 'Look, things are changing and it is going to be different.' Part of bringing Gordon in was his reputation, but more importantly I'd been a student of football and I knew what had gone on at Aberdeen and I thought that he was a potential leader.

"What I needed was someone who would be my leader on the pitch and the person I wanted everyone else to be. I knew that person didn't exist at the club. You are always looking for leaders, they are your bread and butter. They create the energy; then you have followers who feed off that energy; and then, if you're unlucky, you might have one or two terrorists who drain energy.

"I thought to myself, here's a chance to bring a leader in who will set a standard and who will reflect what it is I want to see, in terms of his behaviour, thinking, attitude, application, team-mindedness, etc."

Upon signing, Strachan told the media: "I didn't want to leave Manchester United and go to a club and just tick along and play out my time. I still feel I've got a lot to offer the game and so I'm here trying to get Leeds United back where they belong, and if I can do that in my two years here, I will feel like I've achieved something."

And Strachan revelled in being trusted this way and responded with some influential displays. "Howard gave me what I was looking for, and I probably didn't realise I was looking for," Strachan recalled to ITV. "Responsibility, real responsibility. He said my job was to get the club back into the Premiership (First Division). I thought *that's fantastic* because that showed great faith in me and it's what I was needing."

Wilkinson also brought in the physically combative presence of Vinnie Jones from Wimbledon. The new boss had tried to sign Jones when in charge of Sheffield Wednesday. The hard man and midfield enforcer brawled with Anderlecht players in a pre-season match and, despite fans being delighted to have attracted a player of his calibre to the second tier, there were concerns that his disciplinary record might have an adverse effect.

"What the fuck are you doing? You're not here to kill people, you're here because you're a good player and we know you can pass the ball!" Strachan had taken Jones to one side. "We've got a lot to do this season and we can't have this childish bullshit. We've got to be this force to be reckoned with!"

Consequently, Jones picked up only three yellow cards throughout the entire season and would later pay tribute to Strachan's role: "I was a leader of men, and he was the leader on the training ground and off the pitch. I became a better player because of Gordon. I became a better person because of Gordon."

Mel Sterland had played under Wilkinson at Sheffield Wednesday and, after an unspectacular, short stint at Rangers, was brought to Elland Road on the left side of defence. Another defender, Chris Fairclough, came in from Spurs and Wilkinson reunited himself with striker Lee Chapman, signed for £400,000 from Nottingham Forest, after having previously worked with him at Sheffield Wednesday.

Wilkinson's first game in charge was a second leg League Cup fixture against Peterborough at Elland Road. 2-1 up from the first leg, Leeds ran out 5-2 victors on aggregate and, despite exiting the cup in the next round at the hands of Luton Town, Wilkinson enjoyed success from the start.

"I think, from me starting, we went the next 10 games without defeat in the league," he correctly recalled. "Basically, there were one or two additions, but a lot of them were people that had been there before.

"I said to players at every club that I went to, 'Look, I can make you the fittest, I can make you the best organised, I can give you the biggest return on set pieces for and against. That's not a bad start. And then I will try to think of how I can best employ each one of you with each one of your strengths, so that the net result of all that is we improve and who knows how far we can go.'

In his first season, Leeds revived and finished 10th. The following season Wilkinson's side were promoted as Champions.

The penultimate match against Leicester City was locked at 1-1 with six minutes remaining on the clock. Leeds needed to win to stay ahead of Sheffield United and Newcastle at the top of the table. The Foxes' defence failed to clear Sterland's long throw from the right and the ball ricocheted to Strachan on the edge of the penalty area. The skipper didn't hesitate, hitting a left-footed drive inside the right-hand upright as TV commentator, John Helm, bellowed, "Have you ever seen a better goal, and have you ever seen one better timed?"

Fans had queued for hours to guarantee themselves a place in the ground on the final day of the season as Leeds headed down to meet Bournemouth on the south coast. Everyone wanted to be part of the celebrations and thousands of ticketless supporters had travelled.

When asked if Leeds would win the game, Vinnie Jones answered: "Does the sun come out the sky?" The game took place on the Saturday of a Bank Holiday weekend and temperatures soared. The streets were filled with travelling supporters, some making a long weekend of it.

It seemed almost inevitable that trouble would follow. The police had requested the Football League to change the date of the match and, when running battles ensued, Leeds chairman Leslie Silver suggested that the Football League had been unwise to schedule the game as it had.

"Leeds were against the idea some weeks ago, but we're obviously guided by the Football League," Silver said. "In my view, to have Leeds fans travelling down the motorway on a Bank Holiday Saturday was ill-advised to say the least. We'd have been happy to play it at any other time. If the fixture had been re-adjusted in good time it would have enabled the season to finish on that day."

Wilkinson said: "The Bournemouth thing was an administrative disaster in many respects. Everything about it, Bank Holiday, given the club we were, given the position in the league we were likely to be in, the temperature…"

With English fans banned from European competition because of hooliganism and UEFA preparing to make a decision on readmittance, the Bournemouth troubles had done nobody any favours and was a huge talking point.

On the pitch, Leeds needed to beat Bournemouth to secure promotion as champions and a Lee Chapman header earned a 1-0 win leading to jubilant celebrations.

"It was a massive, massive season that for Leeds United," remembered

Striker Lee Chapman to ITV. "Back in the big time where they belong. They'd been out for far too long for many different reasons, but it was the platform, a springboard to the later success that we achieved."

Wilkinson had signed Vinnie Jones to aid a push for promotion and, with that task complete, had replaced him in his plans with Gary McAllister. The dropped Jones, complete with a tattooed Leeds badge newly installed on his leg, pulled a rifle on his manager as a joke. One final match against Luton and Jones was on his way to Sheffield United. He was named number one in the *Yorkshire Evening Post*'s 'Cult Hero Countdown'.

Wilkinson brought John Lukic back from Arsenal and promoted Gary Speed and David Batty from the youth team in order to provide them with more experience.

In the first season back in the top flight for eight years, Leeds finished fourth, but some way adrift of Champions Arsenal, but the signs were there that they meant business. Chris Whyte was signed from West Bromwich Albion for £450,000 to bolster the defence and the club paid £1million for the first time to land goalkeeper John Lukic from Arsenal and repeated the fee for midfielder Gary McAllister from Leicester City.

It was during the third match of the 1991/92 season that Wilkinson started to think that the league title was not beyond his team. On 28 August, Leeds beat Southampton 4-0 away and the boss began to believe.

"It was a night game at Southampton and Gary Speed scored twice," he told me. "On that occasion I looked at him and thought I have got a player here and at last he's shown what he can do, and this can be a heck of an addition to the team. He could play in their box, he could play in our box, he could play left-back, left wide, left midfield. One game I put him at centre-half, another game I pushed him up front and all of that was done with him demonstrating leadership, because what he said was, 'I will do what is best for the team.' So, I push him up front, he doesn't moan, and one game against Arsenal away I put him to left-back and he didn't moan. He got on with it. And on top of all that he stopped goals at one end, and he scored them at the other.

"You need team-mindedness," Wilkinson added. "And Gary McAllister, after we'd moved on and were reminiscing, he said, 'I learned how to win at Leeds. I was a very good player at Leicester, and I was a very good player for Scotland, but what stands out in my mind that I learned at Leeds was I learned how to win.'

"He is talking about how you manage your way through a game, a set of games and through a season. It's not just this one day, that the next, you've got to think about.

"I remember reading Gary Player's book where he talks about learning how to manage a golf course and that no hole is the same. And that's the skill. And it's the same in football. How to manage the game.

"I saw a game the other night between two top Premier League teams and they were drawing in the last two or three minutes," Wilkinson explained. "One team gets a corner and it gets knocked to the far post, away from home, ball gets cleared and two or three passes later, boom, they've lost the game. That's not good game management. Knock it short, or play it into the near post, but you don't take unnecessary risks if you don't need to. I'm not saying you don't take risks, but the question is: 'Do I need to take a risk here?'

"So, you try and develop them individually and you try and develop this team-mindedness. You try and develop what it is you stand for and what we stand for. Culturally, what are we? They have to have trust and respect in each other, and you have to earn their trust and respect as a manager.

"I talk about the ART of management. Three keys. Authenticity, Respect and Trust. If you are a would-be student of the game, young coach or manager above all, to achieve success, you need to be authentic and true to yourself, and you'll need to get their trust and their respect."

It was Sir Bobby Robson who had originally recommended Wilkinson to Silver at Leeds.

"It was Bob and I've got him to thank for that," Wilkinson laughed. "I had many good years with Bob. We were both recruited by Ron Greenwood as part of his team, scouting for tournaments and so on. We got to know each other through that. Then, when he was made England manager and I was at Notts County, he asked me to be his assistant and I said no, as I didn't think I'd earned my spurs yet.

"We were always frequent chatters, even after he went abroad," Wilkinson recalled fondly. "He'd ring me up about once a fortnight and we'd have a chat. We had a lot of things in common in how we spoke about the game and winning football matches.

"When Bob was at Ipswich and I went there with Notts County we had got promoted playing with a sweeper and playing total football," Wilkinson continued. "There were a lot of passes and we went 1-0 up just before half-time. It was a picture-book goal and not too common at that time. Bobby got out the dugout, stood up, looked across and more or less said, 'I hold my hands up, well done.'

"He was an enthusiast, that was part of Bobby's attraction with people and with players. And he had a very disarming charm about him which was natural. He was constantly getting names wrong and people would giggle and laugh."

The 1991/92 season was on a knife-edge when Leeds went to play Manchester City and got beaten 4-0.

"We got whacked and at that point that was us out of it, or at least that's what everybody was saying," Wilkinson recalled. "I told the players not to speak to the press and talk about whether this, that or the other, and I went home. On the Sunday, I went right through our games and I went in Monday and said, 'We have now got the most important five games in our life and what we've got to do is win four of them and draw one and if we do that Manchester United will have a problem. If we can come off at Sheffield United in the second last game of the season having won three and drawn one of those games, I think we might just give them a problem.'"

The next example he gave me underlines the team-mindedness he held dear, and why Strachan typified what the club was about at the time.

"I told them that I would play the same team every game unless we got injuries, but there was one game where I would change it and leave someone out. And Gordon came in the next morning and knocked on my door early and he said, 'I've come to save you the embarrassment of telling me I'm going to be left out. And I know I'm going to be left out for Liverpool away, isn't it?' And I said, 'Yes.' And he said, 'You want a fucking clean sheet and you don't trust me.'

"He was joking, but that was the reason," Wilkinson laughed. "And I left him out at Liverpool, and we did get a 0-0 draw and we did win four out of five and by sheer luck against Sheffield United we played a lunchtime kick-off. I said to the lads, 'We need for Manchester United to have to go to Anfield and win, or at least get a result, because of the rivalry between them."

Leeds beat Sheffield United 3-2 at Bramall Lane and Wilkinson returned home to share a delayed Sunday lunch with his wife and family. Some friends had also been invited long before the day had taken on such magnitude.

"I had convinced myself that we were going to have to go to the last game of the season," Wilkinson said. "I had prepared myself for another week's work."

Son Ben was watching the game upstairs and updated his father. "He wandered down the stairs into the dining room and said, 'I think we've just won the Championship, Dad!' Everybody left the table and left me eating my Yorkshire pudding.

"The celebrations were quite spontaneous," Wilkinson told me. "We were having lunch that Sunday afternoon with some friends who we'd invited round. There were six of us and gradually people arrived, including Dave Bassett who turned up, knocked on the door bringing a bottle in his hand. He stayed and drank four more. It was just a spontaneous long day."

Wilkinson had told BBC *Look North* a few days after clinching the title: "I never realised how big the trophy was and it's silly little things that start to make an impression. I remember when we got from the Second Division and I got the medal, what an impression that made on me. Right until the minute I opened the box I never even thought about the medal and then as soon as I opened the box and saw the medal it was quite an emotional moment.

"I said to Gordon when I signed him that I would give us two years to get promoted, but I thought we'd do it in the first. And then I said I'd give us three years to get in Europe and I sort of thought we'd do it in the second. But the Championship, given the sort of opposition we're talking about, that was something that was three or four years after we got promoted, even thinking about having a go at it."

Sir Alex Ferguson, interviewed after the Liverpool defeat which handed the title to Leeds, said, "Well it's a terribly disappointing end for us. There's not any point in us analysing our own self. I think we have to say, 'Well done to Howard Wilkinson.'

"It's a marvellous achievement for him and I'd just like to say that people were saying it was an ordinary league, but then others start raving when other clubs start to play well and what you've got to realise about the English First Division is Leeds and ourselves got off to a great start in the season and stayed there the whole season. We were worthy front-runners in the league. And Arsenal got off to a bad start and are now playing well and people say that if they had started right, but that's how hard this league is. If you make mistakes you get punished, as any team like ourselves realise today.

"It's such a difficult and hard league to win and for people to say it's an ordinary league is an absolute nonsense. It's the same hard league it's always been and the same league that Liverpool were winning, Arsenal were winning, the same as Leeds have won this season. I have to say that Leeds deserve their achievement because they've worked hard for it, the manager's worked hard for it and we at Manchester United congratulate them on that."

It's easy to think that the celebration parties would go on for days, but after a long season Wilkinson's battery was running on empty.

"I was clearing out the other day and found a photo of me after we'd been promoted at Sheffield Wednesday," Wilkinson said. "I looked at my face and I looked like I'd been on bomb disposal in Afghanistan for three months. It's tiring!"

Captain Gordon Strachan had been staying in the Holiday Inn, but had not wanted to watch the match: "I told people that the game was on the telly but not to come and see me until the end of the game. Three or four minutes from the end someone came and told me that it's 2-0 Liverpool now. I knew we'd won then."

Lee Chapman recalled: "It didn't sink in until we went into Leeds city centre that evening. It was mayhem!"

A week later, an outstanding solo dribble from Rod Wallace that cut through the Norwich midfield and defence ended with a low drilled shot into the bottom right-hand corner. It was the only goal of the game.

After the final whistle at Elland Road, with Leeds four points clear of Manchester United at the top of the table, Strachan was presented with the First Division trophy on 9 May 1992.

A lot of hope and a lot of chickens were prematurely counted on that day. Dreams and aspirations to conquer English football for many years to come were chatted in pubs and living rooms by anyone who had ever classed themselves as a Leeds United fan.

An enigmatic Frenchman had entered the Leeds first team towards the end of the title-winning season and became an instant hit with supporters. It seems Wilkinson was not as captivated as some.

"If you examine his contribution in the season that we won the Championship, it's nowhere near as significant as has been written since," suggested Wilkinson. "I know some of the boys were slightly offended when it was referred to as 'Cantona's Championship'.

"Eric made a very, very useful contribution, he was a good trainer and he was a good member of the team and one hell of a player, but at the end of the day he made seven appearances that season."

Gary McAllister, however, recognised the significance of Cantona's impact: "That tickly bit at the end of the season when the games were very close, he [Cantona] changed the crowd. The crowd, they loved him. They loved the swagger, the confident air that he brought. When some players were thinking that we were heading for a 0-0, he lifted Elland Road as soon as he came on the pitch. Looking back, Howard Wilkinson used him perfectly."

Cantona would controversially move to fierce rivals Manchester United during the summer. It's not something you do if you want to retain the love that McAllister referred to.

"It was not my decision for him to leave, it was his decision," Wilkinson said. "I was faced with a player who was not going to come back and play at Leeds, so it was irrelevant what he said, I didn't have a choice."

Lee Chapman recalled: "There was a rumour that had started about three different players' wives. And there's no truth in it whatsoever. Eric was not that sort of person.

"I think what happened was the fans had to have a reason why he left, and it wasn't just the fact that him and Howard had basically fallen out.

"Howard had to have people toe the line and Eric wasn't really a great team man."

The next season, Leeds finished 17th in the First Division as the glory of 12 months earlier did not return. In the European Cup, Leeds played Rangers in what the media dubbed the Battle of Britain and went out 4-2 on aggregate after losing both games 2-1.

"We changed as a group," suggested Strachan to ITV. "Our priorities seemed to be elsewhere. People were on telly more, talk of bigger houses, bigger cars. The emphasis wasn't on winning matches every week, I thought."

When I put Strachan's comments to Wilkinson he muttered in agreement as I read.

"It's a lot of things and you can't narrow it down to one," he replied. "One would be, and I say this without being disrespectful at all, that we'd rinsed ourselves dry.

"When I was at Sheffield Wednesday, the season before I left, I went into the dressing room after we'd been beaten or drawn one Saturday, and this was before any of these things got public and there was only Nigel Worthington in there. And Nigel said to me, 'We need to leave Gaffer.' I asked, 'Why do you say that?' I thought, *he knows something here.* And he said, 'You can only get so much juice out of an orange.'

"He was basically saying that we'd all given it as much as we could and would still continue to do that, but it gets harder when you keep having to do that and it does take its toll mentally, emotionally and physically. To never have a day off and to always have to be at it."

I wondered whether there was anything Wilkinson would have changed during that 1992/93 season to steady the ship and regain winning ways. Or perhaps the timescale of five seasons in the top flight that he had originally suggested to the chairman might have been more sustainable. I offered him a magic wand to see what he would have done differently.

"If I had a magic wand, I wouldn't have won it the season before," he responded simply. "I'd have finished second again and, in the summer, recruited two or three more players and the season after I'd have finished a close second and recruited maybe one or two more. Instead of your best team being 11 out of 12, your best team would be 11 out of 18 or 11 out of 20. Then it doesn't matter who you pick, apart from the absolute galactic stars, you can maintain performance.

"That's the basis of what they do now. They monitor players so that they know how every part of their squad is performing. It's alright monitoring players, but if you haven't got anyone better to come in you are struggling.

"If you monitor players these days you know when they need a rest, so your managing becomes a lot more certain. There's a difference between 'do you think he's looking tired' and the sports science people telling you that a player's results are starting to trough physically, or a player might be starting to peak."

That season was followed by successive fifth-placed finishes in 1993/94 and 1994/95, but 13th a season later and things were changing on and off the pitch.

A good run in the 1995/96 League Cup saw the club reach Wembley after beating Notts County, Derby, Blackburn, Reading and Birmingham 5-1 on aggregate in the two-legged semi-final.

On 24 March 2006, the wheels came off for Wilkinson. He found himself alone in the dressing room after being well beaten 3-0 by Aston Villa. The man that had brought the League title back to Elland Road five years earlier had taken them back to their first Wembley final for 23 years. Fans aggrieved by the manner of the defeat were vociferous in their disapproval as Wilkinson walked back to the dressing room.

"Of course, it hurt," he said. "It seemed very personal to me and I don't think that anybody was left in any doubt about what they wanted. I'm the one who has to take the responsibilities when we win and when we lose, but the biggest disappointment of the day was a massive one, we just didn't take enough responsibility out on the field.

"They say that your first time at Wembley passes very quickly, but it didn't for me. I don't think I will ever be able to look back and say I enjoyed it. But Villa got the important early goals, and goals turn games."

Wilkinson had partnered striker Tony Yeboah with Andy Gray, ignoring the claims of Tomas Brolin, Brian Deane and South African Phil Masinga. The 18-year-old Gray, the son of former player Frank, would be one of Leeds's best players.

The irony, given what would come later, was that supporters were annoyed that Wilkinson had not selected Swedish international Brolin.

"If you cannot play in a big game like this one then I have to think about my future," Brolin argued. "I think I will have to try and find another team."

Brolin had signed for Leeds United on 7 November 1995 after excelling at the 1994 World Cup where Sweden finished third. He had been a member of the squad that were beaten in the semi-finals at Euro 1992 and Leeds supporters thought they were recruiting a world star.

Brolin and Wilkinson began to clash when the Swede began to neglect his defensive responsibilities. The relationship worsened when an ill-judged April Fool's Day joke that Brolin was going to see out the season on loan with former club IFK Norrköping got back to the manager as fact.

In 1996, Brolin was given an additional three days by Wilkinson to find a new club, but no club wanted him. By August, Leeds offered him around on the transfer list for around half of the £4.5million they had paid for him a year earlier. When he didn't show for pre-season training ahead of the 1996/97 season, Wilkinson fined him £12,000.

Wilkinson told the media that he would take anyone in his team over Brolin. When Brolin failed to show, Leeds withheld his wages until he joined Zurich on loan on 20 August 1996.

Would a Leeds crowd back Brolin over Wilkinson had they known what each would, and had, given to the club? Definitely not. Sometimes the manager knows more than the fans.

Brolin goes down in Leeds history as one of the biggest let downs. He turned up at Elland Road with a belly bigger than his reputation and, in 2007, was voted second in *The Times* poll for the *50 Worst Footballers (to grace the Premier League)*. He retired from the game aged 28.

That Wembley defeat was effectively time up for Wilko. Chairman Leslie Silver backed him, he continued in the job, but admits that the joy had diminished greatly.

The biggest regret for Wilkinson was that he was not able to see the club through a period of transition and reap the rewards of an increasingly prolific Academy that he had been instrumental in establishing.

"The idea was 10 years and beyond and we set the Academy up and changed it," Wilkinson elaborated. "The season I went there I think they'd recruited 18 boys and only one signed pro. The season I left we'd recruited seven and five signed pro. And so, if you look at the team and bench that played the semi-final of the Champions League, there's about nine of those kids in there.

"But fate intervened, Leslie had his burglary, there was pressure on him, it was the time when clubs were going public and against his better nature he sold the club. The people that came in hired somebody to be manager whilst I was still there, and the rest is history. Unfortunately, and I know because he told me, Leslie lived to regret that.

"I knew the end was coming because the football grapevine is unbelievable. If someone farted in the dressing room in Newcastle, they'd smell it in Southampton the next morning."

And, after contributing so much to the club and planning for much more in the future, the feeling of being a dead man walking at Elland Road was not an easy one to cope with.

"It's an empty hollow feeling and it transmits to the players," Wilkinson confessed. "The players knew. We got a result and won away at Blackburn and the players were going crazy. Even the chairman and the chief exec came in and they were dancing up and down because that was going to be my night to go if we'd got beat.

"You drive to work, and you don't want to go. It's not a good feeling at all. It was time to go and it certainly came at the wrong time as we were 18 months from having a new team. 18 months from Jonathan Woodgate, Alan Smith, Harry Kewell, Ian Harte, Stephen McPhail and Lee Bowyer. We were 18 months from them being ready to compete for the Championship."

Now 75 and living in South Yorkshire, Wilkinson reflects on his time at Elland Road with fondness.

"It was a very enjoyable time," he told me. "I love Leeds as a city. I love their get up and go.

"It wasn't difficult to go into the city to raise money and get people to support and sponsor the club. Even then it had the makings of being one of the country's commercial centres, which it's gone on to be now. It's a very good one-club town and that makes a difference. There's good and bad about that, but there's more good than bad. There are not many cities like that around.

"Of course, you look on from a distance at what has gone on since you left, but you can't do anything about it. You do look with interest, but you have no control. As a manager one of the big factors is control. You must control the areas that are pivotal to the success of the team. You have got to be the decision maker on all sorts of areas that sometimes have nothing to do with football. And by the same token, if you are not manager anymore, then you have no control at all, so you can't worry about it or get too het up about what's going on. You just have to accept it."

Wilkinson brought back the former glories to Leeds United and remains the last English manager to win the top flight in his native country.

18

GEORGE GRAHAM

1996–1998

"I wanted players who wanted to wear the shirt"

Born: 30 November 1944, Bargeddie, N Lanarkshire, Scotland

Matches	Won	Drawn	Lost	Points	Pts/Match	Win %
95	37	27	31	138	1.45	38.95%
				RANK	18th/36	17th/36

When Caspian took over as the new owners of Leeds United, they had sacked Howard Wilkinson after a 4-0 defeat to bitter rivals Manchester United. They had been seeking to install George Graham as their new boss for some time.

Graham had been out of football management for a year after being sacked by Arsenal in February 1995. He'd given the Gunners almost nine years of service from the dugout, plus another six as a player thirty years earlier.

It had been discovered that he had accepted an illegal £425,000 payment from a Norwegian agent after he had bought two of his players, John Jensen and Pal Lydersen. Graham was banned by the Football Association for 12 months after admitting receiving an "unsolicited gift".

As a player, Graham had represented Scotland 12 times (1971-73), scoring three goals. He'd played for Aston Villa (1961-63), Chelsea (1963-66) where he won the League Cup and Arsenal (1966-72) where he lifted the Fairs Cup 1970 and won the League and FA Cup double in 1971. He went on to play for Manchester United (1972-74), Portsmouth (1974-76) and finished his career with Crystal Palace in the 1976/77 season. In all, he played 455 League games and scored 105 goals.

He began his managerial career with Millwall (1983-86) and then enjoyed huge success with Arsenal, where he won two League titles (1989, 1991), the FA Cup in 1993, the League Cup (1987, 1993) and the European Cup Winners' Cup in 1994. That European success was Graham's last with the North London club before his dismissal.

A year spent away from the training grounds and dugouts was a long one for a man who was accustomed to being immersed in the game. It did, however, give him time to reflect on what he had achieved and to prepare himself for his next challenge, despite feeling detached from the action.

"I very much felt like I was on the outside of the game," he told me. "When you'd had the success that I'd had, both at Millwall and Arsenal, you miss it. My first appointment was at Millwall and I did very well there. I learned a lot about how to run a club, how to buy and sell, how to negotiate, how to coach. It was an all-round role, not like today when you're a coach, rather than a manager. So, you were doing a bit of everything.

"I did a bit of work for one of the radio channels during that year out, so I was actually going to a lot of games and studying how teams played, rather than just going to watch and enjoy the matches. It was quite fascinating because I was learning how teams played, the system they used and I was picking up a lot of stuff in that year, even though I was out of the game.

"The game is continually changing all the time. The tactics are changing. There is so much change in every decade of football, it's unbelievable.

"Doing the radio was really interesting," he continued. "Because when you're coaching you are watching a lot of games on television and you're relying on the cameraman. He's the man that dictates what you are watching.

"When I'm watching how a team is playing, or defending, I've got to see it myself rather than someone tell me on the radio or on television. I was picking up a lot of stuff when I was outside the game."

After serving his ban, Graham took charge of Leeds United on 10 September 1996. Five games had been played and the team was in 9th position. Graham bemoaned the lack of first-team experience in the squad and the amount of injuries that had seriously impacted upon results. The season ended with Leeds in 11th place.

Graham had picked up on whispers around football that Howard Wilkinson was on his way out at Elland Road.

"It is one of the difficult things in football that when you are out of the job, and you are looking for a new job, that you know the other managers. Because when you're actually successful you get friendly with the managers, obviously when you are not playing against them.

"I was on the League Managers' Association Committee," Graham said. "I was quite friendly with Howard, because he was the chairman of the LMA at the time and that was his baby. He was pushing it all of the time and he is responsible for where it is today. So, it was difficult for me to take over Howard's job, but that is football and it happens all the time.

"Obviously after winning the Championship title they were going through a bad period. And it was out of the blue and it surprised me that

I was being touted for the job if Howard left. But it's one of those things. I think when I was at Tottenham, Glenn Hoddle was the one being touted for the job before I even got the sack. It's just one of these unfortunate situations that comes up and there's no answer to it really.

"Howard had done a great job winning the title and was the last Englishman to win it," he remembered. "That's how good a job he'd done and that was very good publicity for young English coaches. To think that he was the last one to win it, it's a lovely title for Howard.

"It was a difficult situation, but you get on with it and I think Leeds had a good team, had some good players and a great youth policy. It was superb with some great young players coming through."

The youngsters that Howard Wilkinson would have loved to have hung around, so he could have seen them make their mark, were beginning to do exactly that. They took the 1996/97 FA Youth Cup after beating Crystal Palace 3-1 in the final. That Leeds side contained Harry Kewell, Paul Robinson, Jonathan Woodgate, Stephen McPhail, Matthew Jones and Alan Maybury. Kewell would become a regular in Graham's first team during the 1997/98 season and the rest would follow.

Graham appointed David O'Leary as his assistant. Not only had O'Leary played under Graham for many successful years at Arsenal, he had recently retired as a player after seeing out his days at Elland Road.

"They were a team, when George took over, that were heading for relegation," O'Leary said. "The club needed something discipline-wise off the pitch. It was hard, and George did a fantastic job on that."

When Graham had come to Leeds, I wondered how aware he was of the raft of talent bubbling under the surface?

"Not really, I didn't know much about them at all," he confessed. "I was just told that Paul Hart was running the youth policy at the time and it was well documented around the football world that he was doing an unbelievable job at Leeds United. That was all upfront really, so I knew when I was joining Leeds that there was an opportunity to play some of the youngsters. That was nothing to do with me, it was down to Paul, who brought them into the club."

Graham, a Scot who had made London his home, was enjoying his new life in Yorkshire.

"Going north after being in the south for so long was interesting," Graham recalled. "And that was fabulous. I was living in The Stray in Harrogate and I had a lovely apartment. It was a beautiful place to live. It was really great, and I enjoyed it very much."

He was a man known to build from the back, his tight defence his trademark at the Gunners, and his first signing was Robert Molenaar to assist in that area. He added Gunnar Halle to further bolster the defence. Derek Lilley and Frenchman Pierre Laurent were added as attacking cover.

Graham's approach was simple. He built from the back and he expected his players to be committed to the club.

"No matter where I've been, it's coming from your working-class background in Scotland, you always made sure in whatever you were trying to build, you had to have a good base and then build it up from there," Graham told me. "And I took that into football with me. Wherever I went, I wanted to get a nice solid defence, so we know what we were doing, and we were not going to concede. It's a bit old-fashioned now. Now it's all about pressing and winning the ball early in the opposition's half. As I say, football keeps changing all the time, but at that time a good solid defence was priority and then you could build it up through the midfield and upfront.

"It's all about coaching, it's teaching really, and it's about how you put it over on the training ground, how the players respond," he continued. "You are trying to work with them and make them learn the game. And I did work hard on defending on a daily basis. I would like to think that being a coach is like being a teacher. You get a lot of satisfaction when you see all the work you've put in through the week coming to fruition at the weekend in a match. I worked an awful lot on set pieces as well.

"Even though my reputation is being a defensive coach and you're probably, to a point, one hundred per cent right, but at the time it worked fine. Nowadays it's completely different.

"I wanted players who wanted to wear the shirt and have a bit of sweat at the end of a match. Big Molenaar was another I brought in, the big centre-half, everybody called him the policeman. He was the big guy at the back, and he did a great job.

"But my basic thing, coming from a working-class family, was all about attitude. I wanted someone that was hungry and wanting to succeed, and that's what I've looked for at every club I've been at. You don't get that at most clubs. You soon realise the ones that are really committed, not only to the club but to themselves, having pride in their own performance. That was very, very big with me.

"Invariably, there were people coming in and there was me getting rid of the ones that didn't want to sweat for the shirt."

Lee Bowyer, aged 19 when Graham arrived at Elland Road, and now a manager himself, told *LeedsLive* in January 2019 his new boss's no-nonsense style brought the best out in him.

"I was the kind of player George's approach worked with, because all

I wanted was the truth," Bowyer said. "If I've done something wrong, give me a rollicking and I'll get better. Then I'll get better again. Tell me the truth and I'd give you everything.

"Some players aren't like that, though," he added. "I've witnessed it. Mark Viduka was one who just needed a cuddle; put your arm around him, tell him he's the best, and he will be the best. I've seen it with all different players, including top international ones. They're still people, with feelings. You have to try and figure out how to treat each person."

Lucas Radebe is another former player who enjoyed working under Graham. "He was one of the best managers I ever had," said the South African centre-back. "We had a great relationship. I don't know whether it was because he liked to work with defenders a lot. As a disciplinarian he was straight forward, a fair manager. That's what made me work hard and I think he got the best out of me."

Offensively, Leeds scored a League-low 28 throughout the season, but his first priority of shoring the club up at the back was a success. Leeds conceded 38 goals through the entire season, of which nine had found the back of the net in Howard Wilkinson's five games in charge at the start of the season. Bearing in mind the 38 conceded was the fourth best in the League it shows what an impact Graham had on the backline. It was a necessary evil and not something that made Leeds an entertaining side to watch.

"George's reign at the club was reasonably successful, although people didn't enjoy watching as much as some of the other teams that have played," recalled Eddie Gray. "It's funny when you get people like George who was a flair player and became a manager that concentrated on the other side of the game."

The 1997/98 season dawned, and the young guns were edging ever closer. Harry Kewell was added to the first-team squad as Paul Robinson, Alan Smith and Jonathan Woodgate were given youth deals.

Budgets were tight and Graham cleared out Tony Yeboah, Thomas Brolin, Carlton Palmer, Ian Rush and Brian Deane to make way for Alf-Inge Haland, Bruno Ribeiro, David Hopkins, Martin Hiden and Clyde Wijnhard.

Graham's attention began to turn to attack and Leeds certainly became a more attractive team going forward in his second season, aided hugely by the acquisition of a 25-year-old Dutch striker.

"I had Ian McNeill who had worked at Chelsea for years," Graham recalled. "He was very good on scouting abroad and he saw Jimmy play and told me right away.

"He said, 'George, this guy, he plays for a team that's not very well recognised in Portugal, but he's an out-and-out finisher.'

"We went to see him, and I liked what I saw. He just came alive in the attacking third of the pitch and that's what I needed after organising the guys at the back. What we needed was somebody that could guarantee goals and Jimmy was one of those guys that you just let get on with it in the attacking third. I was never really associated with strikers, but I let him do his own thing and he was a sensation for me. I think they went on to make a vast profit on him and they did well on him.

"Some of the boys were not performing though. I think there was a big problem with Brolin. I didn't have a problem with him, but I think he had a problem with the club. When he joined the club, I just get the feeling he didn't want to be there, and I think a couple of times he actually stayed away in Sweden."

We left the tale of Brolin with him on loan with Zurich in Switzerland when George Graham was Leeds manager. He had played three league matches and one in the cup and had been hoping to stay with them until their December winter break in an effort to find full fitness.

Graham demanded he return to Leeds instead or face legal action, stating at the time: "We have heard nothing from Tomas Brolin. We have not even got a telephone number for him. All our correspondence with him has been done through his agent, Lars Peterson."

Leeds nearly offloaded Brolin to Sampdoria in November 1996, but a loan move with a view to a £2million transfer broke down when the player failed a medical because of a metal staple in his foot.

In December 2006, Brolin paid £500,000 out of his own pocket to fund a loan move back to former club Parma. He barely played and Parma did not want to keep him after the season ended, suggesting they had accepted him back out of gratitude for his previous service.

Loan deals to Real Zaragoza and Hearts fell through and Brolin was fined by Leeds for being absent from training. He missed a Leeds reserve game to attend his father's birthday and publicly criticised Graham in the media and was subsequently fined £90,000.

On 28 November 2007, Leeds United finally terminated Brolin's contract. He signed for Crystal Palace in 1998 and failed to score in 15 appearances for the club, before announcing his retirement on 12 August 1998.

In a BBC poll carried out in 2003, Leeds fans voted Brolin the worst ever player in the club's history.

Meanwhile, Hasselbaink had joined Graham's team from Boavista for £2million and would be sold to Atletico Madrid for £10million in the summer of 1999. Chelsea would bring him back to the Premier League in May 2000 for a British transfer fee equalling £15million.

Bruno Ribeiro joined for £500,000 from Vitoria Setubal. Graham paid £3.25 million to Crystal Palace for midfielder David Hopkins, £500,000 to Rangers for full-back David Robertson and £1.6 million to Nottingham Forest for Dutch utility midfielder Alf-Inge Haland. Martin Hidden, the Austrian international defender came in from Rapid Vienna in February 1998 for £1.3million. The following summer, Dutch striker Clyde Wijnhard was signed from Willem II for £1.5million and Chelsea left-back Danny Granville for £1.6million.

Tragedy was averted when the fast actions of a pilot enabled a plane to crash-land and evacuate 40 passengers, including 18 Leeds players, before it exploded. The aircraft had just taken off from Stansted Airport when captain John Hackett was forced to quickly bring the plane down before a severe explosion in the BA 748 turboprop. Experts later said the pilot had around 30 seconds to ground the flight, which had been carrying the Leeds team home after a game against West Ham.

"I would think that they had another 30 seconds before there would have been a major fire," said Stansted Duty Manager Melvyn Seymour. "I dread to think what would have happened then. You would have been talking about a major explosion and I would think almost certainly fatalities. From the time of the fire and explosion in the engine took place he would probably have had a few seconds to decide to abort the flight. Those are the decisions pilots are trained to make and he made a superb decision."

It had been a miserable day for Leeds in the capital. They had been beaten 3-0 by West Ham and when the take-off was aborted as an engine burst into flames seconds after the wheels had left the tarmac the day threatened to end in major disaster.

The plane overshot the runway and partially collapsed as a full fuel tank began to spill from the wings. Passengers told of how they felt heat behind them as they hastily evacuated fearing a major explosion was imminent. That a Munich style tragedy had been averted was a miracle.

"I was sitting in the centre and just as the wheels started to leave the ground, I saw flames coming out of the engine," Peter Ridsdale explained later that evening. "A few seconds later, as we were leaving the ground, there was a large explosion and the whole engine went up in flames. Everyone on board could see the flames and the explosion and everyone seemed to be shouting: 'Fire! There's a fire!'

"At that stage we were still climbing and almost immediately a buzzer went off and someone, I assume it was a stewardess, said we were going to make an emergency landing, and would we please be braced. We knew we were coming down. The flames were getting worse.

"David O'Leary was in the opposite seat to me by an emergency exit. David opened it very, very quickly and started getting everybody out. Everybody seemed to go pretty quickly to one of the emergency exits. David was superb. He was marshalling everybody out. The cabin crew were superb."

O'Leary, who had sustained a minor shoulder injury when forcing an emergency exit open, said: "The captain said he just had to ditch the plane because if we went up any more it would have been a complete explosion, because he was carrying one and a half tonnes of fuel."

Graham ploughed on and his strategy worked as Leeds scored double the amount of goals in the 1997/98 season as they finished fifth and secured qualification for the UEFA Cup. If it hadn't been for a poor season's end where they won only one of their last five league matches, a higher finish could have been secured.

"That's the way you should do it and I think one of the things I should have done is work more on the attacking side of the game, even at other clubs that I've been with. I should have moved on a bit quicker into the midfield and upfront. But I always believed that if we were organised in two thirds of the pitch the attacking third was always up to the great individuals and you let them get on with it. Let them do their own thing because that's where you score the goals. You rely on the outstanding players and it's very hard to tie them down.

"What they do nowadays is more or less what they want in the attacking third, but when they lose the ball, they've got to win it back quickly."

The rumours started when the Spurs job became available. Graham had gone a long way to mending his reputation and the football world was taking him seriously again with Leeds 7th in the Premier League.

On 1 October, Graham was back in London holding talks with Spurs chairman, Alan Sugar, having been given permission by Leeds to see if he wanted to replace Christian Gross at White Hart Lane.

"I can confirm that we have come to an arrangement with Tottenham Hotspur whereby they have agreed to pay compensation in line with the contract that George Graham signed last December," Ridsdale said. "I have spoken to George and he has asked for permission to talk to Tottenham, therefore we have given George that permission to speak with them."

I asked George if it had been the lure of London that enhanced the appeal of the Spurs approach. His initial denial was heartfelt, but as the answer developed it was obvious that the capital was his home.

"No, it wasn't," Graham jumps in quickly. "There was a situation financially the owners didn't want to invest anymore. I wanted to move the team on after finishing 5th and qualifying for Europe, I said I wanted to take the next step. That next step was to buy better players, or bring better players into the club, but I don't think the owners were willing to do that. I thought I've got to be careful here because if we don't improve after finishing 5th then we're just going to slip down the league again.

"Then the Tottenham situation came out of the blue. I wanted to keep on carrying on with my career and keep on moving upwards all the time.

"Because of my private life as well. I was divorced and on my own for a while and then I met a new lady who is now my wife. She had children and they were living in London. Apart from football, the family life was dragging me back to London.

"Although I enjoyed myself at Leeds, and I really did, I loved the place, I could understand people thinking I might go back to London because my private life was in London. At that time, Tottenham were a potential big club in London, the biggest club in London, more than Arsenal, more than Chelsea, so it was a big move for me as well."

Chairman Peter Ridsdale had moved to keep his manager, telling the media: "At the moment George is still our manager until somebody tells me otherwise. But we now have to anticipate that we will go into Saturday's game [home at Leicester] without him. We have a very able assistant in David O'Leary, and Eddie Gray, and if George is not available to pick the team on Saturday then we will ask them to make sure it is business as usual."

Leeds were in Madeira after beating Maritimo in the UEFA Cup when Graham told Ridsdale he was interested in hearing what Spurs were offering him. They would receive £2.5million in compensation for their man as he liked what he heard from Alan Sugar and the chase was on to find his replacement.

A lot had previously been written about Graham's intent to ultimately move back down south. But was it a wrench to leave Elland Road and Yorkshire?

"Yes, I tell everybody, I enjoyed myself at Leeds, I liked the people and I loved the place where I lived. Harrogate is a lovely town with nice restaurants, everything was nice about it and that part of England is beautiful.

"Funnily enough, I've bumped into a few people when I've been on holiday, Leeds fans, and it's lovely chatting to them actually.

"I had a good time at Leeds," Graham remembered. "I enjoyed it in my career when I look back, I enjoyed it very much. I loved living in

Harrogate, it's a beautiful town and I loved living there and I just enjoyed being at the club. The supporters were very good too, in fact brilliant. I mean how many clubs outside the big cities like London, Manchester and Birmingham can fill a ground. And I knew, because I'd played against them, that Leeds could fill a ground easily.

"And in Yorkshire they'd only Sheffield United and Sheffield Wednesday, so they had the whole of North Yorkshire, so they could fill it, with a decent team, every home match. They were very good the fans, they were fantastic."

The club was rumoured to be lining up former skipper and Coventry manager Gordon Strachan as his replacement. Gary McAllister was also said to be in the frame as Strachan's assistant. Other names on the shortlist were said to be Leicester manager Martin O'Neill and former Norway coach Egil Olsen.

Jimmy Floyd Hasselbaink had been a striker signed by Graham. As always in a period of transition there was uncertainty too.

"If the next man comes in and he wants to build a team to win things then I will sign a six-year contract tomorrow," Hasselbaink stated. "It still all depends on what is going to happen and that not only goes for me but also for everyone at the club. I love Leeds. I'm looking for another house in the city. I certainly don't want the man who brought me to go."

Graham moved back to London and made an attempt to take his assistant, David O'Leary, with him. O'Leary, another man with huge Arsenal connections, later admitted that he could never have worked for North London rivals Tottenham.

"Yes, of course, I made the offer to David," Graham told me. "I said, 'David, I'm going back to London, I'm going to Spurs.'

"I didn't go into any detail why. I think he was thinking about it and then I think Peter Ridsdale talked to David, won him over, he thought David would do a good job and so did I. There was no problem. That's what happens to number twos. If they ever get the opportunity to be a number one, go for it, why not?

"I left hoping David would come, he didn't come with me and went on and did a good job with Leeds," Graham continued. "He was an outstanding player. He's got the record number of appearances for Arsenal and he was a classy centre-half. He wasn't the big physical type, but a reader of the game. He was a very clever boy and although I wished he'd have come with me, he didn't. There's no hard feelings and he went on and did well in Europe."

Meanwhile, Graham was starting his new job at White Hart Lane. Five months later, he was lifting the 1999 League Cup at Wembley after Spurs beat Leicester City, yet as a former Arsenal manager he struggled to get the crowd on his side.

He was sacked by Spurs in March 2001, after the club was purchased by ENIC, allegedly for breach of contract in what the club described as "giving out what was deemed by the club as being private information," and subsequently expressing his disappointment in a "limited budget" for new signings, which led to the club questioning his loyalty.

Graham was "shocked and upset," according to his legal representative, "and could not believe such a flimsy excuse had been given" for his sacking. They went as far as to state that ENIC had "always intended to sack him."

That was to be his final managerial role. He worked in the media as a pundit and slipped quietly into retirement. When I first made contact for this interview he was holidaying in Barbados with his wife, so things are not going too badly.

In November 2003, Graham was rumoured to be on his way back to Leeds after Peter Reid was sacked after 22 months in charge. Graham was favourite with the bookies, alongside Nottingham Forest's Paul Hart, to come back to the club and recue it after a disastrous season. Basically, to do it all again. Graham was seen by many as the better option as he had the capability to shore up a defence that had chronically been leaking goals that season.

"No, I wasn't aware of any of that," he said when I asked him whether a return was ever on the cards. "That was just newspaper speculation. I just don't know anything about that. There was no talk about that at all. They'd got through quite a few managers, so many people."

With Graham safely relocated to White Hart Lane, pressure to avoid relegation and debts mounting to a reported £78.9million, making the right choice was crucial.

19

DAVID O'LEARY

1998–2002

"We lived the dream"

Born: 2 May 1958, Stoke Newington, London

Matches	Won	Drawn	Lost	Points	Pts/Match	Win %
203	101	47	55	350	1.72	49.75%
				RANK	4th/36	4th/36

It was the best and worst of times under the management of David O'Leary. Leeds United experienced some of the most iconic moments in its history under the Irishman.

Whether fair or not, he will be forever tarnished, however, by the financial meltdown and subsequent wilderness years that provided a long and painful full stop to his time at Elland Road.

As a player, O'Leary had been genuinely top-class. He was never sent off in 558 league games for Arsenal over 20 years. A classy centre-back, he was an integral cog in George Graham's title-winning sides of 1989 and 1991.

Signing on as an apprentice with the Gunners in 1973, he made his full debut against Burnley on 16 August 1975. At the tender age of 17, he went on to make 30 appearances during that maiden season. Perhaps it was his early exposure that would see him become known as a Leeds manager eager to trust his own youngsters almost 30 years later.

Over the next decade, he was ever-present in the Arsenal side and was part of the 1979 FA Cup winning side that beat Manchester United 3-2 in a memorable Wembley showpiece. Arsenal were beaten finalists in the 1978 and 1980 Cup finals and also the 1980 Cup Winners' Cup final.

The London-born Irishman was made Arsenal captain in 1982, although he only served in that role for a season-and-a-half. O'Leary won a second League title in 1991 and, although often used as a sub by the time 1993 came around, he saw his team win a League Cup and FA Cup double.

During his time at Arsenal, he broke a number of records. He became the youngest person to reach the 100 and 200 match appearance marks for the club and passed George Armstrong's all-time record of 621 first-team games in November 1989. He continued to set a new benchmark of 722 first-team appearances during his 20-year stay at the club. In a poll to compile the list of the club's Greatest Ever Players, O'Leary was voted 14th.

The highlight of his 68-cap international career came in the 1990 World Cup. With Ireland in a penalty shootout with Romania, Packie Bonner saved Daniel Timofte's penalty and O'Leary stepped up to strike home the decisive final penalty to win the shootout 5–4. The victory took Ireland to the quarter-finals and O'Leary's nerveless penalty has since been voted as the greatest moment in Irish footballing history.

In 1986, he showed his stubborn side when he stood up to former Leeds legend and current Republic of Ireland manager Jack Charlton. He viewed a Big Jack slight as a matter of principle after being dropped from the Irish side for the first time in a decade without receiving any forewarning. O'Leary took it badly.

A spate of injuries forced Big Jack to hand O'Leary a late call-up. The defender refused, telling Charlton he had already booked a holiday. Big Jack suggested he could go on his holidays any time and O'Leary's reluctance to relent led to his international exile for three years.

Charlton recalled: "I phoned David and said, 'Are you coming?' He said, 'No, I'm going on holiday.' I said, 'Cancel it and you can go any bloody time.' And he said, 'Ah, no, the arrangements have been made.'"

O'Leary signed for Leeds United on a free transfer in 1993 and would later describe himself as a "disaster of a player" for the club after running out only 12 times before injury curtailed his career. It would be beyond the white line where he would come into his own at Elland Road after his retirement as a player in October 1995.

When former Arsenal boss George Graham arrived at Elland Road in September 1996, he installed O'Leary as his assistant. He worked closely with the club's plethora of exciting youngsters for the two years that Graham was at Elland Road.

When Graham left to take over at Tottenham Hotspur, he tried to take O'Leary with him, but a legend at Arsenal felt a move to fierce North London rivals Spurs was not in the script. Instead, he stayed at Leeds and fulfilled the role of caretaker manager until a new boss was found.

O'Leary took his chance as caretaker manager with both hands. The club had unsuccessfully attempted to lure Leicester City boss Martin O'Neill to take charge and had also approached a few other candidates, but O'Leary's mild-mannered charm won over the players, public and also chairman Peter Ridsdale.

"Initially I came in and said I didn't want the job," O'Leary would reflect. "I thought the club wouldn't want me and initially I thought the fans wouldn't want me as well. I thought that they'd want me to clear off back because George Graham brought me in.

"I wanted to take Leeds to another level," he added. "I asked the club and they said they had a little bit of money to spend and I said I wanted David Batty back and three of four kids I wanted to put into the team and the injection of five new players. I just wanted a change of style and to make us an attractive team."

Ridsdale finally offered O'Leary the position full-time. Aged 39, he was wet behind the ears in managerial terms. He would endeavour to shape a youthful team to fit that same mould.

He inherited a young side packed with talent. Players he had worked with, knew what they could offer and who he wasn't frightened to throw into the cauldron.

At a club with the pedigree of Leeds United, it takes a strong individual to fit the shirt. Expectation and history can sit heavily on the shoulders of a player not prepared to carry that burden. It takes someone that relishes the challenge and isn't inhibited by the responsibility.

Leeds had won the Youth Cup in 1997 and O'Leary knew the potential that existed in the youth. The club had previously won the Youth Cup in 1993 and failed to reap the benefits. O'Leary was determined not to miss out again.

"The spotlight is bigger and no matter what you do now, on the pitch or off it, it's highlighted now," O'Leary told the cameras as the media became interested in the new manager's approach to his young side. "Football is a big thing now, vast amounts of money. I take calls every day. Every agent can do a better job and this that and the other.

"These lads of 17 don't need agents. I never had an agent and they certainly won't be having agents. I'll make sure of that. There's a time and place for them to get involved with people, the right people.

"They'll get discipline here and that's my job," he added. "I'm a disciplined person. I don't want them to live like monks or saints or anything else, but it's important to have discipline and it's important to have respect. I think they are the main thing when they go on with their career and they become established players.

"Good luck to them, earn as much as they can, but have respect for the people you're working for. Have respect for people in general. Because your earning a lot more money doesn't make you any bigger a person."

Those would turn out to be prophetic words!

O'Leary would often refer to the young crop of talent as his "babies". The majority were graduates of the Thorp Arch academy, a youth system that would become the envy of the Premier League.

Jonathan Woodgate was a refined 18-year-old centre-back and Stephen McPhail a sophisticated 18-year-old that George Graham had compared to Arsenal legend Liam Brady. The midfielder with a stylish left foot who had been handed a debut by Graham would be given a starting spot by O'Leary.

While Woodgate and McPhail were impressive, another academy product encapsulated the times perfectly. Alan Smith was an 18-year-old striker with a fresh face and a commitment level that would endear himself to the home support. Affectionately known as 'Smudger', he came off the bench to make an instant impact on his debut at Anfield. With Leeds trailing 1-0, he equalised with his first touch of the ball, a shot from outside the box. The 3-1 comeback win altered the course of the season as the local lad with a breakneck passion for the cause came to be the poster boy for O'Leary's fledglings.

Harry Kewell was a 20-year-old Australian flying midfielder that O'Leary described as "a wonderful talent". He had debuted under Graham, but struggled for consistency. O'Leary could see the threat the Aussie possessed and gave him his head, roaming the attacking third, creating opportunities to others and scoring goals with a gem of a left foot.

Then there was Lee Bowyer, a combative 21-year-old box-to-box midfielder with an uncompromising work ethic; Irish 21-year-old defender Ian Harte was a gem with a set-piece; 18-year-old goalkeeper Paul Robinson quickly made his mark and was pushing for a first-team start; 22-year-old midfielder, Eirik Bakke, was signed from Norwegian club Sogndal for £1.75million.

To guide the younger players, some experience was needed. This was provided by commanding South African centre-back Lucas Radebe, a player who, while compassionate, caring and constantly smiling off the pitch, was a true competitor on it.

O'Leary added to the spine of his team by bringing David Batty back to the club in December, signing the English international for a £4.4million fee from Newcastle. Batty was another home-grown player, a midfield enforcer to control the centre of the park and offer protection to the developing team.

After an 11-match unbeaten run, Leeds ended the season in fourth place, their highest finish since winning the league in 1992.

O'Leary sought to strengthen the squad with a UEFA Cup campaign to prepare for in the 1999/2000 season. During the summer, Dutch striker Jimmy Floyd Hasselbaink, the main source of goals, left for Atletico Madrid in a £12 million move.

The transfer fee wasn't wasted as O'Leary sought to build on the youthful vitality already present. He brought in Danny Mills, a tough, dynamic right-back for £4million from Charlton; Darren Huckerby, a languid attacker, came in from Coventry for £5.5million; and centre-back Michael Duberry was drafted in from Chelsea for £4.5million.

But it was Michael Bridges who made the biggest impact. Signed from Sunderland, the striker hit 19 league goals in his first season, among them some finishes that fitted easily into the showreel of the season.

The UEFA Cup run ended in a semi-final defeat to the Turkish side Galatasaray, who would go on to lift the trophy.

Leeds finished third in the Premier League after a run of four defeats in April saw their title challenge fade. It was a disappointing end to a campaign that had seen the club produce some stunning and entertaining football. But it had delivered Champions League qualification. It would be the first time Leeds would participate in Europe's premier club competition since the 1992/93 season.

The youngsters were quickly justifying their manager's faith as O'Leary's high tempo play was catching the imagination. The future was bright.

O'Leary's reign would be remembered for many things. The two key positives were his youth development and a tremendous 2000/01 Champions League adventure that captured the imagination.

In advance of the season, Leeds opened their wallet and began to spend big as a reliance on blooding youth was shelved in favour of securing big named imports.

During the summer, Australian striker Mark Viduka and French midfielder Olivier Dacourt were bought for a combined £13.7million. Liverpool defender Dominic Matteo cost around £5million.

It was the signing of West Ham's cultured defender Rio Ferdinand in November 2000 that most signalled the club's intent. Ferdinand was strong at the back, a skilful leader who possessed pace and flair. The fee of £18million was a British record.

Robbie Keane had made his name at Coventry where he had netted 12 goals in 31 games. He had failed to find his feet in Italy at Inter Milan and joined Leeds on loan in December 2000 before his £12million move was made permanent the following summer.

In Europe, the money proved to be well spent. Leeds entered the competition at the third qualifying round stage where they faced strong German opposition in 1860 Munich. Leeds won the first leg 2-1, but with Olivier Dacourt and Eirik Bakke sent off in that match and, with David Batty side-lined through injury, O'Leary had no central midfielders available. The injuries stretched throughout the squad and only four first-team players were available for the second leg in Munich. But a strong performance, capped by an Alan Smith goal, Leeds progressed 3-1 on aggregate. Keeper Nigel Martyn performed heroically in the Leeds goal to keep Munich at bay.

Drawn in Group H, Leeds had the daunting task of pitting their wits against AC Milan, Barcelona and Besiktas. Their tag of third favourites of the four sides appeared optimistic when they were soundly beaten 4-0 in the Camp Nou by Barcelona.

But O'Leary's young side were quick learners. An 89th minute goal saw Leeds claim a 1-0 win over AC Milan at Elland Road. Bowyer scored twice in the 6-0 home win against Besiktas as Viduka, Matteo, Bakke and Huckerby were also on the scoresheet. Leeds were back in the hunt for a top two place and a goalless draw in Turkey was hard earned. They went ahead early against Barcelona through another Bowyer goal, but when Rivaldo scored in the 90th minute to earn the visitors a point it meant that O'Leary needed a point in the San Siro to guarantee finishing above AC Milan.

In one of the most famous nights in the post-Revie era, Leeds travelled to Italy and went in at half-time 0-0. They took the lead in the 46th minute, courtesy of a Matteo header that would become meshed in Leeds folklore and of which terrace songs would be sung. They held the lead until the 68th minute when Serginho levelled on the night.

But Leeds held on to progress to the second group stage as the mighty Barcelona were condemned to settle for a place in the UEFA Cup. They were drawn to face Real Madrid, the side Revie had admired and changed Leeds shirts to resemble. Lazio were an Italian side packed with star talent, such as Pavel Nedved, Hernan Crespo and Juan Sebastian Veron, while Anderlecht packed the upfront punch of giant Jan Koller and diminutive Tomasz Radzinski.

Once again, an opening defeat to Real Madrid at Elland Road was a disappointing start, but Alan Smith's 80th minute strike at the Stadio Olimpico secured a 1-0 win against Lazio. A Stoica goal in the 65th minute had given Anderlecht the advantage in Leeds, but the Whites fired back through Ian Harte and Lee Bowyer to win 2-1 and once again at the halfway stage had put themselves in a strong position to progress.

In the return fixture against the Belgians, Leeds put in a storming display to win 4-1, Koller's 76th minute goal for Anderlecht a mere consolation after a brace from Alan Smith and goals from Mark Viduka and an Ian Harte penalty had secured the points.

With Lazio the main threat to Leeds's chances, a 3-2 defeat in Madrid wasn't fatal as the Spanish sides ensured they would top the group. Leeds had rattled the Spanish giants when Alan Smith's goal put them ahead at the Bernabeu, but their hosts hit back immediately with first-half goals from Raul and Figo. A leveller from Viduka gave O'Leary hopes at 2-2, but Raul popped up again in the 61st minute to take the match.

Lazio knew that a win would see them through. It was a night to remember at Elland Road as both sides gave it their all. Ravanelli put the Italians ahead in the 21st minute, only for Lee Bowyer to equalise seven minutes later. Sinisa Mihajlovic put Lazio back in front from the penalty spot only a minute later and Jason Wilcox ensured Leeds went in at half-time level with a 43rd minute strike. Still all to play for in the second half, the atmosphere was electric as Mark Viduka scored in the 63rd minute to put Leeds in touching distance of the knockout stages. A 90th minute second from Mihajlovic made for a tense finale, but Leeds held on for 3-3 on the night.

The dream was alive. Reigning Spanish champions, Deportivo de La Coruna, were next up in the quarter-finals. Ian Harte, Alan Smith and Rio Ferdinand scored in a commanding 3-0 first leg performance in Leeds and, despite two goals from Coruna at the Riazor Stadium, Leeds managed to see the tie through 3-2 on aggregate.

Valencia stood between O'Leary and a Champions League final. After being held 0-0 at Elland Road, O'Leary was still confident his side could score an away goal and make things tricky for the Spaniards. But 1-0 at half-time turned to 3-0 by the final whistle as Leeds pushed forward to find hope. They were eliminated from the competition. Valencia lost the final to Bayern Munich on penalties.

"I remember we had some unbelievable Champions League nights here where you think to yourself it couldn't get better," said O'Leary, speaking to LUTV in December 2017. "It was just fantastic.

"After Milan, coming out afterwards and seeing all the great Leeds fans behind the goal, and we just stood there and watched and we all just made the most of it," he added, when asked to single out his most memorable moment. "Unbelievable, a great occasion and that's my memory of that Champions League campaign."

The future appeared bright. However, despite losing only one game during the second half of the Premier League season, Leeds missed out on another year in the Champions League, finishing fourth by a single point. Small margins, huge impact. The burden of shouldering English hopes in Europe had seen their Premier League form dip a little.

The loss of Champions League football turned out to be catastrophic for the club, which had banked on prolonged involvement in the competition and Peter Ridsdale had borrowed £60million against predicted future gate receipts, budgeting for prolonged Champions League involvement.

O'Leary's team had to settle for a UEFA Cup place, which yielded far less financial reward. To supporters it was a setback, but hey, the team was punching at the top end of the English game and had shown what it could offer on the continent. What was there to worry about? Leeds United would have to put dreams of going one better in the Champions League to one side for a season, at least. Hmmm.

The consequence of failing to qualify alongside Europe's elite would become apparent later. It was the start of a financial meltdown that would plague the club for the next decade.

It had all begun to unravel off the pitch too. In January 2000, four players, including first-teamers Jonathan Woodgate and Lee Bowyer, were involved in an incident in Leeds city centre where an Asian student was beaten unconscious. All parties had been at a Leeds nightclub before the student became embroiled in a verbal confrontation with one of the footballer's friends after leaving.

The assault led to claims of racism and serious questions about the conduct of the players concerned. It would take until December 2001 for the courts to deliver their final verdicts.

O'Leary was naïve at best when he decided to release his autobiography during the period of the Woodgate and Bowyer court cases. He was foolish to call it *Leeds United On Trial*. Behind the scenes at Elland Road, it was not a happy camp with splits forming inside the club.

Amidst the turmoil, the previously popular O'Leary had begun to alienate the fans, and more importantly Ridsdale. Many suggested that in writing his book he was cashing in on the troubles the club were suffering.

There was little dignity in anything Leeds did during this period. O'Leary found himself at the centre of a row over cash-for-answers. The manager who refused to give media interviews during the period of the trial gave instead an 'exclusive' paid-for article to the *Sunday People*. His book was serialised for a five-figure sum in the *News of the World*. Who was O'Leary looking after?

"The book is not about the trial," O'Leary insisted at the time. "There's only one chapter on that, and anyway I cannot help the serialisation rights of a newspaper that wants to take it. Even though it is my book, I cannot help the timing of it either, and let me just say, I don't get any pennies or monies from what the *News of the World* have printed."

He was technically correct, but despite the cash not going directly into his own pockets, the fact the publishers knew the book would be in serious demand by newspapers would have positively impacted on how lucrative they made his book deal. There is no doubt O'Leary benefitted financially during Leeds's dark times. It was a crass act from the serving manager of a club in crisis.

The family of the Bowyer-Woodgate victim, Sarfraz Najeib, were fiercely critical of O'Leary's insensitivity. They brought a civil action against the players and club and Suresh Grover, the family's spokesman, said: "O'Leary is making money from this incident because he knows there is a huge amount of interest in it. Look at the timing of the serialisation; it was just two days after the court case, and it shows O'Leary is trying to make as much money out of it as possible. The Leeds United manager is accepting blood money."

The truth of the matter is probably somewhere in the middle, but a former teammate of O'Leary's told of a man with quite simply a split personality. O'Leary had been nicknamed 'Jack' by the Highbury dressing room, as in 'I'm alright, Jack', suggesting a solitary and sometimes selfish man in a team sport.

"The main thing is that those who know him are impressed with what he does on the field, but cringe with what he does off it. It's the cringe factor with David — all that 'my babies' stuff," the former colleague stated. "And he's always been an arse-licker. That's why he's so nice about [Peter] Ridsdale. And when he was at Arsenal, he said the same things then. He said the Arsenal chairman was like a second father. What player talks about his chairman like that? He's the kind of person who will move away from you when you're chatting if he thinks someone more important has just walked into the room. He's not necessarily tight with money, but he is always looking to make it."

Things got tragically worse during United's UEFA Cup campaign. After victories against Partizan Belgrade (4-1 on aggregate), Lokomotiv Moscow (7-1 aggregate), Spartak Moscow (2-2 on aggregate, won on away goals), O'Leary's side got past AS Roma 1-0 on aggregate thanks to a Harry Kewell goal in the 2nd Leg at Elland Road.

A commanding 3-0 win over Slavia Prague, in the quarter-final 1st leg, meant that a 2-1 defeat in the away return was enough to set up a semi-final clash with Turkish side Galatasaray. The Ali Sami Yen Stadium was notorious for being a hostile venue for visiting sides. The sign 'Welcome to Hell' hung ominously inside the stadium. The city would live up to that billing. What should have been a wonderful adventure for the 500 Leeds fans with tickets turned into one of the darkest days in the club's history.

On the night before the game, at around 9pm on 5 April 2000 in Taksim Square, tensions were rising. A local hooligan group, 'The Night

Watchmen', arrived and took the opportunity to turn the hostile atmosphere into proper violence between the two sets of supporters and two lifelong Leeds fans were killed and five others injured.

37-year-old Christopher Loftus died at the scene after being stabbed and Kevin Speight, aged 40, succumbed to his injuries after being taken to hospital.

UEFA decided that the match should be played. Leeds lost 2-0, but the result was an irrelevance. The game was United's fourth defeat in a row.

The Leeds United team that took the field in horrendous circumstances in Istanbul: Nigel Martyn, Gary Kelly, Jonathan Woodgate, Lucas Radebe, Ian Harte, Eirik Bakke, Lee Bowyer, Matthew Jones (Jason Wilcox), Stephen McPhail, Michael Bridges (Darren Huckerby), Harry Kewell.

There was every chance that Leeds would have beaten a fairly ordinary Galatasaray side in any other circumstance. Michael Bridges, Harry Kewell and Stephen McPhail all missed clear opportunities and Leeds conceded two sloppy goals to lose the match 2-0. A place in the Copenhagen final had been there for the taking, yet it didn't seem to matter at all.

No players, whether Leeds United or not, should ever have to play a game of football where armed guards with riot shields are required to shield their entry onto the playing surface. Home fans ran their fingers over their throats as they appeared to bay for further blood.

The Leeds fans turned their backs on the play to observe their own two-minute silence. David O'Leary sat in the dugout, dressed smartly in a suit, resembled an accountant waiting for a job interview in a war zone as helmet-clad minders stood guard.

I have never watched a game where I didn't care if Leeds won or lost. When Hakan Sukur headed Galatasaray ahead after 12 minutes, I didn't flinch. All I could think about was wanting the Leeds contingent in Istanbul to get home safely. Just before the break, Carlos de Oliveira doubled the home side's lead.

Leeds desperately needed an away goal to give them a foothold in the tie ahead of the second leg. Leeds had plenty of the ball in the second half, but couldn't convert their chances.

UEFA supported a Leeds request to ban Galatasaray fans from the 2nd leg at Elland Road, despite the Galatasaray vice-president branding the decision "disgusting".

Tributes in the form of flowers, shirts, scarves and messages were laid in abundance outside Elland Road and a black armband was placed on the Billy Bremner statue. A brass plaque was subsequently installed in remembrance of Christopher Loftus and Kevin Speight to ensure they would never be forgotten.

Chairman Peter Ridsdale had visited the Taksim Hospital and said: "It is a tragedy. One minute I was talking to Galatasaray directors to promote the friendship between the two clubs and the next minute I receive a telephone call telling me there had been some problems in town and a fan had been killed. Tonight is going down as one of those black nights in history."

There can never be justice in such circumstances. That arrests were made, and men served time in prison for the stabbings is scant consolation to the families of two men who were looking forward to watching their team play a European semi-final and never came home.

The club entered a period of mourning and, with the shadow of the Woodgate and Bowyer court case never far away from attention, it was a sombre period at Elland Road.

O'Leary reflected on the mood inside the club generated around the trial to the club's website: "Once the implications of the episode sunk in, players were adversely affected. One room at Thorp Arch became a solicitor's office. There was too much going on, too many people missing training sessions, then going off to be interviewed in police stations.

"It's been very disruptive," he continued. "It affects everybody, not just those who have been charged. People have not really appreciated what strain we have been under this season.

"We have that many people going off to police stations to be interviewed and players have missed training here, there and everywhere. I have been planning things only to be told on the morning of the sessions (training) that this person and that person was required to make a statement."

On the day after the first trial at Hull had collapsed, after an article was published in a Sunday newspaper, a TV crew were granted an interview. O'Leary was asked if he would consider quitting his job if such pressure continued and he shot back a quick reply: "Yes, definitely."

O'Leary reflected: "The first couple of years it was a pleasure to manage Leeds and we'd become everybody's favourites and I think over that period we kept qualifying for Europe and doing exceptionally under the circumstances. That (Bowyer/Woodgate affair) put us back a long way football-wise and public relations-wise."

In December 2001, the jury had delivered for over 22 hours before clearing Bowyer of all charges and giving Woodgate community service after he was found guilty of affray.

21-year-old Woodgate had admitted watching the "big free-for-all," but had always denied being involved in the violent assault. Bowyer, by then 24, denied being at the scene and said he had not witnessed the attack.

Woodgate's friend, Paul Clifford, was jailed for six years for grievous bodily harm and affray. Another man, Neale Caveney, received an order to do 100 hours' community service for affray, but was cleared of causing grievous bodily harm.

The trial judge had told Woodgate and Caveney that, "Five young students were caused sheer terror as they were pursued through the streets running for their lives. By joining in that chase you were terrifying both them and other law-abiding members of the community."

Both players were disciplined by Leeds United for being drunk on the streets of Leeds. Woodgate accepted the fine, but Bowyer refused to pay and was placed on the transfer list.

"I have no problem with him [Bowyer] personally, but I think Lee felt let down, but frankly I felt let down because we'd stood by both Lee and Jonathan," said chairman Ridsdale. "Clearly it had done the club enormous harm whatever the circumstances and I thought it was the right thing for the club to do, to be seen to be saying to the world and the players, 'You have to have a code of conduct.'"

Former player Peter Lorimer was not convinced, stating: "You don't just slap massive fines on players, especially when the players had arrived for training that morning to be told by the manager it was solidarity and it was all the players against the press because everybody's going to be against us."

For once, I agreed with Ridsdale. Bowyer's self-interest was not akin to the chaos his actions had caused. He should have been advised to take his punishment and keep his head down.

Back on the pitch, Leeds had begun the 2001/02 season at top speed and regularly topped the table, sitting in first place as we all sang in the New Year in good spirits.

A loss of form in the second half of the season saw them slump into fifth place, again missing out on a Champions League spot and the scant consolation of UEFA Cup football once again.

The failure would lead to O'Leary's sacking as Leeds manager on 27 June 2002. Yet it seemed his dismissal owed as much to comments he had made to Sky about the rumoured sale of Rio Ferdinand to Manchester United.

"I bought Rio Ferdinand for £18million and people said it was a lot of money and I want to keep him, particularly I don't want to sell him to Manchester United," O'Leary said. "They are a great club and we are

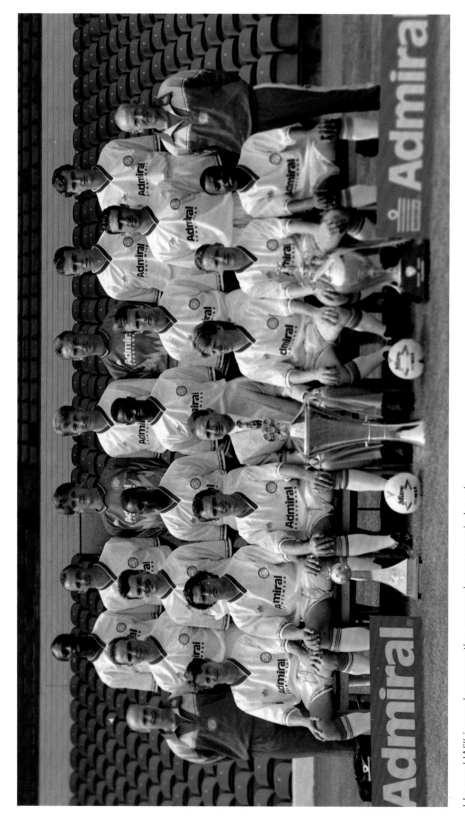

Howard Wilkinson became the second manager in Leeds United's history to win the league title in the 1991/92 season.

Howard Wilkinson, Eric Cantona and his captain Gordon Strachan. One of the players went the right way across the Pennines and the other, despite his success, got his directions messed up.

Howard Wilkinson, Gordon Strachan and Danny Wallace celebrate their title win in 1992.

George Graham took over in 1996 before he was lured away by Spurs two years later.

David O'Leary enjoyed huge success as his "babies" came through the ranks, but the European adventure and period of success would prove costly.

Terry Venables came with a glowing CV in 2002, but his relationship with chairman Peter Ridsdale deteriorated quickly as the financial plight of the club became public and star players were sold.

Peter Reid was a case of right place, wrong time, as Leeds United finances reached meltdown in 2004.

Kevin Blackwell had originally come to Leeds as Peter Reid's assistant, but took charge after the relegation season of 2003/04. He took his side to the play-offs but no further.

Dennis Wise had initial success, but couldn't maintain the momentum.

Gary McAllister was a title-winner with Leeds in 1992 and managed Leeds to the play-off final in 2008, but defeat put the writing on the wall.

Simon Grayson was a
local lad who came close
to restoring the club to
the top flight between
2008 and 2012.

Neil Warnock was
appointed by chairman
Ken Bates in 2012, but
could not replicate
promotion successes
elsewhere at Elland Road.

Brian McDermott took charge in 2013 and was the first manager to fall victim to the Massimo Cellino reign as chairman.

Dave Hockaday lasted eight matches as Leeds boss in 2014.

Darko Milanic didn't win any of his six matches in charge in 2014.

Neil Redfearn had done a great job with the young Leeds players and as a caretaker boss, but when he was handed the job full-time he had to deal with a fly-by-night Italian chairman and lasted 33 matches.

Uwe Rosler has survived the East German Stasi, but could not survive more than 12 matches as Leeds boss in 2015.

Steve Evans became Leeds manager in 2015 and oversaw 38 matches before chairman Cellino decided to ring the changes again.

Garry Monk managed to outlast Massimo Cellino, but left soon after in May 2017.

Thomas Christiansen arrived at Elland Road in 2017, but could not back up a promising start.

Paul Heckingbottom swapped Barnsley for Leeds United in February 2018, but was gone by July.

And then there was Marcelo Bielsa. The Argentine took Leeds to the play-off semi-finals in 2019 and has high hopes that he can lead Leeds United back to the Premier League where they belong.

All photography:
Varley Picture Agency

trying to build a team here, not make them even greater by selling them probably one of the best defenders in the world.

"I'm trying to build a team for the fans and put a squad together for the future of this football club and like any hopefully good manager you don't want to lose your good players, because that makes your job even harder.

"I was very proud that Rio Ferdinand left London to come to Leeds and he's a wonderful lad to deal with, a wonderful person, I always knew what he was going to be and I've tried to bring other players to make the fans proud. Not to lose them, to make them better here, to make Leeds a better team and for us all to do well.

"We're young, get older, get better and, as I say, no matter what money you get, where do you replace a Rio Ferdinand in the squad?"

Ferdinand had returned from England World Cup duty stating that he was happy in Leeds and wanted to stay at the club, but the financial maelstrom that would engulf the club over the coming years meant the club was eager to fill a widening hole in the finances. When the Sky interviewer passed on Ferdinand's comments that he was committed to Elland Road, O'Leary expressed his delight.

"I'm absolutely delighted with that because I don't want him to go," he countered. "I can't help speculation. He's a tremendous player and I want to keep all my best players. He is one of my very, very best. I made him skipper last year to build a base round him. To skipper this club for many years to come. The fans love him, I love him, and like any good manager you don't want to lose your best players."

Then, in recognition that O'Leary was manager and not owner of Leeds United, he moved to recognise that the club was a PLC and therefore the shareholders were also paramount in the process.

"But at the end of the day, I work for people, they are good people to work for, I work for a PLC and I am an employee of them.

"We need to hold on to all our best players and to try to add to that to make us better," he said, when asked what his message to the PLC would be. "We've invested a lot of money, I've been supported with a lot of money, but I think all the money we've spent is like good houses in good locations. They are worth a lot more money, i.e. Rio Ferdinand, and I want to keep them all."

O'Leary had been clever to the extent that he had publicly distanced himself from potential sales, putting the spotlight and pressure firmly on to the PLC.

O'Leary had spent a colossal £96.3million on 18 new players in less than four years as only £29million was recouped in player sales. There had been no reward in terms of trophies, but the team had never finished outside the Premier League top five with O'Leary as manager.

Two days after his comments about wishing to keep Ferdinand, TV cameras ambushed the newly sacked coach as he returned to his Harrogate home.

"I just went in this morning and was told I was sacked, simple as that," he told the media as he removed bags from the boot of his car. "Nothing should shock you in football, I think you've heard that before, but I loved the job, there's great supporters here. I loved the Leeds supporters here; they are good people and they were all very good to me. As I say, I love being here, I love living here and I say, it's news to me.

"I wish them well because it's a place where I was very happy. My family love it here and I wish them all the success. I tried to give it the best I could and I think, under the circumstances of the last four years and what we've had to deal with on and off the field, particularly my family with the problems we've had, I think we've done a good job.

"People saying the money we spent, it's £60million that's worth a lot of money now."

The statement issued by the club to confirm O'Leary's departure had suggested that off-the-field matters had led to their decision to part ways.

"It's news to me," O'Leary suggested. "I'm disappointed, but that's football. I've tried to do the best I can and run a club and take the image of it and raise it. Thanks for everything because you have been fantastic, and I wish them all the best. Great club and a great place to live and whoever gets the job, I think I know who has the job anyway, so that's already in place, I wish them well."

A day later at the airport, as he left for his summer holiday, O'Leary struck a thinly veiled attack on his former chairman Peter Ridsdale.

"They've got a great spin doctor there and I'm sure there will be a lot of spin."

Eddie Gray told me: "George Graham did a good job and then he obviously left to go back to London. When David O'Leary took over I was his assistant and we had a lot of smashing players — the likes of Kewell, Woodgate, Viduka, Bowyer, Dacourt — some tremendous players.

"But up above, the club started spending too much money, and money that we couldn't afford. If you look back at that time we had Mark Viduka, Michael Bridges, Robbie Keane, Robbie Fowler, Harry Kewell, Darren Huckerby and they all wanted to play up front. Who can afford that?

"Football has changed now, but I think we were trying to get a step ahead of ourselves before the big television money really kicked into the game. If it happened now and Leeds United were in the same position as we were then, challenging for the league, going forward in European competitions, it would have been great because the club could have afforded it. It could have afforded to discard players and get others in, but back then the money wasn't in the game to such an extent.

"I think David had the opportunity to be a top manager, but if fell flat. The Lee Bowyer and Jonathan Woodgate thing set the club back," Gray concluded. "That didn't do the club any favours."

O'Leary subsequently suggested that he would like to return to Elland Road at some stage, but those comments are always met with mixed reactions from supporters. Some think he was tremendous, giving them European glory and a young team to cheer. Others believe he was a major factor in the boom-bust nosedive that would see their club floundering in League One within five years of his departure.

Yorkshiremen are known for their pessimism, or realism. Even the most downcast failed to predict what was coming next. The frightening descent had begun.

20

TERRY VENABLES

2002–2003

"If you can't stand the heat in the dressing room, get out of the kitchen"

Born: 6 January 1943, Dagenham, Essex

Matches	Won	Drawn	Lost	Points	Pts/Match	Win %
42	16	7	19	55	1.31	38.10%
				RANK	25th/36	20th/36

In the summer of 1996, the England football team had one of their rare moments in the sunshine. The nation stuck St George's flags on anything others could view, sang 'Three Lions' by Baddiel, Skinner and the Lightning Seeds until they could croak it out no more and it believed. For a few fleeting days in June, football was coming home, until the Germans won the semi-final at Wembley on penalties and normality returned. The man steering England to the edge of glory was Terry Venables.

Roll on six years, and Venables was being unveiled as the new manager at Leeds United. July 2002 saw the former England international and Chelsea, Tottenham Hotspur and QPR midfielder sign on the dotted line for a two-year deal. The robust Londoner took the helm as the financial malaise surrounding Elland Road was only just reaching public consciousness.

"I've had quite a few offers, even getting involved in the World Cup," Venables told ITV. "I just felt this was too tempting to resist."

Expectations were high as El Tel arrived in West Yorkshire. He had the pedigree, his sides played good football and there were reasons to be cheerful.

His CV was excellent. He'd taken Crystal Palace to the First Division via successive promotions. He'd gained promotion to the top flight with QPR too. He'd won the Spanish League with Barcelona, also the Spanish League Cup and led them to a European Cup final. Success followed with Tottenham and the Australia national team and then a short stint back at Palace and also with Boro. When the Leeds job was offered, Venables was hungry to get back into the game.

"Always there was this compulsion within me to go back to being involved in the game in a hands-on role," Venables recounted in his autobiography, *Born to Manage*. "And that is when Peter Ridsdale made his approach. He turned up at our home in Spain all bells and whistles and full of hot air.

"Ridsdale was, I felt, a disaster for Leeds, a man who I believed would have been happy enough to use me as a scapegoat for the storm that was about to engulf the club," he continued. "I will never forgive him for that. I am prepared to admit the mistakes, not Ridsdale, unless he is talking about my appointment in a disparaging way as his one and only major blunder. Ridsdale is a good talker, I will give him that."

Two press conferences perfectly encapsulate the relationship between chairman Ridsdale and Venables. At his unveiling, the new manager was full of smiles, sitting close to Ridsdale, with plenty of cordiality flowing. Scroll on to the twilight of Venables's tenure to another press conference and the two could not have appeared further apart. Not on the same page? They were not in the same library.

It would become apparent much later that Venables was, like most supporters at the time, in the dark to the scale of the problems the club faced and oblivious to the disasters and disappointments just around the corner.

Only two weeks into his reign as boss, club captain Rio Ferdinand was sold to arch enemy Manchester United. Ferdinand had joined the club in November 2000 as Peter Ridsdale broke the British transfer record to land the central defender from West Ham for £18million.

Ferdinand had made 73 appearances for the club and became an integral member of a side that had reached the UEFA Champions League semi-finals, scoring a header in the quarter-finals against Deportivo de La Coruna.

Venables would have undoubtedly seen Ferdinand as a key component of his team, fresh from being part of England's World Cup summer. The £29million move to Old Trafford once again broke the British transfer record, but for Whites' supporters it only fuelled Manchester United's title hopes and was not well received. It was, however, only the beginning of the heartbreak.

Robbie Keane had also been sold to Tottenham for £7million and fans and media alike speculated about prospective big money signings in the knowledge that the coffers had been boosted. Those hopes were short-lived with only Paul Okon, Nicky Barmby and Teddy Lukic added to the squad.

Despite the loss of a key central defender, Venables still had a squad that could compete. But the results were disappointing as they made early exits in the League Cup and UEFA Cup and languished in the bottom half of the table. Opening wins against Manchester City and Bolton and a Harry Kewell header securing victory over Manchester United in front of 39,622 at Elland Road were early season rare highlights.

The youngsters were impressing. In the UEFA Cup, Alan Smith put four past Hapoel Tel Aviv in an inspired display and James Milner became the youngest scorer in the Premier League in a win against Sunderland.

A defeat over two legs in the third round to Malaga ended the team's participation in the UEFA Cup and, to date, Leeds have not qualified for European football since.

As the January transfer window approached, speculation mounted that several clubs were about to table bids for highly rated central defender Jonathan Woodgate.

"Things have changed since I have been here in a very short time, but I'm really dealing in the short-term at the moment," Venables told Sky Sports on 25 January 1993. "It's game-by-game, dealing with the next game and trying to get the maximum amount out of it. We're in the results business at my end of the club. It gets more and more difficult, but only difficult — it's not impossible.

"From my point of view, it's a huge frustration," he continued. "That's why I got the job, I guess, to make sure there's not too much damage to the team while that's going on and maybe next year, financially, we'll be better. During the season I've got to try and stick the whole thing together as best as I can.

"As we sit here now, and there's a lot of talk and a lot of speculation, as far as I know there has not been an offer for Woody (Jonathan Woodgate)," Venables stated. "There's one thing, I will do anything I can to make sure that don't happen.

"It's not just about making the crucial decision whether he goes, it's been going on with other players. I want all the players. I don't just want Woody. I mean Woody is a terrific player and a good lad. I really think a lot of him, but it's all the players and we want to keep them together and then, if we can't, we've then got to do the best we can."

On the same programme, Venables's predecessor, David O'Leary, was asked by Sky's Richard Keys for his opinion: "They seem to need money desperately. They tried to raise it through Robbie Fowler, and it's failed, and Seth Johnson too from what I've been told. It makes other people in there vulnerable for other people to come in," he said. "I bet he's delighted this new system that the transfer window closes in January because, if it didn't, can you imagine what would be going on until the end of the season?

"I hope for the Leeds supporters, and I've got great friends out there who keep in touch with me. The players don't want Woody to go, I don't want Woody to go as he's a fantastic player. If the club are that desperate for money and the only player people want is Jonathan Woodgate, then that makes him very vulnerable for Leeds.

"I can't understand the money, Richard," O'Leary said as he fidgeted with his shirt collar. "They say I spent £100million. Take Ferdinand and Keane, after they'd been sold, that's recouped about £75million, so what's left there now is I've spent £25million. When I left about £40million had been recouped out of the hundred we'd spent, so that's down to £60million. Then Ferdinand has been sold so that's taken it down to £30million, Keane has been sold so that's dropped it down and I think it's probably shocked Terry why he has to sell. I'm sure he came in thinking he had to raise £15million, Ferdinand would be sold, and he would get the rest, but he hasn't got that.

"When I left, I was aware that we needed to raise £15million and that's right," O'Leary continued. "If the chairman wants to raise money you let them do it. I left the club when I got the sack and presumed Terry would have to do the same as I had been told. It's amazed me since that it seems to be one after the other. They've left themselves open. People know Leeds are desperate to bring money in and are taking advantage of them, in my opinion — trying to strike deals knowing that Leeds are desperate for the money. If they get Jonathan Woodgate for £10million after Rio has been sold for £30million, then he's a bargain at £10million, he really is."

Despite his high-profile court case that had engulfed the club in misery for almost two years, Woodgate had remained popular with the supporters. He had stayed loyal, was a fine player and was a local boy.

When Middlesbrough-born Woodgate was asked to fill in a routine Football Association questionnaire, they asked which team's results he looked for first. His reply goes a long way to illustrating his appeal to Leeds fans. He wrote: 'Leeds, Leeds reserves, Leeds Youth teams, Leeds Permanent Building Society Pub Team, Leeds & Holbeck Pub Team, Leeds ice-hockey team, East Leeds chess under-19's, South Leeds Over-75's poker team, anyone else with Leeds in their name, and Middlesbrough.'

A few days after Venables had told the television cameras that he did not want Woodgate to leave, the central defender was sold to Newcastle United for £9million.

Venables found himself in an impossible position, as Lee Bowyer, Olivier Dacourt and Robbie Fowler also left the club. So desperate were they for money in the bank, they accepted a down payment of £3million for Fowler against the total transfer value of £6million and agreed to pay £500,000 of his wages until 2016. Other clubs knew Leeds were on the edge and held all the bargaining power in any negotiations.

At a rather uncomfortable press conference, Ridsdale and Venables sat shoulder-to-shoulder yet miles apart. Ridsdale cited the failure to qualify for the UEFA Champions League had cost the club approximately £30million and therefore costs had to be reduced. He added that the transfer system had imploded with fewer bids being made at far lower levels than had been the case in previous years.

"It is against this backdrop that we have listened to offers where we believed it was right for the long-term financial stability of the football club," an under-fire Ridsdale told the assembled media. "In the case of Olivier Dacourt, he is currently on loan to Roma with a view of a permanent move this coming summer. Lee Bowyer informed us that he would do a Bosman in the summer and we therefore allowed him to go now. This enabled us to recover the money owed to the club in legal fees in addition to a small amount of transfer income, rather than nothing later on in the year. In the case of Robbie Fowler, he was not playing regularly after his recovery from injury, his family had relocated to Liverpool and the offer was significant in a transfer market that was almost non-existent.

"Jonathan Woodgate was a player we did not want to sell," Ridsdale continued, from a prepared statement. "We are, however, a public company. An offer of £9million is significant when set against the backdrop of a company only being valued at £15million on the Stock Exchange.

"By accepting this offer we give financial certainty in a marketplace that is still very fragile. As a supporter, I did not want to take the offer. The manager did not want Jonathan to go and he made that absolutely clear to me and has been consistent with that. As chairman of Leeds United, I have a primary responsibility to the shareholders to take the right financial decisions. However much I agonised, and I did, I am here to make the right decisions and not necessarily popular decisions.

"It is the only decision that could be made to give us peace of mind for the future. Should we have spent so heavily in the past? Probably not. But we lived the dream, we enjoyed the dream and only by making the right decisions today can we rekindle the dream once again in the future. And that's what we intend to do.

"The future is brighter for all Leeds United fans today because we took the tough decisions."

The media quickly jumped from Ridsdale to a bristling Venables who told them that he had yet to make a decision on whether he was going to stay on as manager.

"I don't want to make a kneejerk reaction to something that is as disappointing as what occurred yesterday," Venables said. "I don't want to inflame a situation that is already a very raw position at the moment. But I think it's been stated already that if Fowler went then Jonathan Woodgate wouldn't go.

"I think it's fair for you not to expect me to make such a vast decision on something that has been put on me very, very quickly. I'm clearly thinking about the future position. That could mean I am, or I am not, thinking of going. There is a situation here that is a very difficult one.

"There are six players gone," Venables added. "Four of them wanted to go, two of them didn't want to go. In saying they did when it came to it, but they never started it and I have no problem with those two players. My biggest concern now is that the players who are here and they are the most important of all the players we have spoken about. They are the only people I am considering, and the supporters."

When asked whether he would have taken the job if he'd known the full facts about the players he would see sold, Venables said, "I certainly did not know and I think the chairman will agree to it (he did) and I think he has said certain things have happened in that time, from the time I started to today. There were certain people will tell you I knew about it when I started. He will tell you that is nonsense."

He'd threatened his resignation if Woodgate left and had to be convinced by Ridsdale to stay at the club, but in March 2003 the supporters had lost faith. The results didn't improve, Sheffield United knocked them out of the FA Cup and, with relegation becoming a serious concern and more player sales rumoured, Venables was sacked.

In his book, Venables looked back at his time at Elland Road through gritted teeth.

"United was my hard day in the office. Some day! It lasted all of nine months from July 2012, when I succeeded David O'Leary, until I left in March 2003. There were moments when the clouds parted long enough to let in a glint of sunlight, but for the rest of the time it was infuriating, frustrating and desperately disappointing. Joining Leeds United as manager was my misjudgement, my poor decision and one that still hurts like hell.

"To say it was my monumental error to go there should not be taken as a slur on Leeds United, who had been rightly considered a leading club for decades since the ruthlessly professional one established by Don Revie."

Venables closed the Leeds chapter of his book with these words: "Sadly, the club had still not recovered from those turbulent times where the debris mounted and so many excellent players were sold off. I believe Leeds United will be successful again and that someone will find the formula, but it may not happen for a while yet."

21

PETER REID

2003–2004

"In football, if you stand still you go backwards"

Born: 20 June 1958, Huyton, Lancashire

Matches	Won	Drawn	Lost	Points	Pts/Match	Win %
22	6	4	12	22	1.00	27.27%
				RANK	31st/36	32nd/36

Chairman Peter Ridsdale departed the club in March 2003 after six years in position, just days after Terry Venables's sacking, quitting as financial results were published that illustrated the dire straits Leeds United were in. The interim half-year results to the end of December 2012 showed the club had suffered a loss before tax of £17.2million and an overall debt of £80million.

Professor John McKenzie took over as chairman and told the London Stock Exchange, "Peter has other business interests that he wishes to pursue and we have agreed that it is in the best interests of both parties that he stands down from the board of Leeds United and of the football club.

"The priority for the club is to focus on avoiding relegation, then to balance the obvious need for even greater financial prudence and control with the ability to produce a football squad which has the capability of competing in the top echelon of the Premiership. It will be a very tough challenge to take the business forward in this way, but it is one that I relish."

Peter Reid was handed the poisoned chalice, drank from the cup and briefly survived. He took over from Venables as a headline in a local newspaper proclaimed that he was taking "The Worst Job in Football" and posed the question, "Leeds United, who would manage them?"

Reid did and lived to tell the tale. The football club was lurching from bad headline to potential obituary. The vultures were circling above Elland Road and Reid was operating with his hands treble-knotted behind his back.

He has looked back in his autobiography *Cheer Up Peter Reid* and described his time in Leeds as "an impossible job". But contrary to the song sung in so many football stadia, Reid's persona doesn't need too much perking up. It would have taken the emotional constitution of a saint not to have been strained by his time behind his desk in LS3.

Reid assumed temporary control until the end of the 2002/03 season with the club precariously placed in 15th and only eight games to play. The former PFA Players' Player of the Year in 1985 had one objective, to stave off relegation.

A 3-1 defeat by Liverpool at Anfield was a tough start, but then Reid took his team to Charlton and watched them romp to a 6-1 win. The escape was complete when Mark Viduka scored a left-footed 88th minute curler in the penultimate game against Arsenal at Highbury, to secure a 3-2 win. The victory earned the safety of a 15th place finish and a contract extension for the manager.

Harry Kewell would have been out of contract at the end of the 2003/04 season, so the club were forced to sell, rather than allow him to leave on a free. Barcelona, Chelsea and Manchester United had all been rumoured to be interested in the Australian's services, long before Liverpool joined the queue.

The financial nightmare at Elland Road tested loyalties to the core. There was no doubt Kewell was a player of exhilarating talent on the pitch, but it was the manner of the Australian's £7million move to Liverpool that left officials and supporters feeling hugely let down.

Many players sold by Leeds had forsaken elements of lucrative new deals to give something back to the club in its hour of need. Kewell had taken a more selfish approach and had set his sights on a move to Anfield, despite the fact that a number of other clubs had offered a significantly bigger fee.

Professor McKenzie was left "angry and frustrated at the outrageous situation," and went as far as saying that Kewell had "stabbed the Leeds fans in the back". The £7million fee was divided as £4million to Kewell, split equally from the two clubs, and £3million to Leeds United.

It was appalling that Kewell would receive more money than the club that had nurtured his career. Kewell, who did not appear to care, also threatened to wait until the summer and leave on a free transfer.

McKenzie responded to Kewell's admission that he had been speaking to Liverpool for six months. The professor voiced politely the supporters' view, saying, "It would be impossible for him to play for Leeds ever again. So, sadly, the PLC felt it had no alternative but to accept the paltry sum."

Goalkeeper Nigel Martyn and midfielder Olivier Dacourt also left the club, but Reid had no transfer kitty and was reduced to trawling the loan and free transfer markets.

Jody Morris came in on a free transfer and loan moves were made for

Arsenal's Jermaine Pennant and Didier Domi, Lamine Sakho, Zoumana Camara, Cyril Chapuis and Salomon Olembe from the French league.

Brazilian World Cup winner Roque Junior also came in on loan. The defender flew in after playing two tough World Cup qualification matches and was off the boil, as he was sent off for receiving two yellows as Duncan Ferguson gave him a torrid debut as Everton won 4-0.

Keeper Paul Robinson had gone up for a late corner against Swindon to score with his head to spare Leeds blushes as they drew 2-2 and progressed on penalties in the League Cup.

And then there was Mark Viduka, who had played a key role in the quest for survival in the previous season, was a far more destructive influence in the 2003/04 season. The Australian forward clashed with Reid, often turned up late and wanted a move elsewhere.

Reid would admit to *The Telegraph* in 2017 that his relationship with Viduka taught him that times had changed, and the modern player and his old-school style of management didn't always get along.

"You can't always do now what I did in *Premier Passions*," Reid said about a documentary filmed while he was managing Sunderland. "Effin and blinding at modern players, they'd just down tools.

"I learned very quickly at Leeds, Mark Viduka's reaction told me everything. I've laid into him and I could see in his eyes he's thinking I'm a piece of shit.

"As they're going out for the second half, I've pulled him over and said, 'Hey, listen, I've only made you an example because you're the best player.' I had to think on my feet. But that was the point I realised I couldn't do that anymore."

Leeds loitered in the bottom half for the entire season and Reid was forced to take strong action against Viduka, axing him from the squad that travelled to play Portsmouth on 8 November 2003. The change made no positive difference as Leeds were soundly beaten 6-1.

"There was no desire to play football, to win a tackle," a dejected Reid said after the game. "That second half was the worst forty-five minutes of my managerial career."

He was given his marching orders with Leeds rock bottom after 12 games.

"If I was offered the chance to take over at Elland Road again and the circumstances were exactly the same, I wouldn't hesitate," Reid reflected. "There are only a limited number of truly great clubs and if you have the opportunity to manage one of them, you grasp it with both hands. If things don't work out, then so be it, but you have to give it a try."

Former player and manager, Eddie Gray, finished the season as caretaker manager for the remaining 28 matches, but couldn't help Leeds avoid the drop.

The club announced a pre-tax loss of £49.5million, an unwanted Premier League record and Trevor Birch was appointed chief executive to oversee the finances, but administration loomed large.

Gray was Leeds United to the core and couldn't refuse the position, but would later regret taking on an impossible task. The football was often a secondary issue with the back pages predicting Leeds United's imminent demise. Rescue packages were touted and died, standstill agreements made with creditors, until on 27 February 2003, shares in the club were suspended and the standstill agreement shelved.

"I knew the situation at the football club, and I had second thoughts about going back, but the reason I did was because I quite liked Trevor Birch who was running the club, basically as an administrator," Gray told me. "He was a firefighter. But I liked Trevor a lot and he asked me to go back and then, when he left, the situation at the football club deteriorated."

Birch kept things ticking just long enough for the sale of the club to be agreed on 19 March 2003 when a consortium fronted by accountant Gerald Krasner moved in and reduced the £100million debt to a serviceable £20million and agreements were made with major creditors.

"They were selling all the players, it wasn't a happy camp," Gray continued. "They were asking the players to take wage cuts and that doesn't lead to a happy place.

"I had a fair amount of time and I was disappointed with myself, but, when I look back on it, I think it was a tough ask because the players were not happy.

"Some players were prepared to take a wage cut and some weren't and that led to a break in the camp. Players would come into see me and say, 'The club tried to sell me last night,' and I'd ask, 'How do you know that?' and they'd tell me their agent had told them.

"If I could relive that, I wouldn't have gone back."

At the final game of the Premier League season at Elland Road, the Leeds fans chorused, "'We're going down, but we'll be back!" No one there realised how long it would take.

22

KEVIN BLACKWELL

2004–2006

What might have been

Born: 21 December 1958, Luton, Bedfordshire

Matches	Won	Drawn	Lost	Points	Pts/Match	Win %
114	44	37	33	169	1.48	38.60%
				RANK	13th/36	18th/36

Kevin Blackwell almost did the impossible on 21 May 1996. I remember it as the longest and most disappointing drive home from Wales imaginable. Blackwell recalls the 3-0 play-off final defeat to Watford at the Millennium Stadium in Cardiff as the day his dream of taking Leeds back to the promised land of the Premier League died.

"The disappointment of that final was for everybody, but the club hasn't been anywhere near as close to the Premier League since then, or until 2018/19," Blackwell told me. "After the play-off final, Matthew Kilgallon, Ian Bennett and Rob Hulse were sold to Sheffield United, Simon Walton went to Charlton, Jermaine Wright went to Southampton and I was told whatever I could raise I could spend.

"We raised £5.5million, plus we had £2.5million from the play-off final because the losers get the money from that, but I could only sign five people on deadline day before we played Norwich at home at the start of the next season.

"I felt bitterly let down," he continued. "I was building the team and the club back up. We were only two years out of the Premier League and in that second season we'd finished 5th in the Championship and I knew we were only two or three players off having another good go. So, to lose the players, and the records are all there, they were all sold, that is fact, and then you end up bringing loan players in on the last day.

"At that point I wasn't aware that the club was going to go bankrupt, but at the end of that season it was put into administration."

And in his answer you get straight to the heart of Blackwell's time as Leeds boss. The highs, the so nearly and the huge frustration of doing a job with his hands tied behind his back, as he operated valiantly against a financial maelstrom.

The Luton-born former goalkeeper had begun life in football under the management of Ron Atkinson at Cambridge United, but he had to move to Bedford Town at non-league level to get games as he also worked as a bricklayer. He played for Barton Rovers in the 1978 FA Vase final and then for Middlesex Wanderers, before getting a chance in the Football League again, this time with Barnet.

He moved on to Boston United for £5,000 and saved a penalty in the 1985 FA Trophy final. A brief return to Barnet was followed by a move to Scarborough when he was snapped up by Neil Warnock, which started a long association with his new boss. Warnock led Scarborough into the Football League and over the following two seasons Blackwell played 44 times before following Warnock to Notts County for £15,000 in November 1989, but never played a first-team game. Warnock took over at Torquay in January 1993 and Blackwell moved with him again, playing 18 times as relegation from the Football League was averted.

Again, Blackwell followed Warnock to Huddersfield Town in August 1993, but this time he added coaching duties to his role as he only made three league starts. The pair switched to Plymouth Argyle in August 1995 and took on a player-youth coaching role and this time stayed on after Warnock moved. His playing days were almost over as he added 24 more appearances for the Devon club. Warnock's replacement, Kevin Hodges, was sacked in June 1998 and Blackwell became collateral damage a month later.

He was reunited with Warnock as goalkeeping coach at Bury and then the duo moved to Sheffield United in December 1999 with Blackwell taking the role as Warnock's number two.

Then, in June 2003, Blackwell's telephone rang.

"I was headhunted by Peter Reid and Leeds United because of the fantastic work that myself and Neil had done at Sheffield United," Blackwell remembered. "I think we'd beaten Leeds twice the year before in the quarter-finals of the League Cup and FA Cup and out of the blue I got a phone call after the play-off final against Wolves. It was from Peter Reid and I thought it was a wind up.

"I said, 'If it is Peter Reid you will ring me back,' and put the phone down. And he rang me back. Once I'd spoken to Peter and I knew it was Leeds United, there was no doubt I was going to go. What an honour and what a great place to come to.

"I felt it was my final opportunity to do my last job as a number two before looking to become a manager, but I certainly wasn't thinking that would be at Leeds. I just wanted my last bit of grounding on managing because I'd worked with Neil for a long time and I wanted to look at a different aspect of senior management from someone else.

"I'd turned down about six opportunities to go as a manager to clubs prior to that to stay at Sheffield United, because I knew we were building something really special," he explained. "And that year we'd got to the FA Cup semi-final, League Cup semi-final and play-off final. To go to Leeds under Peter Reid was going to be my last stop as an assistant.

"It was a massive honour for me to go to Leeds United," Blackwell told me. "A lot of my family are season ticket holders who came from the south and still travel up every Saturday.

"It was a club obviously steeped in history and one that had been in the semi-final of the European Cup just a year before. Everything was about going to a top Premier League club and, to that point, Leeds were exactly that. Great players, massive fan base, big reputation. It would be every coach's dream to go and work at clubs like that. And my dream had come true."

But it wasn't long before the gloss on his move to Elland Road lost its shine. Peter Reid was sacked after 22 games in charge and Blackwell had only been around for the second half of that tenure.

"I was bitterly disappointed," Blackwell admitted. "I felt cheated in a way because I only worked with Peter for 11 weeks. Reidy knew there were problems at the club that, to be fair, I wasn't aware of when I first went there.

"The first thing that happened, we signed seven players, I think, all on one day from France because we couldn't get players. It was really strange.

"If I'd known it was going to go into that shambolic deterioration and the finances were in a horrendous condition, I wouldn't have come to the club. There was no point in me trying to build my career at a club that was imploding. The things that you thought you could do, you couldn't.

"We were blooding quite a few youngsters, so Milly [James Milner] came in and Aaron Lennon. They were only teenagers and you are talking about playing for Leeds United in the Premier League at that age. They were playing three, four, five games back-to-back when they should have been given a little bit at a time.

"You were putting young kids into a situation where physically they weren't able to compete against men. You should really bring them in and take them out.

"The great thing about Aaron Lennon, and even more James Milner, his mental capacity was phenomenal, so what Milly's gone on to do is an absolute credit to himself. He always used to stay out and do extra training and I remember him putting cross after cross in and this was at 1pm on a Friday and he's playing at 11am the next day against Arsenal. You'd have to literally drag him off the pitch. I've got nothing but respect for James

Milner for what he's done and how he's conducted himself. Even now he's one of the fittest players at Liverpool."

Eddie Gray had taken charge after Reid's dismissal, but the inevitable fall into the Championship was confirmed when Leeds drew 3-3 with Charlton at Elland Road on 8 May 2004. It was the away game in Bolton prior to that where all but mathematical hope of survival had gone.

"That Bolton game is the one that sticks in my mind because that's when we knew," Blackwell said. "There was the picture of the boy crying his eyes out with his father. That was one of the lowest times ever because we all knew it was over. Eddie resigned after the Charlton game and I took the last game of the season.

"We knew it was coming," he continued. "It had been coming for weeks and weeks. The writing had been on the wall, there was nobody at the top of the club to talk to and we were just a little boat bobbing around on the water and the wind dictated where we went. We couldn't dictate what was happening at the football club. The finances were down with the PLC, it was an absolute shambles and I think whenever you look at a major corporation and it's become so dysfunctional, you need to look at the top. You only have to look at politics right now and that's very much the case."

A statement accompanying Reid's departure highlighted the "club's Premiership status comes under serious threat," and that the "recent run of results has clearly been unacceptable".

Hart had been the fans' favourite to take the job after being touted as a candidate before Reid had been installed. The former Leeds defender had two years left on his contract at the Forest Ground. Hart was seen as a cheap option and was a man used to operating on a tight budget, but Forest were not keen to let their man go.

They turned once again to former player and manager Eddie Gray to take caretaker charge in the interim and, once relegation had been confirmed, Kevin Blackwell was installed as Reid's permanent replacement on 26 May 2004.

Reminding him that he had become the fourth manager inside two years, I asked him if he had any doubts about taking over what others described as a poisoned chalice.

"There was obviously a fear," Blackwell replied. "Any young coach going into management, if you fail in your first job, you never manage again. There's a 75% attrition rate and I thought, 'This is only the biggest club that everyone is going to be looking at, this is the club that everybody wants to beat in the Championship and this is the club that everyone remembers being in the European Cup semi-final only two years before.'

I knew it would be a tough job.

"But then came the realisation that I might look back in years ahead, when I'd retired, and that I could have managed Leeds United. That was really the thing. I did not want to have regrets. Job offers like that don't come around every day.

"And then I took the job and it proved every bit as hard, and maybe harder, than I thought.

"It was ironic because I did a big pro licence course when I'd only just gone to Leeds United. One of the financial courses was through the League Managers Association and the professor had two copies of club statements. One was Manchester United, a very well-run club with £400million in the bank, and he said the other one on the left-hand side was from a club that is 'shagged'. He said, 'Kevin, I've got to ask you, this is Leeds United and if you don't want to know…'. I said, 'You might as well tell me.' And he said this club will never get out of this situation and it will have to go bankrupt.

"I always knew when I took over on the management side that finances were tough, but I'd just agreed to be manager in May and went on that course in June. Last month, two of our people from Cardiff City went on the management course and the financial bloke that did my course said to them all, 'Listen, fellas, I had Kevin Blackwell on this course and I told him his club was shagged,' and my assistants were there giggling and when they came back they said, 'Blacky, I've just been on a course and you were one of the main topics.'"

Ahead of Blackwell's first season in charge, the club had been bought by a consortium headed by Gerald Krasner, with a board comprising former player Peter Lorimer, property developers Simon Morris and Melvin Helme, entrepreneur Melvyn Levi and David Richmond, the son of Geoffrey Richmond, who had been a former chairman of Bradford City.

"I had nothing but problems with them, not because they were bad people, but because they hadn't got a clue about running a football club, as none of them had ever done it before," bemoaned Blackwell. "I think they lasted six months before they went bankrupt and then Ken Bates came in and bought it for a quid, or whatever.

"So, I had to deal with not only the problems on the pitch, but off the pitch, and the club has never been in the state it was when I took it over. It had never been bankrupt, and it had never lost every player.

"It was the toughest thing I have ever done in my career, to manage both on and off the pitch. It was a nightmare, but I went on to turn it around."

Of the Premier League players, only veteran South African defender Lucas Radebe, an injured Seth Johnson, Norwegian Eirik Bakke, a past-his-best Michael Duberry and the Irish stalwart Gary Kelly remained.

A long list of talent had departed and the prospect of life outside of European competition and the Premier League saw the vultures circle above Elland Road. Fans picked up their daily newspaper in trepidation that another story of a prized asset being stripped away from the club would surface.

The club's best talent was being poached by teams that Leeds had until recently been scouring further down the table to find their name. Paul Robinson, Ian Harte, Dominic Matteo, Danny Mills, Stephen McPhail and Mark Viduka had all moved on to pastures new.

David Batty had called time on a long and distinguished career when injuries caught up with him. And then, at the other end of his career, there was James Milner, the wonder kid midfielder. At the start of a glittering career that Leeds fans had envisaged would be played in a white shirt.

Milner had played nearly 50 league games for Leeds after making his debut as a 16-year-old in 2002. "What little money the club owed me I gave up to help them and they got a transfer fee," Milner told *FourFourTwo* in 2018, when looking back at his £5million move to Newcastle. "It was portrayed to me that it was in the best interests of the club due to all the financial difficulties. I thought I was doing the right thing by the club. It was very tough to get relegated and there were a lot of financial things going on."

Another local hero, the player the fans had related to more than any other, was striker Alan Smith. After making his debut at 18 years old, in a 3-1 win over Liverpool at Anfield in November 1998, when he scored his first senior goal, Smith was the epitome to supporters of what it should mean to be a Leeds United player.

"I was just a kid playing football, still living with my mum and dad, so I didn't know what was going on behind the scenes," Smith explained to *Training Ground Guru* in February 2017. "When we sold Rio Ferdinand, it made some sense. Manchester United had offered £30m, so you could understand it.

"It was when Jonathan Woodgate left that I realised something was badly wrong. He had come through the youth team with me, was a big character, our best defender, an England international and I knew he had no desire to leave."

But on 26 May 2004, it was announced that Smith was not only leaving, but the fans' favourite was heading to bitter rivals Manchester United. He had instantly become a traitor in the perception of many.

"I've never spoken about it because I've never felt I had to justify myself," Smith suggested. "By trying to justify the move I would have dragged the name of Leeds United through the mud and been disrespectful to Man Utd, by suggesting I only went there because I had to. I did say on telly that I'd never play for Man Utd. But Leeds always said they'd never sell me, and I thought they'd never get relegated.

"The new owners of the club told me that if I didn't sign for Man Utd, there was a chance Leeds might go under," Smith explained. "Man Utd weren't offering the most, but they were paying up front.

"I understood why people slagged me off, I did it myself when Eric Cantona left Leeds for Man Utd. But I was joining the biggest club in Britain, and it was a massive honour that Sir Alex Ferguson wanted me."

Blackwell could also understand Smith's move. "I had just become the manager when Smithy went to Manchester United and everybody was leaving. Alan Smith wasn't the only one that left that summer. Mark Viduka went to Middlesbrough, Danny Mills went to Man City. Everybody left.

"And Manchester United came in, our big rivals, and Smudger was as proud a Leeds man as you got. You cut him open and he's Leeds United through-and-through. But here was an opportunity to go to the league champions.

"We'd suffered as a club and he'd suffered more than anybody, as he felt it more than anybody else. But what do you do? Do you look at a career, or do you look at a situation where the club is nose-diving? When we went down that year we were red hot favourites to go straight through the Championship into League One.

Everything had to be sold. Players were sold, the training ground was sold, I think the main stadium Elland Road was sold. They had to somehow try and rectify the massive financial catastrophe that had got the club and every player was for sale. James Milner, Scott Carson, Aaron Lennon, it was phenomenal."

As the mass exodus continued, Blackwell was left with the unenviable challenge of piecing together a squad for the 2004/05 season that would be capable of proving the bookmakers wrong.

"From that point onward, it was clear we were in a downward spiral and it was an unhappy club," Blackwell said. "I've never come across a club that was so unhappy and it was a real strain on the staff. It was a terrible place to work, I'll be honest with you.

"I think it became apparent when we played Manchester United at home and it was an early game that was live on TV. On the Friday before, a document on the finances had been produced from London, because we were a PLC company, and it showed we were £121million or something in debt. At that point we all knew we were in the..."

Blackwell paused, but it doesn't take too much imagination to finish his sentence.

"It was every other Friday the club had to go to London to get dispensation from the PLC company to carry on trading. We'd get cleared for another fortnight and then another fortnight and they were trying to find buyers for the club.

"Trevor Birch had come in as acting chairman, but he was an insolvency practitioner and every other Friday he was going down to London to fight the case and say what he was doing.

"It was just incredible and the uneasy feeling within the club that every fortnight we'd wait to see if we were going into bankruptcy. It had a very unsettling effect on all the staff. Perhaps not the players so much, but certainly all the staff around the club. At the end of it, about 200 people lost their jobs.

"It was the first time that a club of our stature had gone into this kind of financial meltdown and it was very difficult to concentrate on the football. The talk was that players were leaving. They were trying to raise money. All the players were available.

"It was so destabilising. It was one of the things that I wrote a dissertation on for a pro licence and it was about the stability of a football club and how it affects the staff and the everyday running of it. And in this particular case, it was shown by the results. With some of the players we still had, the results should have been there, but from day to day players were coming and they were going."

In January 2005, amid rumours that the club was close to going into administration, or worse out of existence altogether, an unidentified group led by former Chelsea chairman Ken Bates moved in with a £10million rescue package.

Blackwell continued in his role as manager and brought in strikers David Healy and Rob Hulse.

I remember clearly sitting in the West Stand as Rob Hulse smashed in a stunning brace on his debut in a 3-1 win over Reading. The goal I remember vividly saw Hulse run on to a ball which bounced up nicely in front of him and he crashed a volley into the back of the net from 25-plus yards. *We are on to something here*, I remember thinking.

The manager recruited wisely, bringing in players on loan and free transfers. He effectively pulled off a miracle. He'd brought in a record number of new faces and Leeds avoided relegation finishing in 14th place.

"I think one of the biggest things I remember was the first game of that first season in the Championship when we played Derby at home live on Sky," said Blackwell. "We won 1-0 and Frazer Richardson got the goal.

"The stadium announcer was still announcing the Leeds United team when the game kicked off because he was saying, 'Welcome to Leeds United — Neil Sullivan. Welcome to Leeds United — Sean Gregan. Welcome to Leeds United — Paul Butler,' nearly all the way through the team sheet.

"Gary Kelly was the only one that played the last game of the previous season at Chelsea. I think I brought in a record number of signings, 16 players that summer.

"I knew I had to sign players that were battle hardened in the Championship. The first couple of years that Leeds United played in that division, 90% of the teams that we played lost their next game. They'd give everything against us. I remember going to Sheffield Wednesday and it was a tight game and their manager Paul Sturrock said in the papers afterwards that he wished his players could play like that every week. That was the problem we had.

"I went and signed players in Sean Gregan, Paul Butler, Shaun Derry, Rob Hulse, Neil Sullivan and Richard Creswell, who knew their way around the division and all of a sudden the club started to change, and we became a force in the Championship."

Blackwell made a record number of signings and concentrated on players he viewed as talented and who knew their way around the Championship, but had never been in the Premier League or at a big club.

Early results disappointed, but a play-off run materialised towards the end of the season until the form tailed off and a mid-table finish had to be settled for. It was enough for new chairman to shelve any plans he may have had to bring in a higher profile name.

Bates backed Blackwell in the transfer market as proven strikers Richard Cresswell, Rob Hulse and Robbie Blake were signed. Former England midfielder, Steve Stone, arrived and American Eddie Lewis as a creative playmaker. But off the pitch things were still looking grim.

"The club was absolutely fucked, no matter which way they did it," Blackwell told me. "Ken Bates came in and to be fair he stabilised the club. At that point, the wages weren't going to be paid, the conglomerate that owned the club just couldn't pay anything.

"Working with Ken in those initial stages was really good as he was a very experienced administrator in football. He was the sort of person Leeds needed at the time as it was haemorrhaging money left, right and centre. You go from fish tanks and full-time drivers waiting in Porsche cars outside the offices. The club had been so badly run; it was unbelievable.

"Ken got people to change their mentality on how they did things at Elland Road and he was lucky because I turned the team around quite quickly and the crowds were up, and we got to the play-off final and that brought in significant money."

Home form was excellent, eight wins in 10 matches over Christmas and by the end of February Leeds were 3rd in the table and automatic promotion was very much on the radar. They appeared hot on the heels of Sheffield United with Reading blazing a trail at the top of the table. Leeds were playing some great football, attacking teams on their travels with Hulse, Healy and Blake scoring regular goals and a defence conceding only 38 goals throughout the entire regular season.

Once again, however, form dipped during the run-in. Only one win was secured in the last 10 matches and 5th in the table threw them into the lottery of the play-offs.

It had been a game in Southampton on 19 November that Blackwell remembers with tangible delight.

"We were 3-0 down with 18 minutes to go and we came back and won 4-3," Blackwell enthused. Chris Moyles on Radio One, every morning that week, played the Adam Pope BBC commentary and you can hardly hear him because his voice has gone. The atmosphere was electric. And that was the point, it turned the season on its head, and we went on to get to the play-off final.

"To be fair to Southampton, they played really well and were battering us," he added. "And the Leeds fans had stuck with us and to be able to repay them with one of the best comebacks ever was special. It was just fabulous; it was away from home and it turned our season on its head. From that point onwards we were the form team of the Championship.

"That year, Sheffield United and Reading ran away early on in the season and with seven-or-so games to go we played Reading at home and were winning 1-0 and with about a minute to go they got an equaliser and that really put Sheffield United up.

"Our next game was Sheffield United away and we drew 1-1. We were the only club then that got anywhere near them."

A goal from American Eddie Lewis had earned a 1-1 draw with Preston in the first leg of the play-off semi-final at Elland Road. At Deepdale in the second leg, goals from Rob Hulse and Frazer Richardson took Leeds to the final. That 2-0 semi-final success would be the highpoint of Blackwell's tenure.

I remember queuing for several hours on a balmy Leeds day to get my tickets for the Millennium Stadium, where 40,000 Leeds fans would join me to watch the Whites take on Watford for the right to return to the top flight. On the same day, ITV's *X-Factor* were holding auditions and some auditionees gave impromptu turns as they left the ground clutching papers that denoted whether they had made it through to the next round.

There is no doubt Watford deserved to win the play-off final against a somewhat subdued Leeds side. As I drove the tortuous route out of Cardiff and back up north, the snail of vehicles were occupied by sombre looking inhabitants or Watford supporters who could not hide their delight. The repercussions of that result could not have been exemplified better.

If anything, despite that play-off defeat, Blackwell had Leeds ahead of schedule in their bid to climb out of their problems. But Leeds at that stage were not a club accustomed to recognising anyone with credit in the bank.

"The club was being rebuilt and it was frustrating to see players leave after that final as well," Blackwell stated. "For that match in Cardiff, Rob Hulse and Richard Creswell were injured and Stephen Crainey had been sent off in the semi-final, so they couldn't play in the final.

"Ahead of the transfer deadline, I had asked the club to bring in two strikers because I knew Rob Hulse had got a hip injury and Creswell was coming back from a knee injury, so we were very much down on strikers. I'd only got them and David Healy and we ran out of strikers in the final and that's a thing you look back on. If we had bought the two strikers it was worth £100million to us to go up and surely it was worth bringing a couple of strikers in and paying a few grand out.

"I had a meeting with Ken Bates straight after the final because he was going away on holiday and I told him that with two or three more players we had a real chance. That never happened, so I do feel bitterly, bitterly let down.

"I knew what I was doing. I went on to Sheffield United and took them on to the play-off final, I've taken Cardiff into the Premier League, so I've done it on quite a few occasions. I know what I am doing and to be let down like that is the biggest hurt of my career by a mile.

"But the disappointing thing for me after the final was that I had just started to build a team. There was no way that process could be finished so quickly. We were rebuilding the biggest club outside of the Premier League and the team everyone wanted to play against."

The disappointment of the play-off final defeat seemed to have been carried into the 2006/07 season, which turned out to be the worst in the club's 87-year history.

Although Blackwell did not survive to see it, the season brought relegation to League One and the first time United had been in the third tier of English football in their history.

Blackwell was sacked on 20 September 2006 after his team lost five of the opening eight matches of the 2006/07 season and were in 23rd in the Championship table. His assistant, John Carver, took temporary charge, but after a 5-1 defeat to Luton in his fifth match, United were in 23rd position in the league and a new manager was found.

A month later, Blackwell made it public that he was taking legal action against the club for wrongful dismissal after it was revealed he had been dismissed for gross misconduct because of "negative comments made in the press about the club's finances."

"It's not a nice way to go out after putting so much into a club," Blackwell added ruefully. "Even now I have a gagging order on me, and I can't tell everybody the things that I would want to say and get out there. So people that are wondering, 'Why did he do that?' can understand and think, 'Ah, now I know why he did that.'

"If you look at my record at Leeds United, it's one of the best of the last 16 years and under the biggest damning time of the club's history, the worst time ever, and I can hold my head up high. I've been in all kinds of places around the world and Leeds fans have come up to me and that's nice.

"So generally, I've got the utmost respect for the club and, like I say, half of my family are still season ticket holders at Elland Road. If I go for Sunday dinner with the family somewhere, one of them will always be talking about Leeds because they've just come back from the game, or whatever.

My relationship with Ken turned into a negative one because I was being asked, quite rightly, by the press guys, 'You've got this £5 or £6million, what are you going to do with it, when are you going to be spending it?' Under Ken's rules, you are not allowed to be talking about finances at the football club, but I was the only one that the press ever spoke to because Ken wasn't there, he lived in Monaco and there were no other directors at the club.

It was the obvious question for the press to ask. The finances of the club had been in the public domain for the previous three years because we'd blown all our money, so I'd always been asked about the finances from the moment I took over. How do you tell the press that you are not going to talk about signing players when you are trying to sell season tickets and inject positive enthusiasm to the fans? I wanted to say that we were not just hanging around, we were going to give it a go.

"That was it though. I knew in my heart of hearts that it was all over,"

Blackwell continued. "The Leeds fans have been great to me. Even when I left and even now when I go to other clubs I always get emails from the supporters' club. I think everybody knew that the club was in such a terrible place. I hope they recognise the job that I did for Leeds United."

Blackwell was enough of a football man to recognise the size of the job he had taken on. Insignificant milestones to others meant a lot to him. He was an early graduate of the League Managers Association certificate in applied management at Warwick University. But more than that, he was a natural student of the sport. After leaving Leeds United, he sought to further his future managerial credentials by visiting teams like Real Madrid and Inter Milan to soak up their training methods and coaching techniques in a quest to build his knowledge base.

"I know it sounds trite, but when I got over 44 days, I knew I had done longer than the great Brian Clough," Blackwell recalled. "It's stupid little things. When people ask me what it was like to manage Leeds United, it was an honour and a privilege, and I just felt like I had earned the respect to be treated better than Ken treated me at the end. But he did it to Ruud Gullit and others, so in that respect I don't feel left out.

"I know what could have been. I know where Leeds should be, its status in the game and I know what it can achieve.

"When you think you've come from the very bottom and you've got the club already close to the Premier League. Two or three players and we've got a chance, and to see that ripped from underneath you, and you can't say anything and yet you're getting hammered by people saying, 'You should be doing this,' and yes, we should be, but if you're not being allowed to do it, there's nothing you can do.

"I don't think anyone thought it would take this long to turn the financial side of the club around to allow it to be sustainable and move forward. I look back at that financial guy who told me that the club would be shagged for 10 years and I thought, 'No, it won't,' not if we can sell him and do this and whatever. He was right."

Blackwell also believed he became very close to becoming the man that Leeds United supporters would have taken to their hearts. For the man that delivers a return to the Premier League would become a legend.

"Oh, I knew that, and I knew how close I was to be that legend at Leeds United," he admitted ruefully. "But the difference between me and Bielsa is, Bielsa has had money to spend and I had no money. I did it all through plaiting sawdust.

"I think when the history is rolled out and people look at who did what, where and when, I think I'll come near the top. And that's not being big-headed, it's because of the situation the club was in, the finances, the direction of travel from the board above.

"I think people will look back and think, 'Okay, I didn't know that, he's done a decent job,' and I think most of the Leeds fans recognise that and they've been very magnanimous towards me and I appreciate it."

Blackwell has been blighted by financial restraints throughout much of his managerial career. He returned to manage his hometown club Luton Town in March 2007 and left the role when the club entered administration. It had got so bad at Kenilworth Road that Blackwell paid some of the younger players out of his own pocket.

He returned to Bramall Lane in February 2008 to replace Bryan Robson as Sheffield United manager. Relegated back to the Championship the season before, Blackwell halted the slump and ended the 2007/08 season in 9th, just four points off the play-offs.

The following season he led the Blades to the play-offs where they were beaten by Burnley in the 2009 final. He left Sheffield United on 14 August 2010 and after a two-year break took control of a Bury side that were seven points adrift of safety, but then again financial problems got in the way. A transfer embargo was put in force, players were sold and Bury were relegated from League One and Blackwell left the club.

He had fallen out with Warnock, such an important figure in his career, when he had moved to Leeds United, but was reunited with him at Crystal Palace in 2014 and then a stint working with Martin Allen at Barnet followed in 2015. Warnock took him to QPR and then Rotherham where they kept the Millers clear of relegation from the Championship.

In October 2016, Blackwell again teamed up with Warnock and Ronnie Jepson, as assistant manager at Cardiff City, where they gained promotion to the Premier League. Despite relegation after one season, Warnock remained in charge after coming somewhat of a cult figure in the Welsh capital.

23

DENNIS WISE

2006–2008

Us against the world

Born: 16 December 1966, Kensington, London

Matches	Won	Drawn	Lost	Points	Pts/Match	Win %
99	47	19	33	160	1.61	47.47%
				RANK	7th/36	6th/36

The biggest rivalry Leeds United have is with Manchester United. The Roses rivalry dates back to the Wars of the Roses in the 15th century. Some would suggest that Leeds and Manchester folk are born to revile each other.

Independent research by the Football Fans Census conducted in 2009 has shown that, within English football, both Leeds and Manchester United were ranked within the top three clubs based on the number of clubs that consider them to be their rivals.

In the report titled 'Rivalry Uncovered!' Leeds fans cited Manchester United as their main rivals, yet supporters of the Old Trafford had different fish to fry with Liverpool shown as their main adversaries, with Manchester City and Arsenal next in line.

The rivalry between the two Uniteds, separated by the Pennines, had begun in the 1960s when Leeds had begun to consistently compete at the top of the English game. With both sides fighting for the League and FA Cup double in 1965, the FA Cup semi-final between the sides had degenerated into a series of horrific tackles and off-the-ball skirmishes. Fans spilled ill-feeling onto the terraces and then into Nottingham and Sheffield after the game.

Under Revie, Leeds had the better of encounters on the pitch with the Manchester side winning only three of 25 games played until they were relegated in 1974. The hatred between the sides intensified.

Joe Jordan and Gordon McQueen moved from Leeds to Manchester in 1978 as "Judas" became a regular taunt from the terraces. Johnny Giles and Gordon Strachan moved the other way, and both made a huge impact at Elland Road.

And then Eric Cantona, a hero of Leeds United's title-winning season in 1992, moved to Old Trafford and played a huge part in landing the Old Trafford side their first league title for 26 years. Cantona's Elland Road return was not welcomed amidst a febrile atmosphere.

Since then, Manchester United have dominated English football as Leeds bounced up and down the divisions. The animosity felt by Leeds fans has often stemmed from an inferiority complex as the team in red regularly enjoyed greater success

And to cap it off, Alan Smith, Elland Road's young badge-kissing prodigy, moved to the 'dark side' as the financial wheels flew from the Leeds bus as the club sank from Premier League status.

Leeds fans believed that their legendary manager, Don Revie, deserved more public acclaim when he died in 1989. The latter years of Revie's life had seen him dogged by controversy.

When Sir Matt Busby died in 1994, the one-minute silence at Ewood Park was marred by hundreds of travelling Leeds fans chanting, "There's only one Don Revie." The incident and subsequent condemnation embarrassed Revie's memory and the club. Elsie Revie, the Don's widow said that her husband would have been "horrified" by the lack of respect shown. A "numb" Leeds Manager, Howard Wilkinson, said that the supporters were "out of touch with the rest of football." Leeds chairman, Leslie Silver, vowed to ban the offenders for life.

The last time Manchester United visited Leeds, the away coach, that usually drops the visiting team outside the West Stand, was driven inside as thousands of Leeds supporters shouted abuse. The team and their supporters are "scum" in each other's eyes.

Despite Leeds falling out of the top flight, the chant, "We all hate Leeds scum," is still sung at Old Trafford. The feeling is mutual, yet Leeds's decline has led Manchester United to largely forget about them as they have more current rivals and bigger fish to fry.

The desire of Leeds fans to return to the top makes that feeling of hostility stronger. It is aspirational. Leeds want that fierce rivalry back because, when it does return in full strength, the club will be back with the big boys once again.

Next in line for the Whites fans' derision in the Census was Chelsea, with Liverpool listed in third. The Chelsea bitterness harks back to the 1960s when the clubs contested some fierce and often contentious tussles. Both teams were in their pomp, facing-off for domestic and European titles. In the 1970 FA Cup final, the feud had boiled over in an overly physical battle. It was stubborn Yorkshire mettle against flash London swank. There had also been numerous hooligan clashes off the pitch, as fan fighting blighted the game through the 1970s and 1980s.

"It always rears its ugly head, even when we're nowhere near them," claimed Rick Glanvill in the *Official Chelsea Biography*, published in

2006. "As predictably as the late plod of Corporal Jones' foot, when Leeds fans gather in any stand, they will sing their song about their Cockney rivals. 'Fetch your father's gun and shoot the Chelsea scum.' Chelsea fans still sometimes reciprocate with an elegy to the hatred of Leeds over the tune of 'The Dambusters March'."

Leeds already had a former Chelsea man as their chairman. Outspoken Ken Bates, who had said during his Stamford Bridge days, "I shall not rest until Leeds United are kicked out of the Football League. Their fans are the scum of the earth, absolute animals and a disgrace. I will do everything in my power to make sure this happens."

Despite iconic former Leeds player, Norman Hunter, saying, "Ken Bates has never been afraid to shirk any responsibilities," and the chairman doing a lot of good work behind the scenes during his time at Elland Road, he was always on the back foot. A man synonymous with an enemy, who has been hugely critical, is never going to be universally supported, whatever he achieved in trying to save the club from extinction.

Bates made his first managerial appointment in the north bringing in his friend from their Chelsea days, Dennis Wise, as the new boss, with Gus Poyet his assistant. The pair had taken charge of Swindon Town on 22 May 2006, winning six of their first seven games and flying to the top of the League Two table.

On 20 September 2006, the former Chelsea midfielder was first linked with the vacant position. Initially, compensation couldn't be agreed, and Swindon offered Wise and Poyet improved deals. The pair had a clause in their contracts that allowed them to talk to Premier League and Championship sides and they could move if compensation was agreed. It proved a tricky negotiation to begin with, but an improved Leeds offer resulted in the appointment being confirmed on 24 October 2007. Wise was the new Leeds boss with Poyet his assistant and Andrew Beasley, the goalkeeping coach. At the time, Swindon were 3rd having taken 31 points from 15 games.

It was certainly not a universally popular move. Some men would have attempted to distance themselves from their Chelsea connections, but Bates was never a man that gave much credence to a PR strategy that pandered.

"After much deliberation the unanimous choice was Dennis Wise and his assistant Gus Poyet," Bates told the media. "I am aware that he may not be everybody's cup of tea, but this is not a popularity contest. It is a question of the right man to resolve a serious situation."

A popular appointment gets much more time to prove himself, whilst someone less fancied is required to hit the ground near top speed. But Bates, who had always been his own man, knew Wise's character and had seen the instant success he had experienced with Swindon.

Wise and Poyet were at Elland Road on the day of their appointment to watch the 3-1 defeat to Southend United in the League Cup. The pair were applauded as they performed a lap of the pitch to say hello to the fans.

Wise took over a side that lay second from bottom in the Championship and told the media that his former association with Chelsea was not a problem and he was intent on taking Leeds United back to the Premier League.

Leeds's next game was against Southend United again, this time in the league, and the new management team got off to a great start with a 2-0 win. It was, however, a struggle from then on and nine wins and six draws from the remaining 32 matches of the season was not enough to escape relegation.

Wise's side would have finished in the bottom three anyway, but a 10-point deduction from the Football League had confirmed their fate with a game remaining in the season and meant bottom spot. The penalty came because the club had gone into administration.

Leeds United were condemned to playing in League One, the third tier of English football, for the first time in their history.

And to make matters worse for Wise, who Bates kept in position, a further 15-point penalty was given ahead of the 2007/08 season after KPMG, the administrators, refused to resurrect the Company Voluntary Arrangement (CVA).

Right-back Radostin Kishishev played 10 games for Leeds United during the 2006/07 season. Despite United's fall down the divisions, the following quote from the Bulgarian showed that the club's name had not lost significance in the world of football: "When I finish with football, I will be able to say, 'I played for Leeds.' No one will ask me which division I was in. They will just know it was the biggest club I have played for."

Starting adrift of the rest of the sides in League One seemed to galvanise the team who won their first seven matches of the new campaign, but the season turned again when Poyet was lured away by Tottenham Hotspur to become their assistant manager.

Many pundits felt Poyet had been the tactical nous of the management team and without him Wise might struggle. To counter that, Dave Bassett, who had managed Wise at Wimbledon, was recruited as the new assistant at Elland Road.

The perfect start ended on 3 November when an away trip to Carlisle saw Leeds beaten 3-1, but remarkably, given the minus 15-point start, the Whites were top of the table on Boxing Day and 3rd as 2008 began.

But as fans began to dream of a rapid return to the Championship, a shock announcement on 28 January 2008 confirmed that Wise had left the club. He had accepted a role as executive director of football at Newcastle United. Leeds were 5th in League One and one point adrift of the automatic promotion places.

Wise was rumoured to have become completely disenchanted with life at Leeds. Poyet's departure had hit him hard and, as with all managers during this period, the financial backdrop was far from encouraging. Without Poyet too, his tactics were often naive. The Newcastle job allowed him to spend a couple of days in the north-east and the rest of his time in London.

But Wise had cultivated an "us against the world" culture which had seen his Leeds side in the frame for promotion, despite the 15-point start it had been forced to give the competition. Despite his Chelsea-heavy CV, Wise was winning over the fans.

Ultimately, anyone that brings success to Elland Road becomes 'one of our own', but that goodwill swiftly disappeared once Wise jumped ship before he'd finished the job.

24

GARY McALLISTER

2008

"Liverpool vs Manchester United is a great following fixture but Leeds vs Manchester United is pure hatred"

Born: 25 December 1964, Motherwell, Scotland

Matches	Won	Drawn	Lost	Points	Pts/Match	Win %
50	25	8	17	83	1.66	50.00%
				RANK	5th/36	3rd/36

After nearly four years out of the game, the Whites appointed club legend Gary McAllister as Dennis Wise's successor at Elland Road. Wise had left the team in sixth place before he'd upped sticks and headed to the north-east.

The Scotsman had been a Leeds United player for six years and had played a pivotal role in the heart of midfield for Howard Wilkinson's title-winning side.

Dave Bassett had briefly served as caretaker before chairman Ken Bates appointed McAllister on 29 January 2008 until the end of the 2007/08 season. Steve Staunton came to Elland Road as his assistant.

After completing a distinguished 19-year playing career, McAllister had moved into management with Coventry City, but resigned 18 months later in December 2003 to look after his wife, Denise, who had been diagnosed with breast cancer. She sadly died in March 2006.

In a move reminiscent of Howard Wilkinson, McAllister's former manager at Elland Road, he was keen to remember former glories, but the pictures of trophy-winning sides from the past had once again been hidden away.

"All the pictures have been put back up, of all eras," McAllister said shortly after his return. "I want to see the team that I was fortunate enough to play in under Howard Wilkinson. They are things that should be around a football club. Is it something for the current crop to aspire to? I hope so.

"I watched as they had a great run in the Champions League," he stated. "Then after that it was all disappointment as it started to go the other way with the financial problems.

"Anybody who has an association with Leeds was in despair when the club was drifting, but it's changed. The analogy is the oil tanker that's stopped. I think it's turned and it's starting to go forward again.

"One day we will return to the Premier League, I just hope it's me and some of the guys that are in this team that are part of it. Leeds will come back. We want it to be sooner rather than later. There is a real feeling of momentum."

McAllister had commenced playing for hometown side Motherwell, making 70 appearances and scoring eight goals. It was enough to impress Leicester City boss Gordon Milne, who brought him to England alongside Motherwell teammate Ally Mauchlen for a combined £350,000 in August 1985. The Foxes were relegated to the Second Division where McAllister's skillful playmaking skills shot him to prominence.

Former Leeds manager Brian Clough had attempted to lure him to Nottingham Forest, but Old Big Head's charms failed to tempt McAllister away from Leicester where he would go on to play 225 matches, scoring 52 goals.

Vinnie Jones had been one of Wilkinson's bigger early buys from Wimbledon at £600,000. Jones had quickly become a cult hero figure in the 1989/90 promotion to the First Division. The robust, ankle-crunching midfielder was sold to Sheffield United as Wilkinson drafted in 26-year-old McAllister for £100,000 to add quality in the centre of the park.

A fourth-place finish in McAllister's first season was followed by the League title in 1991/92, as McAllister and fellow Scot, Gordon Strachan, forged a formidable partnership in midfield. Their dominance allowed younger players like Gary Speed and David Batty to blossom around them, the four players becoming the engine room of Leeds's success. McAllister's set-pieces often provided the ammunition for Lee Chapman's finishing.

McAllister would captain Leeds in two of the seasons that followed, including leading the team out at Wembley in the 3-0 League Cup final defeat to Aston Villa. In all, he played 294 games for Leeds United and bagged 45 goals.

Ron Atkinson's Coventry City stumped up £3million for McAllister in July 1996, before he was reunited with Strachan who took charge of the Sky Blues in later 1996. As captain, McAllister managed to salvage an improbable Premier League survival with a draw against Arsenal and wins against Chelsea, Liverpool and Spurs.

He would play 140 games for Coventry, scoring 26 goals, before Liverpool came calling. It was a surprise signing, a big club snapping up a 35-year-old on a free transfer. Manager Gerard Houllier would class his capture of McAllister as his "most inspirational signing" as Liverpool claimed a treble in 2000/01 of the UEFA Cup, League Cup and FA Cup and also qualification for the Champions League. He was named man of the match in the UEFA Cup final against Alaves after scoring two, including the decisive golden goal, and assisting three others as Liverpool won 5-4 in extra-time.

McAllister had been superb at Anfield and was named as 32nd in the *100 Players Who Shook The Kop* survey in 2008. With age catching up with him, he left Liverpool after 87 games and nine goals on 13 May 2002 to become player-manager at his former club Coventry City.

He had become known as 'The Enforcer' during his career, commanding the midfield, creative and never giving up.

McAllister also played 57 times for his country Scotland between 1990 and 1999 and was captain for four of those years. He should have had more caps than he did. He debuted against East Germany ahead of the 1990 World Cup, but did not feature as Scotland went out in the first round. His first of five international goals came against Switzerland in October 1990.

Unfortunately, he is often remembered most internationally for his penalty against hosts England in Euro 1996. David Seaman's spot-kick save enabling England to win 2-0 at Wembley. Scotland were eliminated at the group phase.

He was key to his country's qualification for the 1998 World Cup, only to miss the tournament because of serious knee injury, which saw him out for a year. When he came back against the Czech Republic in March 1999, he was booed by the Celtic Park crowd during the 2-1 defeat. He retired from international football a week later.

"Last week's result against the Czech Republic was a crescendo of a night which had a major bearing on my decision," McAllister announced. "I am extremely disappointed because I know I am still good enough to play at international level and contribute something to the Scotland side. But there comes a point when that type of pressure from a certain section who are looking for me not to do well, whether that be the fans or in the media, becomes too much.

"It has been a difficult decision to make because it's every player's dream to play for his country and I came into international football relatively late in my career. To give up before my time is very disappointing indeed."

Despite the best efforts of the Scottish Football Association and manager Craig Brown, McAllister would not reconsider.

After leaving Liverpool, his stint as player-manager with Coventry lasted a little over seven months before he resigned to spend more time with his family after his wife was diagnosed with cancer.

Personal grief kept him away from the game. Football can move on quickly without you and there was a danger that might be it for McAllister in the sport. But Leeds United picked up the phone.

McAllister's first game in charge was away at Southend and Leeds were beaten 1-0. He struggled to make an immediate impact, having to wait until his fifth match before claiming a win, 1-0 away at Swindon Town. Leeds had slipped out of the play-off spots, but McAllister began to turn the tide with a first home win in the next game, 2-0 against Bournemouth.

As results improved, just two defeats in 12 games, Bates gave McAllister a new 12-month rolling contract in April 2018 as Leeds secured a place in the end-of-season play-offs.

McAllister had begun to forge a side in the style of his own play. One that passed the ball and entertained.

"There has been change," he insisted. "There's been a different ethos, training has changed. We just gradually fed it to the players, and they've bought into everything.

"I can't honestly say it's my team. Dougie Freedman is the only player I've brought in, and he's a loan signing. But the players are buying into any tactical stuff that's passed on to them. The effort and work rate is something I associated with this group before I started working with them."

United secured a play-off spot with a 1-0 win away at Yeovil on 25 April 2008. Carlisle had led the play-off semi-final 1st leg at Elland Road 2-0 before on loan Crystal Palace striker Dougie Freedman pulled one back in the 96th minute. The visitors had fully merited their victory and John Ward's side were hot favourites to complete the task on home soil.

The Whites were on the brink of elimination when Jonny Howson scored a late goal at Brunton Park, set up by Dougie Freedman, to secure a 2-0 win on the night and a 3-2 aggregate success.

19-year-old Howson had opened his account from close range in the 10th minute when he converted a Freedman cross. Keeper Casper Ankergren saved well from Marc Bridge-Wilkinson just before the break to keep the teams level on aggregate.

McAllister's men pushed forward looking for a second as Bradley Johnson crashed a header against the post towards the end, before Howson secured a Wembley trip with his brace.

McAllister's team had earned the chance to banish the disappointment of their defeat to Watford at the Millennium Stadium two years earlier. They had overcome the odds of a 15-point deficit at the beginning of the season to be on the brink of promotion back to the Championship. Without the points deduction, Leeds would have finished as runners-up in League One and secured automatic promotion.

In the League One play-off final, however, they fell victim to fellow Yorkshire side, Doncaster Rovers, who had finished third in the regular season. It was the Whites' first Wembley appearance for 12 years and the pressure was on to ensure the club's only experience of third-tier football would span just one season.

McAllister was able to name an unchanged side for the final after top scoring striker Jermaine Beckford shrugged off an ankle injury: Casper Ankergren, Frazer Richardson, Lubomir Michalik, Paul Huntington, Bradley Johnson, Neil Kilkenny, Jonny Howson, Jonathan Douglas, David Prutton (Tresor Kandol 69), Jermaine Beckford, Dougie Freedman (Andy Hughes 78). Subs: David Lucas, Rui Marques, Alan Sheehan.

The club had sold its allocation of over 36,000, but with many more Leeds fans attending they were estimated to have outnumbered their Doncaster counterparts by at least 10,000.

"We'll all go onto the pitch together," McAllister said before the final. "In the Treble season I had with Liverpool we had a wee bit of luck; it was the right place at the right time. You've got to draw on these things, it would be foolish not to."

Doncaster owner John Ryan said: "We're not a big club like Leeds United. We're only a pub side having a laugh, you know."

Ryan had purchased Rovers for £50,000 a decade earlier and had been in the Conference just five seasons before. They had played superb attacking football to batter Southend in the second leg of their play-off semi-final.

Heartbreakingly for Leeds, a second-half James Hayter bullet header after 47 minutes, meant that it would be Sean O'Driscoll's Doncaster that would become a 2008/09 Championship side.

Casper Ankergren was kept busy in the first half, denying Hayter and James Coppinger as Doncaster threatened to overpower Leeds. Despite great endeavour after falling behind early in the second half, Leeds failed to trouble former player Neil Sullivan in the Rovers net. The closest Leeds came to a leveller was a late Jonathan Douglas shot that whistled over the bar. The victory secured Doncaster Rovers their third promotion in five years and would see them in the English second tier for the first time since 1957.

"We huffed and puffed, and we gave it every ounce of our energy, but in the final third our final ball or effort on goal lacked quality," McAllister reflected after the defeat. "I didn't think we chose the right execution of crossing, passing or shooting. It goes without saying that it's very disappointing.

"But what I've tried to impress on the guys in the dressing room, who are obviously very low, is that each of those individuals should be proud of what they've done. Myself, and the coaching staff, are very proud of what they've achieved, and I think the Leeds fans are as well.

"To start a campaign with such a hefty handicap and to get right to the final play-off match deserves to be applauded. They've continually got up and got on with it, and it's quite simple — that group of players won 27 games, gained 91 points and barring the handicap they would have been promoted.

"I've got to say that I think the players have got the stomach to come back. They'll go away this summer and regroup, and there's going to be a hardcore of these guys back at Leeds United next season. It's going to be busy for myself and the chairman over the summer trying to recruit people that can make us better. I'm better off myself after 20 games at this level of football.

"We've got to go into next season positive. I know it's difficult to say that at the moment, but we will.

"The fans here are superb. They are second to none, they have backed us all season long … Our average crowd is over 26,500 and there were well over 36,000 at Wembley, and that speaks volumes. We'll be back."

Leeds entered the 2008/09 season as the bookmakers' favourites for promotion and hopes were high. They entered November in second place. 10 wins and a draw from the first 18 league matches, built around entertaining and attacking football, saw them occupying a play-off place. But December saw the form slump and a leaky defence lead to five defeats in six games.

Chief executive Shaun Harvey suggested the players were primarily responsible for the slump, stating, "When the players go out on to the pitch on a Saturday afternoon, they are the only ones who can influence things. We have to get things right and the players have got to start stepping up to the mark.

"Gary is responsible for the players on a day-to-day basis and they work as a unit, but even Gary loses control when it turns over to the players on the pitch," Harvey said. "He is there to guide, encourage and advise, but ultimately if the issue is one of errors of an individual nature there is nothing anyone can do about that."

But it was ultimately McAllister who would carry the can after failing to build on the previous season's play-off exploits. Supporters were not content to settle for the lottery of the play-offs, seeking instead automatic promotion. A section of fans began to call for the manager's head and the Scot could only survive until December, despite telling the media that the situation had not reached "crisis level".

After a 2-1 home loss to Colchester on 13 December, McAllister said: "If we're out of position in the league or unable to pass the ball four feet to each other, then it would be a crisis. I don't think it's quite at crisis level."

He had added that he was at the lowest point of his managerial career. "It's not nice and I'm not enjoying it. We've got a fantastic support here who must be feeling it as well. But I'm going to keep going. When you're in these situations as a player or a manager you've just got to grind it out and get to the other end. There's no point sitting in the corner and sulking."

One sensed he could hear the knives being sharpened. He was right. He was sacked on 21 December 2008 after a run of five successive defeats, including an embarrassing FA Cup exit at non-league part-timers Histon, and ending with a 3-1 loss to MK Dons.

The team had sunk to ninth in the Championship, 15 points behind Leicester at the top of the table and five points adrift of the play-offs. Former Leeds assistant manager, and current Spurs assistant, Gus Poyet, was listed by bookmakers as the favourite to replace McAllister.

"The decision was made to ensure that the new manager has the maximum number of games possible to move the club up the table," a club statement announced. It continued that it wanted to give a new manager enough time to "identify any new players he thinks can strengthen the current squad" during the transfer window.

"Some of the fans were getting frustrated, but it's a minority that start that chanting, and most fans would understand that McAllister tried to bring some flair into the team," said Ray Fell, chairman of the Leeds United Supporters' Club. "I do feel sympathy for the manager, the players have let him down. I sincerely hope whoever comes in is someone with the charisma and personality to lift the players and get them playing."

A little under a year after his Elland Road exit, McAllister had talks with the Scottish Football Association about a coaching role with the national team, but he turned their offer down, holding out for a return to club football.

On 20 May 2010, Gordon Strachan, by now Middlesbrough manager, appointed McAllister his first-team coach. Four months later, he became Gerard Houllier's assistant at Aston Villa and when Houllier was rushed to hospital, McAllister was made caretaker manager for the 1-1 draw with Stoke in the Premier League. His team beat Aston Villa, Arsenal and Liverpool and as a result he was installed until the end of the 2010/11 season.

McAllister seemed in pole position to take over permanently from Houllier when he had to relinquish his job due to ill health, but Alex McLeish was appointed in June 2011 and McAllister was not made part of his coaching team.

He became Liverpool first-team coach at Liverpool under Brendan Rogers in July 2015, but reverted to the position of club ambassador in October 2015 when Rogers was sacked. McAllister then joined Rangers as Steven Gerrard's assistant manager on 4 May 2018.

In the 2001 New Year's Honours List, McAllister was awarded an MBE for his contribution to football and in 2016 was inducted to the Scottish Football Hall of Fame.

25

SIMON GRAYSON

2008–2012

"I knew what every game meant to them"

Born: 16 December 1969, Ripon, Yorkshire

Matches	Won	Drawn	Lost	Points	Pts/Match	Win %
169	84	40	45	292	1.73	49.70%
				RANK	3rd/36	5th/36

For Simon Grayson, managing Leeds United was like coming home. His career in football had begun at Elland Road in June 1986. As a player that could operate in defence or midfield, he only played twice for the club in the four years he was on the club's books.

But what a thrill it must have been to even get the chance to wear the shirt that you'd watched your heroes play in.

"As a young boy, I went to Leeds, Middlesbrough and Southampton for training during the school holidays and, when I got to 14 years old, the age you could sign for a club, Leeds United wanted to sign me," Simon told me. "It was a great thrill.

"On the same day I signed, another 14-year-old signed with me. His name was Gary Speed. We both started our apprenticeships together in 1986. We played in the youth team and the reserves.

"In September 1987, as a 17-year-old, I made my first-team debut," Grayson continued. "A debut in league football was one thing, but to do it for the team you supported was amazing."

It was a fleeting dream, however, as Grayson struggled to break into the first team. Two appearances in four years at Elland Road was a frustration, but one we'd all take off him given half the chance.

"I was in the squad on many occasions after my debut but couldn't quite make the breakthrough on a regular basis," he recalled. "By the time I reached 20 or 21 years old, I realised I had to leave Leeds to further my footballing career.

"In March 1992, I left Elland Road for Leicester City. This was a hard decision, but one I knew I had to make. I needed to play first-team football and three months later I was playing in a play-off final at Wembley. Unfortunately, we lost to Blackburn Rovers, but my career had started.

"Did I think I would ever go back to Leeds in some capacity? My heart would hope to, but my head was realistic that it probably wouldn't happen."

I'd met Simon a few years earlier when I'd been working at Yorkshire County Cricket Club and he was a guest at an evening function. He was the manager of Leeds United at the time and I remember thinking that he was a really nice bloke. I've heard some say he was too genial to make it as a manager. But you don't achieve what he had in the game, both as a player and a manager, without some steel behind the smile.

He signed for Leicester City in March 1992 and played 229 times for the East Midlands club. In five years, he won the League Cup in 1997, Grayson scoring the winner in the semi-final. He was voted the club's player of the season. In 1997, he moved to Aston Villa and then Blackburn Rovers in July 1999, but from there spent much of his time on loan, before signing for Blackpool on a free transfer in July 2002. It was a good move to the 'Seasiders', where he played over 100 times and was made captain of the side and played in the final as Blackpool won the 2003/04 Football League Trophy.

He became a coach at Blackpool in the 2004/05 season, where he managed the reserve squad, before being named as caretaker manager in November 2005. He retired as a player at the end of the 2005/06 season and took Blackpool to promotion to the Championship after beating Yeovil Town in the play-off final at Wembley. That was the 10th successive win of a run of 12 that still stands as the best run of success experienced by Blackpool.

After being linked with the Leeds United managerial job after the departure of Gary McAllister, the Blackpool board refused him permission to talk to Ken Bates. Grayson tendered his resignation, but it was not accepted, and Leeds announced him as their new manager and ultimately settled the dispute for an undisclosed compensation fee.

Grayson took charge for his first game at Elland Road on Boxing Day 2008 against former club Leicester City. His desire to take the Leeds job had been there for all to see.

"Gary McAllister was sacked on the Sunday and on the Monday Leeds United asked Blackpool for permission to talk to me, but they refused to give permission," Grayson recalled. "After talks with Blackpool chairman Karl Oyston, I decided to resign and move to Leeds.

"A legal battle followed, but I knew what I wanted even if it meant moving from the Championship to League One.

"Supporting the club was one reason for taking the job, but managing a club the size of Leeds and where it could go to with its fan base and history was the main reason."

After not making it with Leeds as a player, I wondered if there was an element of unfinished business motivating Grayson's return to Elland Road.

"I wasn't really going back with any unfinished business as managing was a new chapter in my career," Grayson answered before expressing his pride at taking the job. "Walking out on Boxing Day to 'Marching on Together' with my family in the stands was a moment I will never forget. I was so proud to be the manager and remembered all the great managers that had stood in the dugout."

Leeds had suffered five straight losses when Grayson took the reins and were loitering in ninth, but a Robert Snodgrass late leveller secured a 1-1 draw. A 3-1 win over Stockport two days later and Leeds had won their last 11 home games, equalling a record established under Don Revie forty years earlier.

Away from home it was harder work, but Grayson lifted Leeds into fourth place by the end of the season, but promotion hopes were dashed when they lost 2-1 on aggregate to Millwall in the play-off semi-final. One game stands out in Grayson's memory as a turning point in his first season.

"Hereford away was a tough night in my first season," he recalled. "We missed a penalty, played poorly, lost the game and the Leeds fans let everyone know their thoughts.

"I had a long meeting with the players after that game and the players responded by reaching the play-offs. We lost the first leg, but we all felt we could turn the deficit around at home, and we nearly did.

"Unfortunately, an injury to one of their players when we had a strong head of steam and were dominating took the wind out of our sails. We eventually fell short. We felt we had missed an opportunity, but also used it as a motivation to try and go one step further the following season."

That drive bore dividends at the start of Grayson's first full season in charge with Leeds on fire. They went on an unbeaten run that saw them secure seven wins and a draw in League One and progress to the third round of the League Cup where they lost 1-0 to Liverpool.

And Leeds fans, remember this?

"It's Howson, forward towards Beckford, the ball's over Brown and this is Beckford, it just ran away from him, but he'll still get strike in on goal and score at the Stretford End for Leeds United," commentator Clive Tyldesley enthused on the television coverage. "And it doesn't get any better than that for a Leeds centre-forward. Jermaine Beckford gives Leeds the advantage at Old Trafford to the delight of their 9,000 travelling supporters. 19 minutes gone and is Simon Grayson going to spring the shock of the third round?"

Leeds held on against their bitter rivals and secured their first win against Manchester United at Old Trafford since 1981. In the fourth round, Leeds held another Premier League opponent, Spurs, to a 2-2 draw at White Hart Lane, again thanks to goals from Beckford, before losing the home replay 3-1.

"We went to Old Trafford as big underdogs, but within the camp we knew we could cause an upset as we had some really talented and determined players," Grayson told me. "Jermaine's goal seemed to take an eternity to cross the line, as did the last 10 minutes plus injury time. Manchester United had some big players on the pitch, so when the final whistle blew it was a moment of relief, but one of pride that we had beaten the Premier League champions and a big rival in their own back yard.

"We were on a good Cup run, but we all knew that getting promotion was the most important thing we had to achieve," Grayson continued. "There is always pressure on a manager at Leeds United no matter what division you are in or what position you are in the league, but you have to deal with it as it comes with managing such a big club."

And on 8 May 2010, after beating Bristol Rovers 2-1 with goals from Howson and Beckford, Leeds confirmed automatic promotion to The Championship, finishing second.

As the 2010/11 season commenced, Leeds went unbeaten through December, winning three matches and drawing twice, as Grayson picked up the Manager of the Month award. An early dip in form at the start of 2010 saw Leeds finish seventh and slip out of the play-off places.

"We started well and went second when we beat QPR at Elland Road just before Christmas," said Grayson. "We were scoring loads of goals and playing entertaining football, but from my perspective we were conceding too many goals.

"The transfer window opened, and I was keen to buy an experienced player to help us. Unfortunately, the people above decided that we didn't need to add to the squad," Grayson explained. "Unfortunately, we missed out on the play-offs, but I felt we still had a good squad to challenge the following year for promotion to the Premier League."

The 2011/12 campaign stuttered though, and Grayson was sacked by Leeds on 1 February 2012, a day after a 4-1 defeat to promotion rivals Birmingham, which saw Leeds slip to 10th in the Championship table.

"We have 18 games to go this season and are still within touching distance of the play-offs, but felt with the transfer window now closed we needed to make the change at this time in the belief that a new managerial team will be able to get more out of the existing squad of players and make the difference," chief executive Shaun Harvey said.

Grayson left with many supporters believing that he hadn't received adequate financial support from the club, although chairman Ken Bates refuted that charge.

"We have to acknowledge the previous seasons Simon has got us to the League One play-offs, then promotion and then we finished 7th [in the Championship] and we have backed him all the way," Bates told Yorkshire Radio. "We spent over £12million on wages, so why are people blaming me for the recent results? All the money we have received has gone back into the squad. The manager decides who he wants to buy, we as a board just pay for it. I only said no once."

Grayson remembered his sacking came as a shock. "Being sacked was a surprise. Yes, we had lost the previous night to Birmingham with a really young defence, but we still had plenty of games to go and we were only a few points off the play-offs. But the decision was made.

"I was hugely disappointed, but I was also really proud of what I, and my staff, had done at Leeds over the three-and-a-bit years we were in charge.

"We had players leave the club who didn't want to leave, but that was starting to happen too often. Every manager likes to have more players, more money to spend and I was no different, but I genuinely believe if we had strengthened when we were second during the season before we would have got promotion."

Former player, Danny Mills, suggested that chairman Ken Bates could well have had his head turned by the availability of Neil Warnock, who had been sacked by Premier League side QPR in January.

"He [Warnock] got sacked from QPR because he is basically known as a Championship manager who will get you up," Mills told BBC Radio 5. "That is what he has done time and time again and that is what probably swung Ken Bates's decision. Leeds are a big club in terms of tradition, but in monetary terms they are not. They have been out of the Premier League for a long time. They do not have the parachute payments that other clubs have."

I asked Grayson to sum up his time at Leeds and his feelings about his time as manager.

"My overall memories of my time at Leeds are ones of great pride," he answered. "I wanted the fans to be proud of their team and make the players realise what it means to play for the famous club. I wanted to bring the good times back to the club and city.

"From stepping out into the dugout for my first game, to losing at Hereford, to reaching the play-offs, to winning at Old Trafford, promotion on the last day of the season and doing well in the Championship for two seasons, I don't think I could have asked for much more apart from promotion to the promised land.

"My connection with the supporters during my time as a manger, and still now, gives me huge satisfaction. I knew what every game meant to them, and still does now."

26

NEIL WARNOCK

2012–2013

One big challenge

Born: 1 December 1948, Sheffield, Yorkshire

Matches	Won	Drawn	Lost	Points	Pts/Match	Win %
63	23	15	25	84	1.33	36.51%
				RANK	21st/36	22nd/36

When Neil Warnock was appointed as Leeds United's manager on 18 February 2012, with a deal until the end of the 2012/13 season, he promised fans that he had "one big challenge" left in him. Unfortunately for Leeds supporters, it would transpire that Warnock's then unresolved achievement would be to get Cardiff City promoted to the Premier League for the 2018/19 season.

When Warnock secured the elevation of the side from the Welsh capital, he had achieved promotion more times than any manager in English history. He also became the first manager to win promotion to the English top flight with four different teams — Notts County, Sheffield United, QPR and Cardiff.

"I feel I have one big challenge left in me and believe Leeds is a club that should be in the Premier League," Warnock said as he arrived in West Yorkshire. "I want to be the man who is able to deliver this for a set of fans who never cease to amaze me with their numbers and loyalty."

Leeds chairman Ken Bates said: "We believe the appointment is arguably the most important we have made. The objective was to appoint a manager who had a proven track record of getting teams promoted and in Neil we have a man whose record is second to none. We want to be in the Premier League, and we will support Neil in the quest to get us there."

But the man with a knack for delivering dreams could not crack the code at Elland Road. It sticks out on his CV as a high-profile blemish in an otherwise extremely successful career. In mitigation, to achieve promotions, dressing room harmony and for the stars to align, a manager is required to create an environment where various moving parts are pushing for the same end result. At Leeds United, in an era where financial constraints often prevented that happening, Warnock was not always dealt the hand he would have liked to play.

Neil Redfearn had once again stepped up in a caretaker capacity after

Simon Grayson had been sacked on 1 February. As Grayson's time had been coming to an end with Leeds, Warnock had been sacked by Queens Park Rangers for failing to win any of his last eight Premier League matches. The rumours that Warnock's availability had spelled the end for Grayson had not been unfounded.

As Redfearn returned to his job with the Leeds Academy, Warnock swept in to take charge of the Whites with his customary bluster. He'd previously struck me as an individual you loved if he was at your club and detested if he came up against you. Never short of a word, whether that be criticising referees, the opposition or pontificating on something or other, he also had a likeable streak. But he very much had Marmite for blood. You either loved him or loathed him.

Warnock will be remembered far more as a manager than for his playing days. He retired as a winger at the age of 30 after playing 327 league games where he scored 36 goals. He never impressed enough to encourage a big club to consider him. Instead, he operated at the level of clubs like Chesterfield, Rotherham, Hartlepool, Scunthorpe, Aldershot, Barnsley, York and Crewe until, at the age of 30, in 1979, he moved in to coaching.

Warnock began his managerial career at Gainsborough Trinity before leading Scarborough to the Football League and winning successive promotions with Notts County.

Promotions with Huddersfield and Plymouth were followed by spells in charge of Oldham and Bury.

He took control of Sheffield United in December 1999 and his strong allegiance with a Yorkshire rival was always going to be an issue with Leeds supporters further down the line.

Warnock was a Blade, so much so, he said after landing the position with his hometown club: "When I got an opportunity to manage Sheffield United, the club I had been brought up with and watched from a small boy wearing short trousers with my Dad, who was a steelworker there, to then manage the club was unbelievable. I remember driving to the ground at night-time after I had got the job, just to look at the stadium at Sheffield United Football Club, knowing I was their manager and just sitting there."

He led the Blades to semi-finals in both the FA and League Cups. After a play-off final defeat, he bounced back from disappointment with promotion to the Premier League in 2006, his first management season in the English top flight. In May 2007, he left Bramall Lane after a controversial relegation from the Premier League.

West Ham survived after beating Manchester United 1-0 on the final day of the season as Sheffield United lost 2-1 at home to Wigan Athletic. The Blades were condemned by an inferior goal difference. Carlos Tevez had scored the Hammers' goal and his third-party loan deal was subsequently found to be in contravention of the Premier League's rules. West Ham were fined, but many felt they should have suffered a points deduction, which would have secured Sheffield United's safety.

Whilst at Sheffield he tricked his players after being a ten-pin bowling coach in his teens. His break in football came through his ten-pin skills as he coached a Sheffield United player's wife who put in a word and secured him a trial with Chesterfield. He'd worked briefly as an undertaker before getting his break.

Warnock asked each of his players to put a tenner in a pot when they went bowling. Once the cash was collected, the manager took out a personalised ball and cleaned up.

"He convinced us all to put £10 in the pot, winner take all," former player Paul Peschisolido told *The Sun*. "We agreed for some fun, then he pulled out his own bowling shoes and custom ball, shot 250 and took all our money."

Warnock had moved to cash-strapped Crystal Palace, but when they went into administration, he went to QPR in March 2010. He spent 20 months at Loftus Road and led Rangers to promotion from the Championship in the 2010/11 season. He was sacked in January 2012 and was out of work until he got the call from Leeds in February 2012.

A football correspondent's dream, Warnock's aptitude for saying exactly what he thought was gold dust for the media. As the manager of your club he tended to vocalise exactly what the fans thought as he riled, belittled and undermined the opposition. As his Christmas card list shrunk with almost every game, added to what would become four decades in football management, his mind-games brought him plenty of success too.

His most famous quotes fall into four categories: criticising referees, criticising players, criticising other managers and criticising other clubs. Deemed by many supporters as a moaner, the man that is often known as Colin (incredibly his name is an anagram of 'Colin Wanker') can be accused of many things. But having self-belief and backing his own team are traits that have never eluded him.

"There are two or three managers I just can't stand," Warnock had said. "I detest them. So far, I've kept to myself what I hate about them. But what they say gets a lot of coverage. I'd love to come back and give my version. I'd like to tell everybody why I dislike these people.

"The two managers I really dislike are Stan Ternent and Gary Megson," Warnock had said of two rival bosses. "The old saying that I wouldn't piss on them if they were on fire applies."

Ternent appears to rile Warnock more than most. In 2001, the then

Burnley manager had taken his side to play Warnock's Blades at Bramall Lane and believed assistant Kevin Blackwell on listening in to his half-time team talk.

"I had always known Stan Ternent was a dickhead, but when Sheffield United played Burnley in 2001 he behaved like a deranged lunatic," Warnock recounted in his autobiography *Made in Sheffield*. "I'd told my assistant Kevin Blackwell to keep an eye of Ternent. I knew he'd be trying to put pressure on the ref, so when Ternent came around the corner, frothing at the mouth, Blackie told him to leave it out. That was all the encouragement Ternent needed. He launched himself at Blackie and butted him, Blackwell swung a right-hook and smacked him on the nose. He sploshed him good and proper. In Ternent's autobiography, he tells how he gave Blackwell a good hiding. But we saw the incident differently. Blackie had a little cut on his lip. Ternent was in bits."

Warnock had regretted turning down the opportunity to manage Chelsea, saying: "It bugs me when I see other managers getting top jobs and I know they're not as good as me."

In March 2002, Warnock was accused of encouraging his players to feign injury in a league game between Sheffield United and West Brom. The game had to be abandoned when only six United players were left on the field after three had been sent off and two more injured: "The way it has all come out so far, you would think I was guilty of committing more crimes than Osama Bin Laden."

And he wasn't averse to sharing his displeasure at the actions of famous actors either, although he's got my sympathy on this one concerning Sean Bean after Sheffield United had been relegated from the Premier League in 2007.

"He wanted to know where I was. Sharon [Warnock's wife] told him I was doing a press conference and I'd be back soon. So, Sean Bean started swearing at her and my five-year-old son. It's your fucking husband that got us relegated, he's a fucking wanker. That's Sean Bean, the tough guy actor. Some kind of tough guy, eh, reducing a five-year-old kid and his mum to tears."

More often than not, however, it was referees that bore the brunt of his post-match wrath.

"David Elleray was that far away he would have needed binoculars," Warnock said after Sheffield United had been knocked out of the FA Cup in Southampton in 2001. "I really think it's about time we use the means to sort these things out, rather than relying on some bald-headed bloke standing 50 yards away."

And after Sheffield United were beaten 1-0 by Arsenal in a 2003 FA

Cup semi-final, Warnock expressed his frustration at the performance of referee Graham Poll: "I shouldn't really say what I feel, but Poll was their best midfielder in the goal. You saw him coming off at half-time and at the end. He smiled so much, he obviously enjoyed that performance. I think the referee should be banned."

An entire book could be written on Warnock's antics and many had involved Leeds United.

When he had brought his Sheffield United side to Elland Road, he'd reacted to the Leeds crowd's jibes. Let's be honest, Leeds supporters had never been shy at trying to wind him up.

Warnock recalled such an instance: "The Leeds fans chanted, 'Warnock, Warnock, what's the score?' and I signalled to say, '1-0, but there's plenty of time left.' The fourth official came up to me four minutes later and said the head of security has said, 'If you incite the crowd any more you will be removed from the touchline.' They'd probably put me in prison in padlocks."

Warnock's time at Leeds United was never going to be easy. He had never courted popularity with Leeds fans, who would require being won over quickly. Instead, bitterness ensued.

Ken Bates had never been shy of making unpopular appointments and the chairman since 2005 was under pressure to bring success to Elland Road with the crowd having never been fully in his corner from the outset.

Warnock took over a Championship side in mid-table. It had to be said, he was working with one arm tied behind his back as he set about revitalising the side through the summer of 2012. He suggested that he was going to perform "major surgery" on the squad but, with Bates reluctantly negotiating his sale of the club, money was in short supply.

Warnock tried to buy right-back Joel Ward from Portsmouth, but Bates kept his cheque book closed.

£500,000 came into the coffers when Adam Clayton was sold to Huddersfield Town and, when keeper Andy Lonergan was moved on, Warnock brought in Paddy Kenny who had played for him at Sheffield United.

Scottish international Robert Snodgrass was sold to Norwich City as Leeds pre-seasoned in Cornwall. Warnock admitted years later that losing the influential midfielder sounded the death knell for his time as manager. He had planned to make Snodgrass his captain and build his new-look Leeds around him.

"I was so disappointed," Warnock told TalkSport in 2018. "I thought I could have turned that club around. In pre-season, I thought we've got a chance here. And a week before (the season started), Norwich came in for Snodgrass and Ken Bates said to me, 'You've got to sell him for £1 million as we need the money.'

"In the end they got £3 million, and he said, 'You can have half of whatever we get.' Then, unfortunately, two days later Ken told me the bank had stopped him from spending any money.

"Snodgrass. I could have cried. He was the one chance we had. He came to see me, and I said, 'I don't want you to go.'

"He said, 'Just for the family gaffer, I've got to go.' And he was right, and I had to let him go. That just about finished me off up there. I had no chance."

Portsmouth's financial plight allowed Warnock to circle above Fratton Park and swoop for Jason Pearce, Jamie Ashdown, David Norris and Luke Varney as a replacement for Snodgrass.

As Warnock embarked on the 2012/13 campaign, he signed El Hadji Diouf in a short-term deal to add some sparkle to an otherwise one-dimensional attack.

It was a bizarre signing of a player Warnock had publicly slammed in January 2011. Diouf was playing for Blackburn Rovers and Warnock had watched him break the leg of his QPR player Jamie Mackie.

"For many years I have thought he was the gutter type," Warnock had said angrily after the game. "I was going to call him a sewer rat, but that might be insulting to sewer rats. He's the lowest of the low and I can't see him being at Blackburn much longer."

With Diouf now a Warnock player the signing smacked of desperation. Bates, meanwhile, appeared to have lost interest as he bargained for a takeover by Gulf Finance House, a Bahrain investment bank.

Leeds were struggling on the pitch and by November 2012 Warnock admitted: "I get frustrated because if I was 10 years younger then there's always tomorrow, but I want to do it today. You're almost in a straitjacket. The club's got to move on, the sooner the better."

Supporters were as disillusioned with Bates as they were with the constant lurching from drama to crisis that had plagued the club since before relegation from the Premier League in 2003/04. They could see that Warnock was not able to manage in top gear.

Bates agreed the Bahraini sale on 21 November 2012 and Warnock was able to recruit Alan Tate and Jerome Thomas on loan. The form improved as Christmas approached and a League Cup quarter-final run lifted spirits.

Warnock wanted to move for West Brom striker Chris Wood in the January transfer window, but the New Zealander moved to Leicester City instead with Leeds unable to meet the transfer fee.

In January 2012, the writing was on the wall as Leeds slipped to a 2-0 defeat to Yorkshire side Barnsley. The away support let their manager know that the performance was a long way from expectations.

Warnock spoke of a rift between his coaching staff and the Academy staff at Thorp Arch who he believed took pleasure in first-team defeats. "It's like a cancer in the club," he reported in his autobiography.

Leeds have enjoyed two decent cup runs. They'd seen off Shrewsbury, Oxford and then Premier League Everton and Southampton before being ousted by Chelsea 5-1 in the quarter-final. A two-legged win against Birmingham saw Leeds handed a tough FA Cup fourth round tie against Premier League Spurs where goals from Varney and McCormack saw them through 2-1. Drawn against England's top club Manchester City at the Etihad Stadium on 17 February 2013, City comfortably progressed 4-0.

Argentinian striker Luciano Becchio had become a cult figure at Elland Road with timely goals. It had been rumoured throughout January that he was on his way out.

"You've just got to see what happens," Warnock told TalkSport on 28 January 2013. "The transfer window is a nightmare for managers. I've seen players in this situation go and I've seen them stay and whatever happens we can't let him go unless we get a replacement in. We haven't got a guaranteed replacement coming in just yet."

It did nothing to boost public support when he was sold at the end of the transfer window in a deal that took him to Norwich City and brought Steve Morison and £200,000 back in the other direction. Warnock moved to appease criticism by suggesting that Morison would become "a legend", but the new man found the net only five times in 41 games for Leeds.

Ahead of a 0-0 draw in Blackburn on 23 February 2013, Warnock told a press conference: "If we don't go up I won't be here. They've known that, I think the fans have known that all along and we're eight points off now, so it's not rocket science, really.

"I think the club will be sensible about it," he continued. "I don't want to leave them in the lurch. It's a great club and in the next couple of years I'm sure they will be back in the big time. And they'll make some noise I'm sure.

"It's my contract. There's no way I want to stay in the Championship again next season. The club's known that all along. And that's why I've been living away from the family, to let me have one go at trying to get Leeds United promoted.

"What's gone on behind the scenes over the last 12 months, I deserve a medal if I'm honest," he added with a wry smile.

Future England player, Ross Barkley, came in from Everton on loan but was returned to Goodison Park when he was deemed surplus to Warnock's requirements.

Youngster Tom Lees, United's much-admired centre-back, had been promoted from the youth team along with equally impressive Sam Byram.

Lees was still finding his way into the side, but received a vocal mauling from his manager when he was sent off in a 3-0 defeat to Ipswich Town on 20 March 2013. Paddy Kenny had sold him short with a goal kick and Warnock told the media that the youngster was "stupid" and had been guilty of "letting everyone down". Ken Bates, by then club president, was moved enough to phone Lees to put a metaphorical arm around him.

Striker Ross McCormack then gave Warnock a four-letter volley after he had come on as substitute in a 2-1 home defeat to Derby County. It painted a picture of disharmony behind the scenes and a manager that was losing the goodwill of his players quickly.

Warnock, 64, had previously admitted he would leave Leeds if they failed to win promotion to the Premier League and would probably go once it had become mathematically impossible for the Whites to clinch a return to the top tier. Warnock had also spoken to GFH Capital about his successor.

"I don't think they should rush into a permanent appointment because there are no outstanding candidates at the moment, but there will be in the summer," he said after the Derby defeat. "I have been a manager for 33 years and these last 12 months have been the hardest. I have given it my best shot, but, being honest, we haven't been good enough in the final third of the pitch."

New owners GFH had already privately agreed that a loss to Derby would be the last straw and Warnock was sacked straight after the game. In a career of promotions, highs and achievement, Leeds is the black mark, where Warnock, hamstrung by a lack of financial backing, was unable to keep the wheels on the bus, let alone steer it to its destination.

The 69-year-old departed along with his assistants, Mick Jones and Ronnie Jepson. Leeds were only five points clear of the relegation zone with six games of the season to play.

"We would like to thank Neil for his efforts during his time as our manager and share his disappointment that we could not achieve promotion," said chief executive Shaun Harvey. "We would also like to thank Mick Jones and Ronnie Jepson, who will leave the club with Neil, for all their hard work.

"We need to look to the future and the search for his replacement is under way," added Harvey. "There is no fixed timescale, as securing the services of the right person is the primary objective to give us the best chance of promotion next season."

Owen Coyle, Brian McDermott and Roberto Di Matteo were immediately touted in the press as Warnock's replacement. Until Warnock's replacement was installed, youth team boss Neil Redfearn was once again tasked with taking temporary control of first-team affairs. Under Redfearn, Leeds won three and lost three of the remaining Championship matches to finish the season in 13th position.

As promised, Warnock did have one more job left in him. After leaving Leeds, he had brief returns to Crystal Palace and QPR before taking over at Rotherham and saving them from Championship relegation. He then took charge of Cardiff City on 5 October 2016 and miraculously led them from second-to-bottom of the Championship to finish 12th in his first season before gaining promotion to the Premier League in the 2017/18 season. He described that success as "the biggest achievement in my 38-year career by an absolute mile."

In an interview when at Cardiff, Warnock, who has always been able to laugh at himself as well as dish it out, spoke about Bristol City, rivals of Cardiff and former club Plymouth.

He said: "I joke with their fans that, when I do pass away, I hope they all have a minute's applause for me at Ashton Gate and remember the good times I've given them. I don't want silence. I want them all to be chanting, 'Warnock's a wanker' over and over again. For a whole minute. That would be my ideal."

Warnock failed with Leeds, yet is viewed as a managerial genius to fans of a large number of other football teams where he masterminded the fulfilment of their dreams. His desire to operate alongside his big-named managerial rivals in the Premier League has been fleeting. Sheffield United and Cardiff City were both relegated from the top tier after just one season.

At the age of 70, Warnock was still suggesting he still had the hunger for more adventures. Whether it is with Cardiff or some other side, there seems little doubt he will bounce back. He always has.

When I had spoken to Kevin Blackwell, I had also asked him about Warnock's time at Leeds United.

"Neil and I fell out when I became number two at Leeds United and I left Sheffield United and Neil didn't take that very well," Blackwell told me. "When he took the Leeds job we'd not really spoken, but he did ring me the second or third day he'd gone in. I said, 'There's only one problem you've got, and you better look above you.' And that proved to be the case. Promises that were made were never kept. That was the big thing.

"I know he will have been frustrated. We talked about things afterwards, but both of us seem to have had the same frustrations that our plans and ambitions at the club couldn't be met by the club, and promises made by the club couldn't be kept by the club either."

BRIAN McDERMOTT (2013 - 2014)
DAVE HOCKADAY (2014)
DARKO MILANIC (2014)
NEIL REDFEARN (2014 - 2015)
UWE ROSLER (2015)
STEVE EVANS (2015 - 2016)
GARRY MONK (2016 - 2017)

"Coaches are like watermelons, you only know how good it is when you open it" — *Massimo Cellino*

Brian McDermott   Born: 8 April 1961, Slough, Berkshire

Matches	Won	Drawn	Lost	Points	Pts/Match	Win %
55	21	9	25	72	1.31	38.18%
				RANK	24th/36	19th/36

Step up Brian McDermott, who replaced Neil Warnock on 12 April 2013. The former manager of Reading signed a three-year deal and became the club's sixth permanent manager since relegation from the top flight in 2004.

"This is probably the only club I would come to at this stage of the season and I just want to get going now," he told BBC Radio Leeds. McDermott had intended to give himself a break from the game until the summer of 2013, only to be convinced by the chief executive at Elland Road that he could not pass up the opportunity.

"I've gone on a lot of goodwill here," McDermott added. "Shaun Harvey told me that I will be supported, and I've had a good conversation with the owners. The most important thing is the fans and we want to do right by them. We want to give them a side that is exciting to watch and first and foremost gets results. A prerequisite for any team I put out is that every player gives their all. I know the supporters here will respond to that."

McDermott brought his assistant Nigel Gibbs with him and the pair had a track record of promotion from the Championship after taking Reading to the Premier League the previous season, but had been dismissed at the Madejski after a run of four straight defeats.

He had been promoted from scouting and coaching roles at Reading to caretaker manager in December 2009, before taking permanent charge in January 2010.

Relegation was averted that season and then a run to the play-off final the following season was tarnished by a 4-2 defeat by Swansea. McDermott then steered his side to the 2011/12 Championship title, but they failed to notch their first Premier League win until late November. A decent period of form took them through January with four straight wins and McDermott departed with Reading four points adrift of safety at the bottom of the table.

With Leeds only five points clear of the Championship's relegation zone and without a win in seven games, McDermott's first task was survival with five games to go. Life began with two games and six points. A 2-1 derby match win over Sheffield Wednesday was followed by a 1-0 defeat of Burnley and safety was assured. Defeats to Birmingham and Brighton and a final day away win over Watford brought the season to a close. McDermott's next job was to build a squad and a mentality that could punch at the other end of the Championship table in the 2013/14 season.

Midfielder Luke Murphy was signed from Crewe for £1million and Scott Wootton recruited from Manchester United. Strikers Noel Hunt and Matt Smith were added in July and Lithuanian Marius Zaliukas was added to the backline in October.

There were few fireworks as the season began, but momentum gained as the team gradually pushed as high as fifth in December. But form deserted them through Christmas and into January as they lost five games straight, including being dumped out of the FA Cup by Rochdale and thumped 6–0 by Sheffield Wednesday. McDermott's side dropped down to 12th place.

Massimo Cellino was known as Il Mangia-Allenatori, the Manager Eater, during his 22-year tenure as owner of Cagliari Calcio in Italy, during which time he got through 36 managers.

When the Italian billionaire entrepreneur sold Cagliari in June 2014, his interest in acquiring Leeds United was already known by supporters. Cellino was larger than life, a sharp dressing, whisky drinking, heavy smoking, Italian wannabe rock star, who had moved to London in 1975, aged 18, to become a famous rock legend, but instead washed dishes at the Regent Palace Hotel.

That desire was still within him as he still played guitar in a band called Maurillos and at Leeds United's end of season awards dinner he joined The Pigeon Detectives on stage for a rendition of 'Hey Joe' by Jimi Hendrix.

Cellino had a colourful past. He'd been arrested in February 2013, along with the mayor of Quartu Sant'Elena, Mauro Contini, and the public works commissioner Stefano Lilliu. The charge was attempted embezzlement and fraudulent misrepresentation following an investigation into the construction of the Stadio Is Arenas. Cellino had been held in custody for over two weeks and the case remains unresolved.

On his arrest warrant, Cellino was described as a person of "marked criminal tendencies ... capable of using every kind of deception to achieve his ends."

Cellino also had two criminal convictions, for deceiving the Italian Ministry of Agriculture out of £7.5million in 1996 and for false accounting at Cagliari in 2001.

He was also a little bit crazy. His suspicion of the Italian unlucky number 17 had dictated his life as a football owner. The number had been removed from all seats at Cagliari's stadium and been replaced by 16B. He would retire the Leeds United number 17 shirt on 15 May 2014.

Leeds fans welcomed the prospect of the Italian's money, but were nervous of his reputation. Lovers of the chaotic would not be disappointed by Cellino's arrival and the writing was on the wall for McDermott too.

Prospective owner Cellino instructed his friend and former Middlesbrough defender Gianluca Festa to sit in the Elland Road dugout as Leeds drew 1-1 with Ipswich. Media reports of mistrust from the top were confirmed when McDermott was sacked on 31 January 2014.

It was transfer deadline day. Striker Ross McCormack had called up the Sky Sports coverage to confirm he would stay at Leeds United if Brian McDermott was staying as his boss. Then when the news broke that McDermott had been dismissed, McCormack picked up the phone again to say he was ready to listen to offers.

Leeds fans went down to Elland Road and a taxi sent to collect Cellino was blocked. For a while the owner was imprisoned inside his own football club.

The League Managers Association confirmed that, "Brian received a call on Friday night from a solicitor informing him that Leeds United were terminating his contract as manager. On Saturday morning Brian received a further phone call from a director of the football club stating that the company on whose behalf the solicitor had contacted Brian are not the owners of Leeds United. In the circumstances, Brian was asked by the directors of the club not to take the match and we are awaiting clarification of the situation over the weekend."

Festa was the obvious centre of replacement speculation, but Gulf Finance House then attempted to have McDermott reinstated, insisting that Cellino, who was still technically a prospective owner, did not possess the authority to hire and fire.

McDermott's assistant, Nigel Gibbs, took temporary charge for the 5-1 home win against Huddersfield. Supporters expressed their support for

McDermott during the game and the club issued a statement immediately after the match stating: "The club would like to make it clear that Brian McDermott remains our first-team manager. He has not been dismissed from his post as has been suggested. We look forward to him continuing in his role with us in taking Leeds forward."

At the start of February, McDermott was back at the club, taking training and telling the media that he was grateful for the fans' backing during the Huddersfield match. Understandably, speculation was rife about his future as Cellino's purchase of Leeds United was pending approval by the Football League.

Cellino may not have yet officially taken charge, but his hands were all over club affairs. Festa had picked the team that had played Huddersfield, only for it to be changed by Gibbs ahead of the match. Festa was present at team training sessions, this time under the guise of translator for new signing Andrea Tabanelli. The Italian had been signed from Cagliari in the period where it had appeared McDermott had left the club and the Football League cancelled the transfer a week later, as it 'did not comply with Football League regulations.'

On 7 February 2014, Eleonora Sport Ltd, Cellino's family consortium, officially became the new owners of Leeds United, acquiring 75% of the club, subject to Football League Approval. Former majority shareholders GFH Capital retained the remaining 25% of the company.

Jump on seven weeks, and the Football League would reject Cellino's ownership on the basis that he had failed their Owners' and Directors' Test. They barred his ownership bid because of his conviction in a court in Italy.

The agreement between Cellino and GFH Capital said that even if he failed the test, he would have to provide funding until Leeds qualified for the Champions League. GFH withdrew their funding and staff and players went unpaid.

Cellino answered his phone in Miami to a Leeds fan known as ToeNailSoup. The recording was released on social media. Cellino called the managing director David Haigh "a son of a bitch, dangerous, a fucking devil". He complained about wages, called some of the players "shits" and referred to himself as "the sheriff".

When an independent QC overturned the decision on 5 April 2014 and Cellino took over the club, he said: "Justice has been done. I'm happy for the Leeds fans. A lot of hard work has gone into this. We need to start winning games!"

The QC ruled that Cellino's conviction in Sardinia had not involved conduct that would 'reasonably be considered to be dishonest' based on all available information.

McDermott publicly welcomed Cellino's confirmed purchase of the club and role of club President: "I would recommend the stability of a man who has got clout. I've spoken to him on a number of occasions and, for me, the most important thing is not the position of the manager, or any individual player, it's Leeds United Football Club and that going forward.

"I can work with Massimo, we'll just wait and see what the outcome is," McDermott added. "It's a prerogative of any owner, in any situation, to choose the manager he wants to work with. I absolutely respect that."

Cellino was embittered by the process the Football League had put him through. "They made trouble at a time when I couldn't walk away and I submitted myself to a trial, a humiliation.

"I don't want to be here if the Football League don't want me, but who are they anyway? They are acting for what's right, the principles, the ideal. Me, I sort out the fucking problems at Leeds. I prefer to play by the rules, not to cheat."

When Cellino arrived at Elland Road, he had been critical of former owners GFH's running of the club, saying: "You can see what's been happening here. It's been done by people who knew they weren't staying. And now I have to clean up the shit. GFH made big mistakes, but not on purpose. That's why I don't go against them for the moment. But the men who were here in GFH's name did a really, really bad job. That's not GFH's fault. They trust people they shouldn't."

McDermott signed keeper Jack Butland and striker Connor Wickham after consulting Cellino, but Leeds's slide on the pitch continued and they ended the season in 15th place.

Cellino gave an interview to ITV on 14 May when he questioned McDermott's priorities in taking a holiday, stating the club "have no manager" and asking, "Who's managing this club?"

McDermott's power at the club was diminishing daily. Cellino and Benito Carbone handled the retain and release list of players and Neil Redfearn picked the Academy players list. Carbone was announced as being 'involved with all football matters, including both the first team and the Academy'.

On 30 May 2014, Brian McDermott was sacked as Cellino announced he was looking for a head coach as opposed to a manager. And Leeds entered an era where we all came close to landing the job as Leeds manager, or so it seemed.

McDermott left with the indignity of effectively having been fired twice. He went back to Arsenal later in 2014 and worked there as a scout. He then returned to Reading as manager, but was sacked after six months.

With all due respect to the incumbents throughout this period, there was barely a ripple of excitement upon their appointments. Only football anoraks instantly recognised the names of some of them, as the common response when telling a friend of Leeds's new man was a frown, a snigger or "Who's he?"

I've always been of the opinion that you give someone a chance to shine. They may not have been A-listers, but then the club wasn't either anymore, apart from in our hearts. The general opinion is that none of them were good enough. In truth, we never got time to properly judge them as their heads rolled away from the guillotine after a paltry number of games in charge.

The manager makes his decisions and lives or dies by results, but when you only get the introductory credits of your feature film, how on earth can you stamp your own image on the team?

If a Leeds chairman phoned up and offered any one of us the job of Leeds United manager, very few would turn it down because of a lack of experience, quality or desire. In the same way, regardless of fitness and skill, if we were named in the Leeds side for Saturday's big game, would we say no? Probably not. Most of us would run around like a fool for five minutes before the dugout realised their mistake.

We'd all jump at chances to wear the shirt. We'd also walk over hot coals to experience managing the great club.

I can never fault any wannabe manager for taking any job. If it's the Leeds United job, then there can never be any blame whatsoever. But if he's sackable after a couple of months, then it's the board and chairman that should be sacked too for their misjudgement for appointing the wrong man. Instead, the manager skulks away and the chairman retains his seat in the gods as if nothing happened.

And that's why I have huge respect and a large element of pity for the men appointed by Cellino. Being appointed as a manager by the Italian was akin to being handed the keys to your own paradise desert island, only to find it was due to sink beneath the ocean in a matter of weeks.

Enter David Hockaday.

David Hockaday Born: 9 November 1957, Sedgefield, County Durham

Matches	Won	Drawn	Lost	Points	Pts/Match	Win %
6	2	0	4	6	1.00	33.33%
				RANK	33rd/36	26th/36

Hockaday's time at Elland Road barely registered a blip on the radar. Yet it was significant in how it shone a spotlight on the muddled, foggy thinking of the regime he briefly served.

As Hockaday arrived, Benito Carbone left the club after just two months, publicly due to family reasons, but as rumours grew that his relationship with Cellino had become untenable.

Under-18s manager, Richard Naylor, and Under-16s coach, Leigh Bromby, were sacked, Neil Redfearn returned as development coach.

Hockaday had been sacked by Forest Green Rovers, at that stage a non-league team, only a year earlier.

To most Leeds fans his appointment on 19 June 2014 was the equivalent of asking for a bike for Christmas and receiving a pair of socks. He brought Junior Lewis with him as his assistant and signed a two-year deal. He had met owner Massimo Cellino three times and impressed the Italian with his thoughts on how football should be played.

Fans on social media ridiculed 'The Hock', as he became known. He came cheap, reported to be earning a salary of around £80,000 in comparison to the £750,000 paid to Brian McDermott.

But this was Massimo Cellino's new Leeds. A head coach as opposed to a manager. Someone that could be more easily influenced from the board room.

Hockaday's regime was farcical from beginning to end and the pre-season tour to Italy was a sign of things to come. The 16-0 win against FC Gherdeina, an amateur side, can have reaped few rewards as new signing Marco Silvestri swapped nets in a bid to make the opposition harder to break down. The second match of the tour had to be cancelled when the opposition didn't turn up.

Much of the pre-season back home was against non-league standard sides and when the real action got underway, Leeds went down 2-0 away at Millwall.

The only league win of Hockaday's tenure came against Middlesbrough at Elland Road on 16 August 2014, as new forward Billy Sharp scored the only goal of the game on his debut.

Leeds then lost 2-0 to Brighton at home and suffered a 4-1 drubbing in Watford as they ended the match with nine men.

Cellino had come to Leeds with a trigger-happy reputation as a chairman and his gun was out the holster. He was on the brink of sacking Hockaday, but instead he publicly shouldered the blame. Five days later that all changed.

Bradford City then saw off their West Yorkshire rivals 2-1 at Valley Parade on 26 August 2014, after Luke Murphy was sent off early in the game, the fourth red sustained in six matches under Hockaday. Leeds had been leading 1-0 with eight minutes to play and subsided.

Two days later, both manager and his assistant also saw red after being in post for just 70 days.

"I was going into Championship games blind, it was crazy, and I've seen Marcelo Bielsa going on about all this data, but we had nothing," Hockaday candidly told *The Guardian* in 2019. "We had just one match analyst, one strength and conditioning coach, and it just felt unprofessional.

"I was thrown to the dogs, just scrambling to get information on the opposition by phoning up other managers who had played the teams. I went in at ground zero. There was virtually nothing."

Hockaday had been manager of Forest Green Rovers and recalled the Leeds squad's underwhelming reaction to his credentials and admitted he was as surprised as anyone how he got the job without formally applying for it.

"I'd done my homework on Cellino," Hockaday recalled to the *Daily Mail*. "I saw his record with managers. I thought he would be bringing in an Italian-based head coach. I thought he either wanted me to give support to this head coach, or as an Under-23 coach.

"I got on really well with him, he has a lot of knowledge about the game. We talked about tactics and he asked me a few good questions.

"After about three hours, he said, 'I like you. Would you like to be my head coach?'

"The fella beside me nearly fell off his chair," Hockaday joked.

"I turned to Cellino and said, 'Do you know what you're asking? In the game, I've got a good reputation, but the fans won't know me from Adam. You're going to leave yourself open to some stick.' He said, 'That doesn't bother me, does it bother you?' I said, 'No, I'm a good coach. I can handle that.'

"He was going to do all of the finances, all of the recruitment. What he did say was you will pick the team. Having said that, he kept on signing players that I wouldn't have signed.

"I can see why he wanted to pick someone like me. Someone who wouldn't demand things."

He was presented to the media before signing a contract and had a reasonable degree of scepticism about the task ahead, the time he would be given and his relationship with Cellino, who had sacked 36 managers in 22 years as owner of Cagliari.

"It was just surreal, so cloak-and-dagger," Hockaday recalled. "I knew his record with managers and I was thinking, 'Does he want to get an Italian-based manager in and get somebody who knows the English game to support him as the first-team coach? Or does he want an under-23s coach to bring through players, which is really what I'm about.'

"He said, 'Go and get me a young, unproven striker that will score goals and we can sell on,'" Hockaday continued. "I said, 'Andre Gray.' A few days later, he said, 'No, I've spoken to him and his agent, he's too much.' I said, 'From Luton to Leeds United, and he's too much?' Later in the season, he goes and gets [Mirco] Antenucci for millions of pounds."

Hockaday suggested bidding for Virgil van Dijk, then of Celtic, who would go on to be considered one of the best defenders in the world during his time at Liverpool. He was told 'no' for the Dutchman, as well as for Craig Cathcart, Mark Hudson and a free transfer suggestion for Conor Coady.

"I was scratching my head being told 'no' about those I had recommended while we were getting in these Italian-based players who were nowhere near it and, I have got to say, that's what killed me.

"He'd send me a video and say, 'Here's who we want to sign.' I'd look at the video and go, 'No, I don't like him.' He'd say, 'Well, we're going to sign him anyway.'

"He got this centre-half. He was a giant Scandinavian, playing in the Italian league. He said, 'What do you think of him?' I said, 'No good.' His face dropped. He was raging. I said, 'Watch him in training.' The next day we had training, he watched him, and by lunchtime he said, 'He's gone.'

"I basically had an under-23s team and a lot of disenchanted senior players. It was the most dysfunctional squad I've ever played with, trained with, coached — whatever. It was a terrible environment.

"I don't know what they are doing with the swimming pool at Thorp Arch now, but you know when you see the westerns with all the tumbleweed? It was like that, because none of it was being used. It was a massive facility that was 'too expensive to run.'

"He kept on bringing in these lads who all reported to him. He was seen as the manager; they'd all call him up after training and tell him how it went.

"The players he was bringing weren't good enough for the Championship and weren't good enough for Leeds United."

Hockaday and the goalkeeping coach, Neil Sullivan, took the goalkeeper Marco Silvestri away from the rest of the squad to work on his kicking.

"I found out quite quickly that the Italians reported back to the president ... I had a phone call from Cellino to say, 'Get yourself down to Elland Road.' I get in there and he says, 'What are you doing, embarrassing my goalkeeper?' I said, 'Right, hang on a minute, what's he like with the ball at his feet?' He went, 'He's not that good.' I said, 'Does he need to work on it?' He said, 'Yeah.' I said, 'Do you know what we've done? We've taken him to another field and worked on it.' He said, 'Good work, well done.' That sort of thing went on every day."

Cellino would phone Hockaday at all hours and suggested, "You're not a good English coach," before adding, "You're a good Italian coach, three times [training] a day. I love it. Keep it going."

Hockaday was delighted to have been offered the chance to manage Leeds, so was more inclined to swallow the owner's madness than other more high-profile managers would have been. He suggested that was part of the plan: "He wanted a vulnerable, if you like, good coach. He told me he'd let me down and I have talked to him a couple of times since, when he has phoned out of the blue.

"It was a brilliant experience; I learned a lot about myself. 'Can I handle the shit?' Yes, I can. 'Can I handle players at that level?' I think so. I'm such a massive Leeds fan now; I love them to bits. It was only three months, but it is a massive part of my life.

"I'd have bet money that being head coach of Leeds would have been a good thing for my career. It hasn't turned out that way."

Hockaday had been in position at Elland Road for only 70 days. After leaving, he briefly managed Swindon Supermarine before taking a job as youth coach at Coventry City youth set-up, but only stayed there for six months. Kidderminster Harriers appointed him as manager in October 2015, but he was out of the door the following January. He then worked as Head of Male Football at South Gloucestershire and Stroud College.

Darko Milanic   Born: 18 December 1967, Izola, Yugoslavia

Matches	Won	Drawn	Lost	Points	Pts/Match	Win %
6	0	3	3	3	0.50	0.00%
				RANK	35th/36	36th/36

Cellino had set the target of buying back the Elland Road ground in 2014 and to gain promotion to the Premier League by the culmination of the 2015/16 season.

The man he hired to help him achieve those goals was a break with tradition. Slovenian, Darko Milanic, signed a two-year deal in September 2014 and became the first non-British or Irish manager to be in charge of Leeds in their entire history.

He was sacked 32 days later, after drawing three and losing three of his six matches in charge.

As a player, Milanic began with hometown side Izola before signing for Partizan when aged 17. He transferred to Austrian Bundesliga side Sturm Graz where he enjoyed tremendous success.

Internationally, he won five caps for Yugoslavia. After the split, Milanic played another 42 times for Slovenia, captaining them at the Euro

2000 Championships. In a quirk of fate, they faced Yugoslavia in the Group phase and drew 3-3.

He retired as a player at the age of 32 due to injury and began to pursue a coaching career. He began back at Izola before moving on to Primorie and then the job of assistant coach with Sturm Graz in Austria for the 2006/07 season. He impressed enough to be appointed head coach of Gorica in Slovenia and led them to third place in the 2007/08 PrvaLiga.

In June 2008, he became head coach of Maribor and won the PrvaLiga in his first season in charge. His team lifted the Slovenian Cup in 2010, adding that to the Supercup and becoming the first manager to win three domestic trophies. He added another Supercup and league title in the 2012/13 season and was named Slovenian Manager of the Year.

Milanic led Maribor to their 11th PrvaLiga title in 2013 and also won the Cup, but left in June 2013 to take the head coach role with Sturm Graz and secured a fifth-place finish in the Austrian Bundesliga in 2013/14, but left on 21 September to become manager of Leeds United, taking with him his assistant Novica Nikcevic.

After leaving Leeds, he had 23 months remaining on his contract and enjoyed some time away from the game.

He returned to Maribor in March 2016, where, at the time of writing, he remains head coach. His team won the league title in his first season back and also reached the group stages of the Champions League.

Neil Redfearn Born: 20 June 1965, Dewsbury, Yorkshire

Matches	Won	Drawn	Lost	Points	Pts/Match	Win %
33 (10)	11 (5)	7 (1)	15 (4)	40 (16)	1.21 (1.60)	33.33% (50.00%)
				RANK	28th/36	27th/36

(BRACKETED FIGURE IS CARETAKER SPELL IN 2012,2013,2014)

Cellino moved on to appoint former caretaker manager and academy coach Neil Redfearn in November 2014. Redfearn signed a one-year deal with an option of another 12 months. The contract he signed also included a route back to the academy upon leaving his role as manager.

He'd enjoyed a long and distinguished football league career, where he had played a mammoth 790 games for 15 different teams, including two seasons in the Premier League for Barnsley and Charlton. He had scored 176 goals from midfield.

Redfearn had been tried and tested by Leeds as caretaker manager on two occasions. The first time came between Simon Grayson and Neil Warnock, the second between Warnock and Brian McDermott. Of the five games as caretaker manager, he'd won two and lost three.

He'd first arrived at Leeds as Academy boss at the end of 2008 and had become a popular figure at the club. Wholehearted and determined, as he was when a player, he enjoyed success with the young Leeds players, including Sam Byram, Alex Mowatt, Lewis Cook and Kalvin Phillips, who all progressed to play first-team football.

When his appointment as manager was announced, it was welcomed by Leeds fans as he took the helm, initially until the end of the 2014-15 season. But, as was becoming the norm, his period in charge was largely overshadowed by events away from the pitch.

Redfearn famously said: "There are only three results in football and only two are good. At Leeds Utd, only one is acceptable."

Leeds finished 15th again and fractures had emerged in Redfearn's relationship with Cellino. The Italian had been disqualified by the Football League on 1 December 2014 and asked to resign. Italian court documents showed that Cellino was guilty of tax evasion. His appeal, on 19 January 2015, was turned down. He had also taken too long by Football League rules to produce the necessary documentation, which resulted in his ban being extended until 8 May 2015.

Cellino proclaimed he would be back as President when the season was over. In his absence, his sporting director Nicola Salerno looked after his affairs and caused a stir when he suspended assistant manager Steve Thompson for "internal matters", seemingly out of the blue. It was particularly strange as Leeds had won six of 10 games and the general mood at the club was positive. Redfearn complained about being kept in the dark as to what was going on.

At the same time, it emerged that the manager was under pressure to leave top goalscorer Mirco Antenucci out of the side. The striker's contract contained a clause giving him an additional year if he scored 12 goals in the season. Redfearn started Antenucci against Wolves on 6 April and Salerno blamed the manager for the striker's lack of football.

Cellino told the media on 9 April 2015 that Salerno had left the club. Confusion reigned as to who was making the important decisions. With Premier League sides sniffing around young talent like Alex Mowatt, Lewis Cook, Charlie Taylor and Sam Byram, Redfearn demanded the club fight to keep them at Elland Road.

Leeds lost 2-1 to Charlton on 18 April 2015 after Mirco Antenucci, Giuseppe Bellusci, Souleymane Doukara, Dario Del Fabro, Marco Silvestri and Edgar Cani, all signed by Cellino, pulled out of the squad with supposed injuries the day before. They became known as the 'Sicknote Six'.

Cellino returned as chairman and president on 2 May 2015 and 12 days later confirmed Adam Pearson as the club's new chief executive. At that infamous hour-long press conference, Cellino disappeared midway to have a cigarette. When questions were asked about the role of Redfearn as head coach, the Italian was evasive. He also stated that he would sell the club if he felt he could not take it to the Premier League by the end of the 2016/17 season.

On 16 May 2015, Cellino told the *Daily Mirror* that Redfearn was "weak" and "a baby". Four days later, former Brentford and Wigan coach, Uwe Rosler, was unveiled as the new head coach on a two-year deal.

No announcement was made on Redfearn's dismissal and it emerged that he had been offered his previous role as academy director. He accepted that position on 10 June 2015 and resigned it six days later. The suggestion being that the club's owner had not expected him to take the role and had therefore not made his return easy. Redfearn had remained popular at Elland Road and the supporters were not pleased by his departure, or the manner of it.

I contacted Redfearn to ask if he would chat about his time at Leeds. He gave me a very courteous refusal. I got the impression the wounds were still raw. I understand how people don't want to be defined by that period in time. It cannot have been easy.

Doncaster Rovers Belles signed Redfearn and were rewarded when they won the Women's Super League 2 title. He managed Liverpool Ladies for just one heavy defeat against Arsenal and then moved to work for Newcastle Under-23s. He can often be heard working as a radio pundit.

Salerno's strange tenure with the club officially ended on 24 June 2015 after he had assisted in the signing of defender Sol Bamba from Palermo. The club issued a statement: "Leeds United would like to thank Nicola for his efforts over the past year and he will always be welcomed back to Elland Road in the future."

Then Cellino had a public spat with youngster Sam Byram, saying he was "deeply offended" and "hurt" that the player had not signed a new deal. The *Yorkshire Evening Post* then claimed that the new contract offer was on a lower wage.

Leeds as a club had held its head up with dignity during the financial crash. The wider world of football thought there but for the grace of God because Leeds's meltdown could happen to others. But Cellino had turned the once great bastion of English football into a laughing stock. And then he began to turn the hardcore support against him.

The Cellino family moved to London after daughter Eleonora was verbally abused by fans while attending the local university. "It hurt me to see my daughter so depressed, so unhappy, because they didn't respect her. Now she never wants to live in Leeds. She won't even come back to see a game. A young man shouted, 'Bitch, you are a hooker, tell your father that he has to keep Neil Redfearn.'"

Cellino began a protest against kick-off changes for television matches where he would cap away ticket allocation to 2,000. Supporters who wished to travel to support their side were not happy. Ultimately, Cellino changed his mind, but the damage had been done.

Uwe Rosler Born: 15 November 1968, Altenburg, East Germany

Matches	Won	Drawn	Lost	Points	Pts/Match	Win %
12	2	6	4	12	1.00	16.67%
				RANK	32nd/36	34th/36

Uwe Rosler had beaten cancer and the East German Stasi to land the job of Leeds United manager. He had turned down an offer for 1860 Munich in an attempt to continue working in England after previously managing Brentford and Wigan.

He brought Rob Kelly with him as his assistant, Richard Hartis as goalkeeper coach and Julian Darby as first-team coach and came to Leeds with a reputation for playing high pressure football in the mould of Jurgen Klopp. Supporters never really experienced that in practice. Perhaps, he would argue that Leeds didn't have the personnel to deliver his style, but a clever manager surely adapts. But to do that he needs time.

Rosler was born in East Germany and was playing for Lokomotive Leipzig as the politics of divided Germany changed and the wall came down. He had been interviewed by the feared Stasi secret police, who had ordered him to divulge details of anyone he knew to be considering defecting to the west.

The Stasi told him that they would make his life easy and help his promising football career. The Leipzig manager intervened, and the secret police turned their attentions elsewhere.

His most successful period as a player came with Manchester City, where he became a fans' favourite between 1993 and 1998, scoring 50 goals in 159 matches as the Citizens slipped out of the Premier League.

He was diagnosed with non-Hodgkin lymphoma in 2003. He credited his full recovery to the Manchester City supporters who he heard singing his name on a game he was watching on a hospital television.

His first match at the helm saw Leeds draw 1-1 with Burnley, but his tenure never caught fire and he was sacked after five months after securing only two wins from 12 games. To remain that long can only be deemed as a success in the Cellino era.

Rosler's last game was a 2-1 home defeat to Brighton on 19 October 2015, which saw his side dwelling in 18th position in the Championship. It was immediately announced that former Rotherham boss Steve Evans would take over with immediate effect.

That same day the Football League announced they had disqualified Cellino from being Leeds United owner for a year. This time it was because of an issue over tax legislation in Italy which meant he failed their Owners' and Directors' Test.

Cellino issued a swift response that he would sell the club to a fans group called Leeds Fans United, saying, "100%, I will sell to the fans, if they want to buy it and look after the club. The fans are the only asset the club has."

After Leeds were beaten 2-0 by Blackburn Rovers, Cellino was upset by the abuse he received from fans in the ground and said he would not attend another game. He had levied a 'Pie Tax' by adding £5 to ticket prices and providing attendees a voucher that could be exchanged for a pie and drink.

He was rarely seen at Elland Road after that. He met Evans occasionally and, bizarrely, took his guest Mini-Me actor Verne Troyer to a game.

By the beginning of November, the Italian retracted his previous statement that he would sell the club to the supporters and described their ambition as "fairytales".

Cellino had appealed his ban and the Football League confirmed on 13 November 2015 that his disqualification had been deferred. Cellino banned Sky Sports from Elland Road, but U-turned that decision when he realised that possible financial sanctions would impact heavily on the club.

Steve Evans   Born: 30 October 1962, Glasgow, Scotland

Matches	Won	Drawn	Lost	Points	Pts/Match	Win %
38	14	13	11	55	1.48	36.84%
				RANK	14th/36	21st/36

Steve Evans took over from Rosler with Cellino saying: "He's a tough coach and I want that character in my team," but the P45s were piling up and any manager taking the Italian as a boss surely needed their head testing.

Evans was another appointment that did not fill me with huge enthusiasm. He'd not been particularly complimentary about Leeds United when managing Rotherham and I didn't feel he had the credentials to succeed. I have to say, by the time he left, he had won me over and I was sad to see him leave.

He was a surprise appointment, but then again, the queue to work for Cellino was shortening by the day. Evans, pretty feisty in nature, had made a career of ruffling feathers.

He had played as a striker for Scottish teams, including Hamilton Academical and St. Johnstone. At Albion Rovers he had scored 28 goals in 76 games, but a serious knee injury ended his dreams when only 24 years old.

After eight years away from football, he became manager of non-league Stamford. He took them to promotion to the Southern Football League before leaving for Boston United in 1998. Four years with Boston saw him secure two promotions to reach the Football League.

However, with Boston, Evans' achievements were clouded by accusations of off-the-field 'contract irregularities' that led to his suspension in 2002 for 20 months by the Football Association. He returned to Boston in 2004, often creating stories because of his up and at 'em, aggressive approach to management.

In 2007, he was found guilty of tax evasion, was fined £1,000 and given a one-year suspended sentence. The 2006/7 season ended in Boston's relegation from League Two as the club struggled financially. He joined Crawley Town two days after resigning as Boston United manager at the end of that season.

With Crawley receiving new investment, Evans was able to get them promoted to League Two in the 2010/11 season, but he was never far from trouble. In the 2008/9 season, he received a 10-game touchline ban after being repeatedly sent from the dugout. In the FA Cup, they also beat Manchester United 1-0 in the fifth round.

Rotherham came calling in April 2012 and once again Evans enjoyed success taking them to League One in 2012/13. The following season, Rotherham beat Leyton Orient 4-3 on penalties, after drawing 2-2 in normal time, to secure promotion to the Championship.

Evans promised the Rotherham fans that if he kept them in the Championship he would wear a sombrero, T-shirt and shorts for their final game at Elland Road. He was good to his word.

He left Rotherham on 28 September 2015 as the board's intention to manage by committee did not gel with Evans' approach. The managerial merry-go-round was epitomised in October 2014, when Evans was replaced by Neil Redfearn and on 19 October 2015, he became the new Leeds boss.

He'd been watching a game between Coventry and Blackpool when he received a text asking if he would be interested in becoming Leeds manager. Evans thought it was a joke. A second text contained a telephone number. When Evans asked whose number it was he was told it was Cellino's. Evans and his wife burst out laughing. It was time to meet the Italian.

"It was the Sunday, I usually go out for Sunday lunch with the family at 1pm, but I told my wife we'd go at 4pm because I didn't think I would be spending too long in Leeds," Evans told the *Daily Mail*. "I got there and drove around the stadium twice; I was so excited."

With Rosler still in the role, Evans had been understandably sceptical.

"I met with Mr Cellino, but said I wouldn't talk about anything with him unless I knew there was a vacancy," he recalled. "He assured me the situation had been dealt with, so I felt my conscience was clear. I'm not the kind of guy who treats fellow managers badly."

After a five-hour meeting, where Evans was assured that he would have the final say on transfers, hands were shaken, and a new manager was ready to be announced.

"If I get the time, I'll make Leeds United successful, I believe that 100 per cent," Evans said shortly after taking the position. "Just give me a chance. I'll never be Don Revie, I know that, but I just want people to look back and say, 'He did a good job there,' because that's what they say everywhere else I've managed."

Evans was never short of comment and some would come back to haunt him. He had stated in October 2014 that he could never work for an owner who interfered in squad selection and transfers like Leeds owner Massimo Cellino, referring to Leeds United as a "sinking ship like the Titanic" and "not a big club".

At his first press conference, Evans described Leeds as a "humongous club", but gave the caveat, "The day the owner picks the team is the day I leave the club.

"If you look at Leeds United and Massimo Cellino, where would they be if he had not have stepped in with his millions of pounds?

"If you work for Massimo Cellino, you coach the players and get the results from the players he brings in or you pay with your job, that is the way it is."

It was no surprise that as the sixth manager in Cellino's short reign that the talk was always about how long he could survive. Speculation grew over whether Evans would be retained as head coach for the 2016/17 season.

Cellino told *The Daily Telegraph* on 18 April 2016, that Evans "talks too much" and that he had to learn to "shut his mouth". His disqualification was removed when on 9 May 2016 he was acquitted after appealing his conviction for tax evasion for not paying VAT on a Range Rover he had imported into Italy from the USA.

On 13 May 2016, Cellino told *The Times* that he had regretted buying the club and was open to offers.

Evans' role was further cast into doubt when it became known that MK Dons boss Karl Robinson had turned down an offer for him to replace him at Elland Road. Cellino was also turned down by Bristol Rovers manager Darrell Clarke.

Evans' time ran out on 31 May 2016 when he was sacked with Cellino, stating the club "needed a different approach in order to achieve targets for the new season." Evans moved on to manage Mansfield from November 2016 and then moved to Peterborough United until being sacked in January 2019.

Cellino seemed to walk from one storm to another. In April 2016, ex-Leeds women's striker and former Education & Welfare officer, Lucy Ward, had won a twin unfair dismissal and sexual discrimination case at an employment tribunal. Ward, a partner of former manager Neil Redfearn, had been sacked in 2014 and her victory cost the club £290,000 plus legal costs.

Cellino had been in court in June 2016 to defend himself against the tribunal panel's April accusation of sexism, but did not take the stand because of the huge press attention. Allegations that Cellino had told a colleague that women belonged "in the bedroom or beautician's" went unchallenged, although the Italian strenuously denied it.

Ward also alleged that Cellino had seen a female conditioning coach working with the Under-21 side in 2016. He reportedly said: "I can't have a fucking woman doing that. She a woman. She sleep with players."

Cellino had sacked all of the cleaning staff at the Thorp Arch training ground, deciding the U18 players could assume the duties. A sickness bug broke out, caused by spores from the swimming pool which Cellino refused to pay £25,000 to maintain.

As Redfearn's partner, Ward also alleged that after his sacking as manager Cellino assumed that she would have to go too.

Garry Monk   Born: 6 March 1979, Bedford

Matches	Won	Drawn	Lost	Points	Pts/Match	Win %
53	25	11	17	86	1.62	47.17%
				RANK	6th/36	7th/36

Cellino's seventh manager was Garry Monk, appointed on 2 June 2016, signing a one-year rolling contract. Monk had played for Swansea for 10 years as a centre-back before taking over as manager in February 2014.

Far from selling the club, Cellino increased the ownership of Eleonora Sport to 100% on 8 September 2016 when he acquired the remaining 15% of shares from GFH Capital.

But his sole majority shareholder status gave Cellino increased ability to find a new owner and on 4 January 2017, Milan-born entrepreneur Andrea Radrizzani purchased a 50% stake in Leeds United. Radrizzani was said to be worth an estimated £450 million, earned from trading television sports rights.

Meanwhile, Monk was settling in nicely and would become the only one of the Italian's managerial appointments to see out a full season. For a while it appeared that the former Swansea boss could be the man to finally end the Whites' stay in the Championship.

During a period of relative calm in the otherwise fraught Cellino era, Monk led the team to their highest league finish since 2011. For the majority of the campaign, Leeds mounted a serious play-off challenge, but a run of only one win from the final eight games saw them miss out.

Despite the late slump, Monk had won 48% of his league matches, the fifth highest win-rate in the club's history. It seemed extremely likely that Monk would remain for at least another season.

That anticipation increased when Radrizzani completed a 100% buyout of the club on 23 May 2017. And that was the end of Massimo Cellino's ownership and a period of unparalleled havoc. He departed with the message to Leeds fans: "If you can survive working with me, you can survive anything."

Cellino went back to Italy to buy Brescia who were playing in Serie B. In his first season he made four managerial changes.

The change of owner and the hope of a more tranquil future seemed the ideal time for Monk to sign on the dotted line and celebrate outlasting the Manager Eater. But it transpired the Monk preferred the supposedly greener pastures of Middlesbrough. He was gone less than 48 hours after Cellino's departure had been confirmed.

The club and its outgoing manager told different versions of the talks. Monk tendered his resignation before Radrizzani activated a clause to extend his stay until the end of the 2017/18 season. The Italian businessman had immediately signalled his intention of keeping Monk at Elland Road for another 12 months. Monk was reported to want a longer-term deal.

Leeds United suggested that Monk's head had been turned before he had met with the new owner on 24 May 2017. Radrizzani claimed that Monk had not discussed wanting a longer contract.

"Shocking news from GM," Radrizzani tweeted. "We were keen to do 3 years deal. We never receive any request from him and his agent. No regrets, we did our best."

An earlier club statement read: "We are shocked and disappointed by Garry's decision, but his resignation has been reluctantly accepted by chairman Andrea Radrizzani. Andrea made it clear to the media yesterday that his intention was to exercise the club's option to extend the manager's contract for another 12 months and immediately begin negotiations for a longer-term deal.

"Mr Radrizzani has met with Garry twice since taking over at Elland Road earlier this week and during the second meeting yesterday it became clear that Garry was considering life beyond Leeds United as at no time did Garry wish to discuss terms for a longer contract. Following that meeting yesterday Garry's agent requested that the option was not exercised, and his resignation was received this morning.

"Whilst we are deeply saddened by Garry's decision, there is no individual bigger than our club and we will now begin a process to identify and appoint a new head coach to take the club to the next level. We thank Garry for his contribution during his time at Leeds United, we are disappointed that we could not continue on this journey together."

Monk tweeted: "My intention was always to remain at Leeds, and I saw myself at this fantastic club for many years to come. However, ultimately, no agreement could be reached."

The media talked of a scramble for Monk's signature with many clubs touted as being in the frame. The early favourite to replace him was outgoing Boro boss Aitor Karanka.

None of the men appointed by Cellino were bad managers or bad men. Many have achieved success since. All were football men seeking success at a club that they knew offered their dreams a home if they could unlock the box marked 'success'. That none were given time to establish their credentials is appalling. Six matches. 32 days. It was a period of utter nonsense.

Monk had been the only man to outlive the Italian. And that appeared to be enough for him.

34

THOMAS CHRISTIANSEN

2017–2018

"Always been a dream"

Born: 11 March 1973, Hadsund, Denmark

Matches	Won	Drawn	Lost	Points	Pts/Match	Win %
38	17	6	15	57	1.50	44.74%
				RANK	11th/36	9th/36

On 15 June 2017, Thomas Christiansen was announced as Leeds United's new head coach after being appointed by new owner Andrea Radrizzani to replace Garry Monk.

The Whites announced they wanted "to appoint someone who can help us create a winning culture at the club and unite everyone connected with Leeds United, from the players to the supporters". Four days later, it was revealed that the 44-year-old would be joined in Leeds by assistant Julio Bañuelos, fitness coach Iván Torres and goalkeeper coach Marcos Abad.

Christiansen hailed from Jutland in Denmark and had Spanish heritage on his mother's side. He enjoyed stints as a teenager at a number of clubs, including training with the Real Madrid academy, before signing with Barcelona as an 18-year-old in 1991, playing for their B side. The young striker failed to make a first-team appearance during five years at the Nou Camp.

After several loan spells, he moved to Oviedo in 1996 and then Villarreal a year later. He returned to Denmark for a short stint with Herfølge before securing a move to German side Bochum.

Christiansen finished his career at Hannover in 2006, having played 15 years as a professional. His most successful season was as the Bundesliga top scorer in 2002/03 when he netted 21 goals for Hannover.

Despite being born in Denmark, he represented Spain on two occasions, scoring his only international goal in a 5-0 win over Lithuania in a 1994 World Cup qualifier.

Christiansen began coaching in the United Arab Emirates under the management of Luis Milla at the Al Jazira Club in February 2013. When Milla was sacked eight months later Christiansen left too. In April 2014, he took his first job as a manager with AEK Larnaca in the Cypriot First Division. He had been recommended for the role by his former Barcelona B teammate Xavi Roca, who was acting as director of football.

In his first two seasons in Cyprus, he took his side to their best ever league finish with consecutive runners-up spots. During the 2015/16 season, Christiansen's team reached the third qualifying round of the Europa League, where they lost 4-0 on aggregate to Bordeaux.

His performances with AEK earned him the respect of reigning Cypriot champions APOEL. He moved to manage them on 21 May 2016. As a student of the great Johan Cruyff, Christiansen received praise for the Barcelona-style football his team played. They knocked Rosenborg out of the Champions League 4-1 on aggregate in the third qualifying round. They lost to Copenhagen in the following round and subsequently reached the last-16 stage of the Europa League for the first time ever.

The 2016/17 season saw the club lose only twice in the Cypriot league as Christiansen won his first title as his team collected 27 clean sheets. They reached the final of the domestic cup. But after a stellar season and a meeting with the club, the Dane's contract was not renewed.

Christiansen was clearing out his desk on 25 May 2017 as Gary Monk was handing in his resignation at Leeds United.

"I'm very excited and believe we can do good things here," Christiansen said after accepting his third managerial job with Leeds United. "I believe in my possibilities. This is why I'm here and Leeds also believe in my abilities and we all want the same.

"Last year we finished seventh. At least the promotion should be there and of course we hope to do better."

Christiansen impressed the club's owner Andrea Radrizzani and his new director of football Victor Orta, recruited from Middlesbrough, with a presentation during an interview in Madrid.

"I don't know if it was the presentation, of course it always helps," Christiansen said. "It's more the idea, the way you think, what you want to do, how you analyse the whole situation in Leeds, the team and the whole environment. But I think it is important how you work day-by-day, your ideas, because if you want to come here and change everything you will have more problems than success. And I will be very flexible.

"The most important is that you know where you're going, what you want to do in the new club and have an idea of work, that was what I presented," Christiansen said. "My ideas, how I saw the team, what I want to do and that was in the presentation and it looks like they liked it.

"I'm in a big club with ambition and also one of the things that inspired me to come here after having a talk with Victor and the chairman, it's a big club which deserves and has to be in the Premier League.

"I believe with good work we can achieve that. Since I was a boy, I've followed the English league and know how they play and how they have advanced.

"Being in England is something important," Christiansen added. "It's always been a dream for me. I've always followed English football. It's been a big target and now I have this big opportunity to come to Leeds."

When Leeds beat Birmingham 2-0 at Elland Road on 12 September it was Christiansen's fifth win in his first seven league matches in charge.

With Leeds top of the table after keeping six successive clean sheets, Christiansen said: "I think it is very important that this is the way we can take the results if you keep the goals to zero and take the opportunities that you get and put them in. Today was a team win. That when we play bad, everyone puts their shoulders together and fought for the same goal, which was not to concede any goals and keep the 1-0 we had. And then, in one of the last situations of the game, we managed to score the second.

"It's a team who believe in their possibility, a team who fight until the end to take the three points and when you believe in what you do, and do it with passion like they did, then things are easier to achieve."

However, a run of four defeats in five in October checked their promotion charge. Critics suggested Christiansen didn't possess a Plan B when tested. Injuries mounted and four red cards in five games had fans tearing their hair out in frustration at a lack of discipline shown by the players on the pitch.

Christiansen came across as a really nice chap, always conducting himself with dignity, but there seemed to be an underlying problem. Perhaps his message was not getting through, or more likely the players did not respond to what they heard.

It resulted in the squad being stretched to the limit and seven games without a win, culminating in a 4-1 defeat to Cardiff on 3 February 2018. Christiansen had also watched his team beaten in the FA Cup third round by League Two opponents Newport County and the writing was on the wall.

Leeds dropped to 10th in the Championship table. When striker Pierre-Michel Lasogga was substituted during the Cardiff match, annoyed fans chanted, "You don't know what you're doing." The touchline had become a lonely place for the man who had been all smiles only a few months before.

After the loss to the Welsh side, Christiansen had resigned himself to losing his job: "If it's their decision that they want to find somebody better, I cannot do anything about that, this is their decision and I will then go away, but with my head high that I have done the best for the team, for the club."

On 4 February 2018, Leeds sacked Christiansen after eight months as head coach. The club were without a win since Boxing Day.

The media had dubbed the job of Leeds United manager as 'the hardest outside of the Premier League'. Whatever the reason, the players were not performing, and the manager seemed unable to steer the ship back on course. Not a recipe for success, resulting in the club hunting for yet another managerial replacement.

After his sacking, Christiansen posted on Instagram: "I didn't want to leave without saying goodbye to you, the fans. You are the most precious treasure of this wonderful football club. Managers, players, directors and presidents may change, but you are the ones who remain, together and united. Your passion and requirement for success symbolises your strength. Thank you for all your support."

Leeds were seven points shy of the play-offs; the bare minimum target set by owner Andrea Radrizzani at the beginning of the season.

As always, rumours circulated about who the club would target to replace the Dane. Some said they had seen former England manager Steve McClaren at Elland Road during Christiansen's last match in charge. Former boss Simon Grayson was touted for a return and even Reading manager, Jaap Stam, was in the frame after being interviewed for the role prior to Christiansen's appointment.

McClaren and Stam both had history with the wrong United on the dark side of the Pennines. They would have been up against it from the start.

Instead, Leeds were looking 23 miles down the M1 toward Oakwell, Barnsley.

35

PAUL HECKINGBOTTOM

2018

"I loved it"

Born: 17 July 1977, Barnsley, Yorkshire

Matches	Won	Drawn	Lost	Points	Pts/Match	Win %
16	4	4	8	12	0.75	25.00%
				RANK	35th/36	33rd/36

Paul Heckingbottom replaced Christiansen for only four months in what appeared to be Radrizzani's nod to the Cellino era. It didn't encourage confidence.

The Cellino blueprint: Pick a manager from a rival Yorkshire club, with no experience of gaining promotion to the Premier League and no track record at a club with big expectations.

I've come to the decision during writing this book that 'big expectations' is better than continuously saying 'big club', which I think sounds too conceited a means of describing a club that had not operated in the top tier of English football for over a decade. Big in expectations, aspirations, history and heart, but can a team in the second tier be classed as big in the present tense? It's not a debate I have invented, so I'll leave that with you.

Heckingbottom left Barnsley to take over as head coach at Elland Road on 6 February 2018 and signed an 18-month rolling contract. The 40-year-old had only extended his deal at Oakwell the previous week and Barnsley were clearly confident they had nailed their man down, stating they were "shocked" when he told them of his intention to head north on the M1 motorway after Leeds activated a £500,000 release clause in his deal.

Under Heckingbottom, Leeds won four of 16 league games, ending the season in 13th position in the Championship. They were 15 points short of the play-offs.

Heckingbottom had handed debuts to a number of academy graduates, including goalkeeper Bailey Peacock-Farrell and Tom Pearce. He also took a number of academy players on an infamous close season tour to Myanmar. But he could not halt the club's slide down the table, winning just one of his first eight games.

The campaign ended in controversy with a much-criticised post-season tour of Myanmar arranged by owner Radrizzani. The trip was sponsored by AYA, a private Myanmar bank implicated in ethnic cleansing against the Rohingya.

Heckingbottom's last two games in charge of Leeds were friendlies against an all-star team from Myanmar's National League and the national side, which were held in Mandalay and Yangon.

There have been many occasions during my time supporting Leeds that I have been disappointed to the point of devastation. I've also walked on air after witnessing a big win, screamed 'Yes!' and punched the air at traffic lights when hearing a Whites winner on the radio.

There have only been two times when I have been embarrassed to be a Leeds supporter. The unveiling of a ridiculous new club emblem that looked more like a right-wing political emblem as it incorporated the Leeds salute was one time. The other was watching my team fly to Myanmar.

The AYA Bank, owned by a tycoon blacklisted in the USA for his links with the military regime accused of the ethnic cleansing atrocities and human rights abuses against the countries Muslim Rohingya minority. The United Nations had described violence in the northern state of Rakhine since August 2017 as ethnic cleansing and genocide.

The tycoon's bank was alleged to have been one of the biggest funders of the controversial programme to rebuild Rakhine, which was thought to offer little benefit for the Rohingya community even if they were allowed to return.

Over 700,000 had fled to neighbouring Bangladesh as the military killed men and abused the women and children. A UN human rights official had demanded Myanmar be referred to the International Criminal Court.

An organisation representing the Rohingya community in the UK said: "Leeds United FC is going to play football on the grounds soaked in the blood of innocent Rohingya children, women and older people."

It smacked of a stunt to boost Leeds as a brand in Myanmar and bolster Radrizzani's personal business interests in sports media firms operating in south-east Asia.

Kate Allen, Director of Amnesty International UK, said: "The last year has seen the human rights situation in Myanmar deteriorate dramatically, far too often sporting events have been used as a cheap PR tool to 'sportswash' the stain of a country's human rights record. We're not going to tell Leeds United where they should and shouldn't visit, but if the tour does go ahead, the club should use its leverage to call for an end to the crackdown."

Furthermore, there had already been rumours about Heckingbottom's future. He viewed the Myanmar trip as an opportunity to spend time with his squad and take a look at some of the younger players with the following season in mind. In that regard, his removal soon after the foreign tour was a missed opportunity.

Heckingbottom was sacked by the club on 1 June 2018 after only four months at the helm.

"Leeds was a big job and a big club, and I loved it," Heckingbottom told the *Yorkshire Post*. "There were lots of things we needed to do and change behind the scenes and lots of big, tough decisions needed to be made.

"But Barnsley was a lot more all-consuming as you felt you were on your own a lot of the time," he continued. "In the couple of years I was there I took on a lot of roles and responsibilities and was driving to get things done. At Leeds there were lots of staff there and decision makers and it was totally different. The value of both experiences has been really good, definitely.

"Leeds wanted a head coach, but I just felt that the decision-making around the first team had to change and the atmosphere, make-up, recruitment strategy and staffing, and they have done it.

"I took a lot of positives from Leeds when I look back. But the disappointing thing was that they came and got me because they wanted X, Y and Z and spelt it out and said, 'This has got to happen'. But within a couple of weeks it was not happening.

"I took people on and had arguments over it and tried to make changes and did. It maybe quickened my exit a little bit. But the worst thing I could have done was sit tight knowing it is going to fail 10 months down the line and then get the boot."

Heckingbottom was unfortunate that, despite inheriting a side that looked good on paper, the squad was beset by injuries and his tenure further highlighted the impatience of Leeds supporters and the need to give managers a chance to shine.

It is naive to think that a fresh approach hit the ground running. If Leeds had used the same strategy, Don Revie would not have survived to enjoy the great success he did. As Theresa May was banging on about "strength and stability", in message if not delivery, as the country became embroiled in Brexit, it was something Leeds had been needing for many years.

Aspects regarding how his departure was handled plainly did not sit well with him at the time. But he has quickly "moved on" and returned to Oakwell as a Sky TV pundit for the recent home game with Luton

Town.

"The club [Barnsley], to protect their own back, fuelled it a little bit, which I did not like," Heckingbottom recalled. "I do not think there was any need for it but understand why they did it."

Chief Executive, Angus Kinnear, who had been former West Ham managing director, said: "Our objective is to bring in a head coach with more experience who can help us reach the goals we have talked about since we became custodians of the club last summer. Paul came to us during a difficult period in the season and has conducted himself in an exemplary manner despite results not going as any of us had hoped"

Heckingbottom appeared on TalkSport on 19 July 2018 and said: "I really wish everybody at Leeds United well. It was a great experience for me, I had a good time there and I worked with some really good people.

"It was just a change of direction from the club — they've gone with an experienced manager who is known all over the world.

"I just hope they back him [Marcelo Bielsa] and give him the support to make changes and give the fans there what they are crying out for.

"For me the Championship this season is wide open," he added. "There are no stand-out teams. All three relegated clubs are going to do really well. I see those three being really strong. But I think if Leeds invest and bring the players in, there's no reason why not.

"There is lots wrong with management in how crazy it is. It can be an impossible job, but it is a drive," he observed. "I have had a taste of it and three good years at it and have learned a lot and that all-consuming challenge is what I miss. Until that changes, I will keep doing it."

And he did. After eight months out of the game, Heckingbottom was announced as Hibernian's new manager up in Scotland on 13 February 2019.

"He's a manager who, at Barnsley, was known for trying to play football, trying to play through the thirds of the pitch," McAllister said on Rangers TV. "I thought when he went to Leeds United he just never got enough time. I thought he was unfairly treated there. He's a footballing man. So, he will run alongside the Hibs tradition of trying to play good football."

36

MARCELO BIELSA

2018 to present

El Loco

Born: 21 July 1955, Rosario, Argentina

Matches	Won	Drawn	Lost	Points	Pts/Match	Win %
51	27	8	16	89	1.75	52.94%
				RANK	2nd/36	2nd/36

(FIGURES FOR SEASON 2018-19)

As Marcelo Bielsa crouches on his bucket and studies his team, the intensity is there for all to see. The Argentine, known as one of the greatest tacticians and innovators in world football, offered Leeds around 30 years of experience as a coach across the world. It was a major coup for the club to lure him to Elland Road and supporters, many after a few minutes on Google, recognised the magnitude of the signing.

Known as 'The Professor' to some and also 'El Loco', meaning 'The Crazy One', for those of a different linguistic tendency, he possesses a death stare that could shrivel the largest of dressing room egos. But then there is a genuinely charming smile and an obsessional love of the sport in which he plies his trade. His nickname derives from his homeland and is a nod towards his renowned eccentricity, but that perceived 'madness' derives from his single-minded drive, determination and desire to do things the right way.

The man in the dugout, or more often perched on his upturned bucket nearer the touchline, is 62-year-old, Marcelo Bielsa. He became the club's 36th manager and its 10th since 2014 and, of those, only Garry Monk has survived a full season.

CEO Angus Kinnear recalled: "Andrea [Radrizanni] and Victor [Orta] suggested his name as someone we should be looking at. I had a wry smile because, neither of them lack ambition, but sometimes their ideas aren't rooted in reality."

Kinnear and Orta travelled to Buenos Aires in Argentina and met Bielsa in a hotel as they opened 12 hour talks to bring him to Elland Road. Bielsa was attracted by the challenge of turning Leeds back towards greatness. Leeds had shown their ambition and landed their big name. Shaking hands with their new manager before heading home.

"I considered the strength of the institutional sports project," Bielsa recalled to the Amazon 'Take Us Home' documentary. "I analysed the sporting possibilities and that made me make the effort to be the one they chose in the end. As managers we have no choice but to impose what we think, because we can't convince by proposing something that we don't believe in."

Bielsa arrived in Leeds with a huge reputation, particularly admired by revered people within the sport. Tottenham manager Mauricio Pochettino referred to him as his "football father" and Manchester City boss Pep Guardiola was a huge admirer. Both men call Bielsa the "best coach in the world".

Defender Luke Ayling was excited. "All of us thought 'wow', we are about to work a whole season with one of the best managers. Everybody speaks so highly of him. Straight away, no matter what he wants done, the answer was 'yes, absolutely, no problem'."

Guardiola had written a supporting letter when Bielsa had applied for his work permit so he could work in Leeds. "It is good for football, I think, that we have Marcelo here in English football," the Manchester City manager enthused.

Bielsa had done his research on more than football when he came to Leeds. He had learned about the city, taking interest in how much money an average fan earned. He passed that information on to his new squad and had them picking up litter for three hours, so they knew how much a fan had to put in to purchase a ticket.

He has a bed in his office. The man literally lives, breathes and sleeps the beautiful game.

He had been in charge of Argentina, Chile, Athletic Bilbao, Marseille and Lille. His haul of titles and trophies would not compare well with other coaches given that tag. Yet his influence on football had been huge and far-reaching.

He won the league three times in Argentina and took his country to Olympic gold in 2004. His Argentine side were Copa America runners-up in 2004 and he took Athletic Bilbao to the finals of the Europa League and Copa del Rey in 2012, but didn't take the trophy.

"We are judged by that, how much success we have, how many titles we have won, but that is much less influential than how he has influenced football and his football players," suggested Pep Guardiola. "Still, I didn't meet one guy, a former player who speaks no good about him. They are grateful about his influence on their careers in football."

As manager with Athletic Bilbao, Bielsa pitted his wits in La Liga against Guardiola, who was then Barcelona boss. Guardiola had flown to Argentina in 2006 to pick El Loco's brain about becoming a coach and had been in regular contact since. "My admiration for Marcelo Bielsa is huge," Guardiola had said. "He makes the players much, much better and helped me a lot with his advice."

Argentine Pochettino had first come into contact with Bielsa when 14 years old. Jorge Sampaoli, Diego Simeone, Gerardo Martino and Eduardo Berizzo were all followers of Bielsa's every word and have attributed some of their success to him.

"We are a generation of coaches who were his disciples," Pochettino told SFR Sport. "How he feels football, the passion he had for football, I think we all took that from him."

"My relationship with him started when I was 12 or 13 years old," Pochettino has said. "I love him, and will always love him, because he was a very important person for me in my career.

"My desire and my wish, my hope, is that he changes the reality of Leeds," Pochettino added when his mentor arrived at Elland Road. "Bring to the Premier League, bring them to the Premier League and he will do a fantastic job there. Of course, that is my wish."

Bielsa's scouting tactics led him towards controversy in Leeds, but he had always used everything at his disposal. A perfectionist, a man that devoured information, read every newspaper before breakfast and used what he had learned to his advantage.

Pochettino tells of when he was a teenager making his way with the Bielsa-managed Newell's Old Boys. Bielsa gave his players homework, to read three newspaper reports of their opposition's games and report to the squad on their findings.

Benjamin Mendy, who signed for Manchester City for £52million in July 2017, was a youngster with Bielsa at Marseille. In 2014, Bielsa said of the then 19-year-old: "You may think I'm joking, but Mendy will be one of the best full-backs in the world."

He had an eye for talent. He recognised the potential a 13-year-old Pochettino possessed when he was asleep. At 2am he arrived at his home and requested that Poch's parents allow him to measure the length of their son's legs. Bielsa then signed Pochettino for Newell's Old Boys because he had measured up and looked like a footballer. The story would appear sinister if relayed about anyone but Bielsa.

Pochettino confirmed the tale to *Sport Magazine*: "Yes, that was the reality, I woke up in the morning and my mum explained the story. I said, 'Yeah, come on, it was in your dream. What did you drink before you went to sleep?'"

Some will point to Bielsa's CV and lack of titles and trophies. Then you have Leeds United, perpetually invited to a less glamorous party.

Many younger supporters only witnessing glory days through tales from their fathers, YouTube videos and books like this.

There is sometimes no rhyme or reason in football. Some managers do well at one club and fail dismally at another. They have taken the same approach, used similar methods, but the time and place has been different.

With most relationships, it's the invisible chemistry. Two separate entities combine to lift each other to fresh highs. The stars align and what was previous frustration and regular despair takes a seamless transition into everything that is wonderful.

Pancho Aquilano, the kit man at Newell's, spoke of Bielsa, who remains a legend at the club. "He doesn't get motivated by money or comfort," he said. "He is motivated by big challenges. It's the way he handles himself and how honest he is, how much of a great manager he is. I think he is one of the best managers in the world."

I would love to have sat down and chatted with Bielsa. I knew he hated giving interviews. You could see his unease during the pre- and post-match interviews that he was contractually obliged to attend.

If I'd been granted the chance to meet him, I would have been somewhat nervous about how he would have been with me. The one consistency with Bielsa seems to be his unpredictability. That encounter was denied me, like many other journalists, when a one-on-one interview request was turned down.

He left his job at Lazio after only two days because his transfer targets were not being pursued. He left Athletic Bilbao because he was irritated by delays in training ground developments. His stay at Lille was cut short when he grew antagonistic toward the board. And he walked away from Marseille after only one game of his second season due to contract issues. In Bielsa's favour, none of those parting of the ways was for self-interest, they were symptomatic of a man that could not accept things not being dealt with properly.

When manager of the Chilean national side, Bielsa had delighted fans with a fresh style of attacking, high-pressing, passing football. Playing the ball out from the back, utilising an attacking 3-3-1-3 formation, it was attractive football designed to entertain, and win.

"He always caught my attention with the way that he worked," recalled Harold Mayne-Nicholls, former President of the Chilean Football Association. "The way that he worked on the full aspect of the game. He wanted to be part of a show. He didn't want to win by winning, he wanted to win because he did things better than the other one.

"He always says, 'We need the best bed for the players, so they don't get injured when they are sleeping,' Mayne-Nicholls continued. "His biggest success is that he has been able to build his own philosophy behind the game."

"My first impression was his personality," recalled Fabian Garfagnoli, who played under Bielsa at Newell's Old Boys where they had won two league titles. "I will always remember that strong personality. Willing to progress, to train every day, to improve every day. He wanted everything to be perfect.

"Marcelo convinced us that the key was in the intensity of training," Garagnoli added. "The intense 'suffering' during the week, in order to enjoy Sundays.

"I think he has left his presence, his style and his mark everywhere he has been. He was always straightforward, loyal to us and he always convinced us that this was the right way to understand football."

Enrique Ballester, a Spanish journalist, recalled how Bielsa made his initial mark with Athletic Club against lower league opposition. "Marcelo Bielsa made his debut at Athletic Club in a friendly against Third Division side Alzira. Before the game, Bielsa's coaching staff got in touch with Alzira's with a really clear message, 'I'm Marcelo Bielsa. My players expect great speeches from me and I need you to help me as a fellow manager by letting me know how you are going to play, how do you usually play, if you have any injured players, etc.' And the Alzira manager, Frank Castello, told him that they had some injured players, that the right midfielder was going to be a player from the youth side. He basically gave him a complete analysis of Alzira's team. Bielsa thanked him and then gave a speech to his players going through the strengths and weaknesses of their rival. And he, of course, achieved the effect that he wanted. He had won over his players."

When he started at Lille, he asked for 20 very basic bungalows to be built at their headquarters and the players moved in to eat, sleep and train two times a day. Bielsa was creating a team environment.

The director general of Lille had appointed Guardiola as head coach during his stint as vice president of Barcelona and could see similarities between the two: "He reminds me of Pep Guardiola sometimes in the way that he has an extreme intensity," said Ingla. "Playing at extremes always generates stress in the systems, but I think it's good to push everybody and every single point or lever that can make us better. The players, the club or the infrastructure at the training ground."

The appointment of Bielsa was a gamble. My worry had been whether the Leeds players were up to the task. Could the team that had stuttered for so long delight this new manager and the way he wanted to play the game? This was a man that accepted nothing less than ultimate commitment.

"Marcelo was very specific on the additions we needed to make," recalled Kinnear. "And was actually much more focussed on what we could get out of the existing squad. Players who had potentially been written off by the fanbase, like Liam Cooper and Kalvin Phillips, they were specific players that Marcelo said, 'I will make them the best players in the league'."

Bielsa moved to bring in striker Patrick Bamford from Middlesbrough in a deal worth up to £10million. It was the most the club had spent on a player for 17 years. Left-back Barry Douglas signed from Wolverhampton Wanderers for £3million.

It became clear that Bielsa's brutal pre-season preparations had his players buzzing. The new manager worked his team hard, made them fit and the results followed. Leeds fans too were learning how to smile again.

Bielsa's ethos was to play fair and to score more goals that the opposition. It was simple and effective. Bielsa came to Leeds with a reputation for being fiery, but quiet and not a man to be the darling for the media. He expected 100% from everyone that plays for him. His training methods largely represent match scenarios. To succeed, players have to be physically and mentally strong. He had a clear vision for how football should be played, and the Leeds United players bought in.

An opening 3-1 win against relegated Stoke, pre-season favourites for the Championship title, was a great start. Mateusz Klich, Pablo Hernandez and Liam Cooper scored the goals against Stoke and supporters for who their glass is generally half-empty, suddenly wondered whether it was time to believe again. When it was followed with a stunning 4-1 win away at fancied Derby, the Whites faithful were pinching themselves. Klich had opened the scoring with a long-range strike, Kemar Roofe restored a 2-1 advantage and he doubled his tally with a sharp left-footed strike in the second half before Ezgjan Alioski headed the fourth. Bielsa's Leeds were a breath of fresh air.

Leeds picked up wins against Bolton and Rotherham before dropping their first points of the campaign in a 2-2 away draw against Swansea. After eight games Leeds were undefeated and top of the Championship table. Spirits were high. But could this level of performance be maintained?

It was the movement and intensity that stood out. It was different and the Leeds supporters loved it.

"The most valuable thing is the happiness that we are able to provoke," Bielsa said. "In those that struggle to find happiness in other ways, away from football."

It was a defeat away at Birmingham towards the end of September that broke the run, but only two further defeats came before Christmas.

Bielsa's sides had a history of training so hard at the start of each campaign that they would run out of steam towards the end of the season. Could Leeds hang on to an automatic promotion berth? It was clear that the high-pressing, high-energy style was going to be tough to maintain. Injuries mounted but the positive results continued with a never say die attitude often taking points at the death.

But Bielsa's team responded with seven straight league wins to ensure they were top of the Championship table of Christmas Day. For the previous 10 seasons every team in that position had gone on to secure automatic promotion.

On Boxing Day Leeds went 2-1 behind in added time to Blackburn Rovers at Elland Road but Kemar Roofe scored twice in the dying seconds to secure another win. It was written in the stars. Leeds were heading back to the Premier League.

"It was emotional for everyone," Bielsa said. "I think that football has these impacts that originate from feelings and reach high peaks of expression. In this sense, as a trigger of emotions, football is incomparable."

But four defeats in the next six games began to burst the bubble as 2019 dawned. In the January transfer window goalkeeper Kiki Casilla was recruited from Real Madrid. The three times Champions League winner signed a four-and-a-half year contract to become the highest paid member of the side.

"For sure we needed an alternative for the goalkeeper position," Bielsa said. "For a goalkeeper to come from Real Madrid and choose Leeds, my conclusion is that the owner of the club should feel proud to own an institution that is worthy of such a decision."

For a club that has longed for the sustained success that the team experienced under Don Revie, there were parallels there too. Revie was known for his obsessive preparation. His dossiers on opposition teams were legendary. Bielsa, if anything, is even more meticulous in his nature. His obsessive use of videos to prepare for matches and no-stone-unturned-preparation hit the headlines in January 2019.

'Spygate' was all the football world was talking about as Leeds prepared to play Derby at Elland Road on Friday 11 January 2019. Radrizzani apologised to Derby owner Mel Morris as Bielsa admitted he had sent one of his coaches to observe a closed session at Derby's Morley Road training ground the day before the game. Police were alerted when Derby officials reported a suspicious looking man lurking in the area.

Bielsa was accused in some quarters of cheating and going against the spirit of the game. Others defended the Leeds boss, suggesting it was a further example of his detailed and thorough nature.

Leeds released a statement on the Saturday saying the club will "look to work with our head coach and his staff to remind them of the integrity and honesty which are the foundations that Leeds United is built on".

Bielsa couldn't understand what all the fuss was about. It was what he had always done.

"Yesterday I talked to Frank Lampard [Derby manager] and he told me I didn't respect the fair play rules," Bielsa told the Sky Sports coverage after Leeds had secured a 2-0 win. "I have a different point of view, but the important thing is what Frank Lampard and Derby County think. I didn't ask permission from Leeds United to do it so it's my responsibility.

"Without trying to find a justification, I've been using this kind of practice since the qualifications for the World Cup with Argentina [in 2002].

"It's not unlawful, it's not illegal. We've been doing it publicly and we talk about it in the press. For some people it's the wrong thing to do, and for others it's not."

On 16 January 2019, the Football Association confirmed that they had opened an enquiry into the 'Spygate' affair. Bielsa called a press conference. Those who knew his history feared the worst. He tended to resign at press conferences.

But within hours, Bielsa was holding fort at his impromptu media gathering, not to beg forgiveness, but to give a thorough reveal on how he worked. It was a masterclass and the Argentine's way of putting a full-stop behind 'Spygate' and getting back to what was important to him.

He told the media, in a much-shortened version of his lengthy presentation, that he had not broken any rules or laws.

"When you watch an opponent, you are looking for the starting 11, the tactics, the approach on set pieces. These are the three main axis that the coach analyses. When you watch the activity of the opponent, you get this kind of information the day before the game or you confirm the information you already have."

Bielsa explained that he wanted to convey how his coaching team's analysis was incredibly in-depth, without watching training sessions.

"This information I will give you is that this analysis has been done using 360 hours of work," Bielsa said. "When I say that I know that people laugh at you when you create this much data. When you have strong data, it allows you to make a caricature of the one who is saying that. I am good at giving others the opportunity to characterise myself. I will tell you the info we gather from opponents.

"Of each opponent we watched all of the games from the 2017-18 season. The 51 games of Derby County. We watched them. The analysis of each game takes four hours of work. Why did we do that? Because we think this is professional behaviour. We try not to be ignorant of the competition we play in. We watch the players in the 51 games, those who are still playing for Derby County.

"The other thing we do is point out the chances to score, the half chances to score and which team dominates every five minutes. That's why it takes four hours to analyse each game.

"I can't speak English, but I can speak about the 24 teams of the Championship."

Bielsa gave a PowerPoint presentation that went into incredible detail about how he, and his coaching staff, had analysed Derby, used the data to assess which formation Derby found most difficult to play against. He broke the game into five-minute sections in incredible detail.

"I'm going to tell you a story," Bielsa told the room, breaking away from his statistics for a moment. "When I was Bilbao coach, we played the final against Barcelona, who won 3-0. They were generous with us because after the third goal they stopped playing. I was very sad to lose this game.

"When the game finished, I sent to Guardiola this analysis as a gift expressing my admiration for him. He told me, 'You know more about Barcelona than me.'

"But it was useless because they scored three goals against us. I do this to feel well, I see that this information does not allow you to win games.

"What I want to tell you is that I want to be judged for my intentions. I don't need the information I gather.

"In my eyes, I feel I am innocent. I don't feel I'm trying to get a moral advantage. I feel I have done something not forbidden."

It was an extraordinary presentation. It was Bielsa's way of telling the world that, if anything, he did too much. He had every piece of available information on his opposition each week, regardless of his spies.

A tweet from Bielsa's first club, Newell's Old Boys, simply read: "I hope that press conference helped you to understand why we named our stadium after him."

The Football Association fined Leeds United £200,000 for the spying controversy, a sum that Bielsa paid out of his own pocket.

Benjamin Mendy, left-back under Guardiola at Manchester City from 2017, who played under Bielsa at Marseille, told *Onze Mondial*: "He made me devour videos like never before. To begin with he put me in front of the videos, and I'd fall asleep. But he was happy! I was shocked. After a while I stopped sleeping and told myself, 'Go on, I'll watch two minutes of this thing after all.' After that he talked to me, I talked to him and we'd go over moves together. He told me, 'See, that's why I let you sleep. You slept, you slept, you slept, but the day you decided to watch you got interested on your own. If I'd pushed you to watch you wouldn't have been interested' ... Marcelo is just too good."

When he arrived at Athletic Bilbao, he watched all of their matches from the previous season intently, making files full of notes on each game. It is reported that, at Marseille, he watched all of their games from the previous season as many as 13 times.

Leeds lost 2-0 at home to Hull on 29 December 2018 and 4-2 away at Nottingham Forest as the New Year arrived. They began a run of four losses in six games, the last a 3-1 Elland Road loss to Norwich City, who were beginning to take a hold on the top of the table.

A late Phillips goal secured a point away at Middlesbrough and a run of eight wins in the next 11 games kept Bielsa's side in the hunt for automatic promotion to the Premier League.

"I think that from now until the end of the Championship, all of the games will have heavy consequences," Bielsa said. "It's a big dream [to win promotion] and it gets bigger with each passing game and one sees how hopeful the fans are. "

Just one away defeat in the next seven league games, 1-0 to QPR, which saw them miss the chance to go back to the top of the league, suggested they still had the legs for the challenge.

But a 1-0 home defeat to promotion rivals Sheffield United on 16 March, where Leeds had controlled the game, meant a nervy run-in was likely. It meant defeats at Elland Road to their main adversaries for promotion, having lost 3-1 to Norwich at the start of February.

"We lost playing at home against the two teams in front of us, these are important facts," Bielsa stated. "At home, with our fans. For us, the support of the fans is vital, but the support from the fans is earned and no demanded. We have a responsibility to keep this linked to us."

The good run leading up to the Sheffield United defeat had begun with a 2-1 home win over Swansea where Leeds fans sang the name of opposition player Dan James and saw leading striker Roofe hobble off with a knee injury that would keep him out for two months.

Leeds had missed out on signing Swansea's left-winger James for £7million on deadline day in the January transfer window. The Wales international, who would ultimately end up at Manchester United in the summer of 2019, had posed for photos with his new Leeds shirt, but the Swansea owners, who had given James permission to have a medical, did not sign the papers.

A game at the end of March saw Leeds come from behind in the dying embers to secure at 3-2 win over Millwall as Sheffield United lost and

Leeds were back in an automatic promotion berth.

Former Leeds manager Garry Monk was in charge of Birmingham City during the 2018/19 season and ahead of Birmingham's home game against the Whites on 6 April 2019, Monk said: "The foundations were always there to kick on, it's a huge club, I've said it all along, that type of club needs to be in the Premier League.

"Obviously being an ex-manager there, it's good to see that they've decided that this season is the season. As I said, they've had the core, they've invested in the squad and they learned from some mistakes they made last season, invested really well in the squad this season and decided that this is the one for them."

Monks' side won the game 1-0 and it would become a wonderful season for Bielsa but without a Hollywood ending.

"The loss was unexpected and to be sad for a loss is completely natural," Bielsa said. "It's my job, my obligation, to overcome the sadness, and hope for the next game works as a cure for that.

"The fans have always had a positive impact on the performance of the team. And, without the support of the fans, we wouldn't be the team that we are now.

"I came to be part of a programme that has goals and of course we are aware of the goals wanted by the city and the club, the players, the fans, everybody. But I also can't say that my only interest is winning. What also interests me is the way we build to the victory."

After the defeat in Birmingham, Leeds beat Preston away and Sheffield Wednesday at Elland Road, but a horrendous Easter changed the complexion of the table.

Leeds entered the Easter weekend with automatic promotion in their own hands, but defeats to 10-man Wigan and Brentford, a home draw with Aston Villa and a 3-2 away defeat to relegated Ipswich, saw Bielsa's side finish in 3rd place, a solitary point behind Sheffield United and two behind champions Norwich City.

Leeds and the play-offs don't tend to mix well and drawn against an in-form Derby County in the semi-finals was no easy task. Frank Lampard and Marcelo Bielsa had previous bad blood after 'Spygate' earlier in the season, yet Leeds had maintained bragging rights after following up their 4-1 Pride Park victory with a 2-0 win at Elland Road in mid-January.

A first leg 1-0 away win, courtesy of a second half Kemar Roofe goal, eased Leeds's nerves and the crowd sang 'Stop crying Frank Lampard' to the tune of 'Stop Crying Your Heart Out' by Manchester band Oasis:

All of the spies – Are hidden away
Just try not to worry – You'll beat us some day
We beat you at home– We beat you away
Stop crying Frank Lampard!

Frank Lampard was outwardly unfazed by the fans' ribbing and described the song as "good fun" as the second leg, for the right to play Aston Villa in the Wembley final, approached.

I remember laughing when hearing the song, but also had a horrible feeling that the complacency would bite Leeds hopes on the backside. Sadly, it did.

In a dramatic second leg at Elland Road, played in front of a 36,326-strong expectant crowd, Derby were determined to overhaul the one goal deficit.

With seconds left of the first half, Leeds had doubled their advantage. A 24th minute Kalvin Phillips free kick rebounded off the post and a grateful Stuart Dallas stabbed home from six yards to send Elland Road into raptures.

But then Lampard pulled a masterstroke by introducing forward Jack Marriott in place of Duane Holmes up front. Marriott was on the scoresheet 33 seconds later as he pounced on a mix-up between defender Liam Cooper and goalkeeper Kiko Casilla to guide home into an empty net just before the half-time whistle.

Derby came out of the traps quickly in the second half and a right-footed strike from Mason Mount (46) and a Harry Wilson penalty (58) put them ahead in the tie by the hour mark.

Leeds were not prepared to roll over and die and Dallas levelled the tie after 62 minutes, as he skipped inside and curled a drive into the bottom right of the net. Gaetano Berardi was sent off for a late challenge that earned him a second booking and Leeds were a man down as the tie was 3-3 on aggregate. The season hung in the balance.

Wilson hit the post and soon after Marriott was fed inside the area, chipped the outrushing keeper and Derby had secured a 4-3 aggregate win.

Derby would lose to Aston Villa in the Wembley final, but by then Leeds were pondering a season of heartbreak.

"It's a painful situation and we are very disappointed," Bielsa admitted. "It's not necessary to analyse, during the season the games that could have allowed us to find a solution to all possibilities.

"In the first half, we should have finished with two goals more, but we finished [level] and in the second half it's a game that broke immediately.

"The chances of the opponent ended in goals and ours not. It's meaningless explaining that we had as many chances as the opponent in the second half and in the first we made more. It should have made a difference."

One season in and Bielsa has taken a mid-weight Championship squad and, with few personnel changes, has coached them to the edge of the Premier League.

For a short period, it seemed that Bielsa would leave. The man that had reinvigorated the city had a reputation for not hanging around in the same place long. But there is something about Leeds United and the Argentine that fits and he agreed to stay at the club for an additional season.

Kemar Roofe was sold to Anderlecht for £5.4million and defender Pontus Jansson joined Brentford for £5.5million as the club sought to balance the books. But big money offers for Kelvin Phillips were rejected.

The 63-year-old is unconventional, a little mad and has a death stare that would wither anyone with a contrary opinion. But he is the man tasked with taking Leeds United back to the Premier League in their 100th season.

"I have been working here in Leeds for a year," Bielsa said. "And there are many things that happened to me this year, that have given me nice surprises. I am responsible for the sporting results, and for the process, it is the most important thing I do.

"I have received the support of Victor Orta and the chairman. They have allowed the plan that we devised to be realised. I really appreciate that they could fulfil what they had promised.

"Regrettably, the goal we pursued, we did not reach," he continued. "That takes weight off everything we did. Of course. We should provide the promotion of the team, but anyway, this was not possible, and we all suffer for this, especially me, because I'm responsible.

"I was very sad that the team did not go up because so much effort from so many people that work at and love the club and this workforce, this human tide that accompanies the team all year, deserved a different ending.

"I was very grateful that I was able to be here this year and I hope that I can also complete a second year," Bielsa concluded. "I am proud to be part of an organisation like this one."

The Whites had taken 13 points from their opening six matches of the 2019/20 season when I had to sign this book off for print.

Has the crazy man woken up a sleeping giant? Can they unleash the potential in one another?

The pride is back. The club is looking upwards again. Promotion a century after rising from the ashes of Leeds City and becoming Leeds United would be a fitting full stop to a hundred years of drama, controversy, guts, trophies, despair and glory.

Whatever the outcome. Wherever they play. We are Leeds. And we love it.

LEEDS UNITED MANAGERS RANKED

RANK		POINTS PER MATCH	WIN %
1	Don Revie	1.86	53.30
2	Marcelo Bielsa	1.75	52.94
3	Gary McAllister	1.66	50.00
4	David O'Leary	1.72	49.75
5	Simon Grayson	1.73	49.70
6	Dennis Wise	1.61	47.47
7	Garry Monk	1.62	47.17
8	Jimmy Armfield	1.60	44.90
9	Thomas Christiansen	1.50	44.74
10	Howard Wilkinson	1.58	43.25
11	Bill Lambton	1.33	41.66
12	Dick Ray	1.46	41.64
13	Raich Carter	1.48	41.47
14	Billy Bremner	1.46	41.26
15	Jock Stein	1.50	40.00
16	Major Frank Buckley	1.45	39.11
17	George Graham	1.45	38.95
18	Kevin Blackwell	1.48	38.60
19	Brian McDermott	1.31	38.18
20	Terry Venables	1.31	38.10
21	Steve Evans	1.48	36.84
22	Neil Warnock	1.33	36.51
23	Jimmy Adamson	1.41	36.46
24	Eddie Gray	1.44	36.30
25	Arthur Fairclough	1.32	35.62
26	Dave Hockaday	1.00	33.33
27	Neil Redfearn	1.21	33.33
28	Jack Taylor	1.22	33.33
29	Billy Hampson	1.18	32.26
30	Allan Clarke	1.21	32.14
31	Willis Edwards	1.00	27.66
32	Peter Reid	1.00	27.27
33	Paul Heckingbottom	0.75	25.00
34	Uwe Rosler	1.00	16.67
35	Brian Clough	0.86	14.29
36	Darko Milanic	0.50	0.00

*NB. Points across all games assumed as 3 for a win,
1 for a draw and 0 for a defeat.*

ACKNOWLEDGEMENTS

Writing this book has been a really enjoyable experience. Delving from the start of Leeds United through to present day has made me appreciate what an amazing football club I support.

This book could not have been written and completed without the help and support of a number of people.

First and foremost, to the managers that gave me their time, both on and off the record, to add their viewpoint within their respective chapter. A special thanks to Kevin Blackwell, George Graham, Eddie Gray, Simon Grayson and Howard Wilkinson for extensive interviews and their help.

Thanks to Great Northern Books and particularly David Burrill for help, understanding and for publishing this book. This is my fourth book and the second sports book I have published with Great Northern and they make the process enjoyable and give me the kick up the backside when I need it. Thanks to Ross Jamieson for his work in proofing the book.

Thanks to a few mates too. Mark Wilson gave me a few excellent contacts. Ben 'Wurzel' Barrett loaned me some books for research purposes that helped a lot.

Thanks to the current Leeds United team who gave me a great season during 2018/19 which kept me thinking good things and excited about getting to the final chapter. Although, I had hoped it would finally lead to the Premier League.

Thanks to all the successful, and less so, teams down the years that gives Leeds United such a fantastic history to delve into.

And, last but not least, thanks to you for buying this book. It really has been a labour of love travelling back through the years and I hope you enjoy it.

Good luck to Leeds United for the next 100. May it be full of celebrations, heroes and trophies.

James Buttler
August 2019